Sir John Shorter 1624-1688, Lord Mayor of London.
Photograph of an engraving in the Sutherland collection at
The Ashmolean Museum, Oxford, from the original at Strawberry
Hill, now in the possession of the Earl of Waldegrave.

THE SHORTER FAMILY

ENGLAND, AMERICA AND AFRICA IN THE

HISTORY OF A FAMILY

by

Aylward Shorter and Maggie Price Taylor

HERITAGE BOOKS, INC.

Published 2003
by
HERITAGE BOOKS, INC.
1540E Pointer Ridge Place
Bowie, Maryland 20716

1-800-398-7709
www.heritagebooks.com

ISBN 0-7884-2293-6

TABLE OF CONTENTS

PART TWO

The Shorter Family in America 1635-2001

by Aylward Shorter with Maggie Price Taylor

APPENDIX ONE

Maps

APPENDIX TWO

Tables

Photo Credits

Index

ABBREVIATIONS

D.N.B.	-	Dictionary of National Biography
G.L.R.O.	-	Greater London Record Office
G.R.O.	-	General Register Office
I.L.N.	-	Illustrated London News
P.C.C.	-	Prerogative Court of Canterbury
P.R.O.	-	Public Record Office

NAMES AND SYMBOLS

Throughout this book, whenever Christian or given names are not followed by a surname, it is to be presumed that the surname is **Shorter**, except in the case of some early wives, whose maiden surnames are not known. As a general rule, the surname **Shorter** is not repeated in the text and tables. An exception is made in Table Ten to emphasize a Shorter intermarriage, that between Henry (3) and Eleanor Shorter. In other cases, the surname/maiden surname is given, where known. Many Christian names, such as **John** or **William**, are repeated. To avoid confusion - both in the text and in the tables, numerals are placed in parentheses behind such names. For example John (12) William (8). This applies only to those whose surname at birth is **Shorter**. N.B. Numerals referring to footnotes are not placed within parentheses.

INTRODUCTION

The Shorter Family

This is the story of a family spanning more than 700 years of history. It begins in 1298 with the earliest known makers of glass in England and with one who became a medieval royal official. A 17th century member of the family was made Lord Mayor of London, a ship builder who crossed the Atlantic many times in search of timber, who did business with the famous diarist Samuel Pepys and who had the celebrated John Bunyan, author of **Pilgrim's Progress**, as his private chaplain. It was the Lord Mayor's granddaughter, Catherine Shorter, who married Sir Robert Walpole, the first Prime Minister of England and the mother of the brilliant essayist, Horace Walpole. The late Princess Diana of Wales, mother of Prince William and Prince Harry, was a descendant of this Catherine Shorter and of her sister Charlotte. In England the family continued with a long line of farmers and financiers and with a well-known Egyptologist from the British Museum.

Several of the family - besides the Lord Mayor - crossed the Atlantic at different times and settled in America, the earliest in 1635. The family developed in Virginia, one of its branches moving to Georgia and thence to Alabama as cotton planters. It counted among its members lawyers, generals and a Governor of Alabama. Another member was the founder of Shorter College, Rome, GA.

Many African American bearers of the name became famous in their own right, counting in their ranks a Methodist Bishop, Baptist pastors, television stars and an internationally renowned jazz musician. The white Shorters can also boast of a learned 19th century Catholic priest from Kansas, a digger in the Klondyke gold rush and the champion of the marathon at the Munich Olympics. England, America and Africa all played a role in the story of this remarkable family.

Aylward Shorter

Aylward Shorter became interested in the history of his family at the age of fifteen, and had a memorable interview on the subject with Archibald Russell, then Lancaster Herald, at the College of Arms, London, in April 1948. His father, Alan Wynn Shorter, died when he was six years old and as he grew up, he heard more about his mother's side of the family, than about his father's. He therefore treasured the nuggets of information that he obtained from his grandfather, Wilfred Wynn Shorter, on his occasional visits to London. At the same time, some family papers belonging to his great-grandfather, Henry Shorter (3), came temporarily into his hands, and he was able to construct an incomplete pedigree from the information they contained.[1]

The visit to the Lancaster Herald, and subsequent correspondence with him, convinced Aylward that research into the history of the Shorter family was beyond the means of an impecunious schoolboy. The project, therefore, had to be postponed. On leaving school, it receded still further into the distance. Military service, theological studies, fieldwork in anthropology and finally twenty years of missionary work in East Africa, rendered it impossible. Long acquaintance with African tradition, however, convinced him even more strongly of the importance of ancestors and prepared him for the study of African American Shorter families. At length, at the age of fifty-six, Aylward Shorter received a teaching appointment in London in 1988, and the project could be resurrected.

Circumstances demanded that it be no more than a spare time activity, and from 1989-1992 Aylward's weekly free

[1]. The papers were loaned to him by his cousins Molly and Eileen Shorter, the daughters of George Shorter (3) and his wife, Elizabeth Louise Shorter (née Shorter) his great aunt.

afternoon was devoted to family research. To these afternoons were added occasional excursions during the holidays to county record offices and to places of family interest. Fortunately, in England the Shorters have always lived in London and the south east, and no lengthy journeys were required. The result was an account of the family in Chiddingfold (Surrey), Staines (Middlesex), London and Mountfield (Sussex), which was printed privately in 1992.[2]

In 1995 Aylward was appointed back to East Africa, but he still managed to conduct intermittent family research on visits to Britain and to carry forward the story, especially of the earliest Shorters in Chiddingfold (Surrey). Then a remarkable breakthrough occurred which opened up a whole new field of research in the United States. This not only provided information about Shorter families in America, but revealed new dimensions in the history of the family in England.

Aylward Shorter had been aware of the existence of Shorters in the United States: Frank Shorter, the Olympic Marathon Champion; Wayne Shorter, the Jazz Musician; and the names of Shorters on the Viet Nam Memorial in Washington, DC. In 1998, he learned by chance of the existence of Shorter College, Rome, GA, and made contact with Dr. Alice Taylor-Colbert of the Social Science Division at the College. Through this contact, he was introduced to Lisa Shorter-Hilton, Michael W. Shorter and William J. Shorter, Shorter family descendants in Virginia - all of them interested in the history of the family, who kindly provided him with initial materials. William J. Shorter, in particular, had produced an unpublished history entitled **The Shorter Family in Virginia - The Early Years**, which he was then revising. Then in 1999 Dr. Maggie Price Taylor of Washington, DC, a descendant of African American Shorters in Georgia and Alabama, contacted Aylward and thus began a fruitful collaboration over three years, resulting in the

---

[2] Aylward Shorter, **The Shorter Family - A Preliminary History**, London 1992, ISBN 0 9520839 0 6. A hundred numbered copies were distributed.

re-writing of the entire Shorter Family History. Dr. M. P. Taylor did most of the research on the American side, and furnished Aylward with an extensive archive of the Shorter Family in America.

Thanks are due in the first place to Aylward's mother, Joan Shorter (née Dove) for much valuable information and many reminiscences. She lived to see the appearance of the first book, dying on March 14th 1993; Dr. Harwood Stevenson was the friend of Aylward's father, and provided information concerning the origins of the Shorter family, and recollections of Aylward's father and grandfather. He died in 1999. Dom Philip Jebb, Prior of Downside Abbey, kindly proposed Aylward's membership of the Society of Genealogists in London. Aylward is grateful to Michael Gandy for several helpful indications, and for proposing his membership of the Catholic Family History Society. The Garter Principal King of Arms, Sir Conrad Swann, kindly allowed a consultation of several manuscripts at the College of Arms in London, and Aylward's nephew, Damian Hutt, researched the burial place of Arthur Shorter (died 1750) in Bath Abbey. Acknowledgements are due to Rev. Colin Preece; David and Barbara Martin; Robert J. Charleston; Rev. Pol Vonck; Michiel Maertens; Mrs. Helm, owner of The Banks, Mountfield; and the Saunders family, owners of Bybrook House.

Acknowledgements are also due to the staffs of the following libraries, archives and research institutions in England: Downside Monastery Library; the Library of the Society of Genealogists, London; the Guildhall Library, London; the College of Arms, London; The John Harvard Library, Southwark; Westminster Central Library, London; The Public Record Office, Chancery Lane, London; The Public Record Office, Kew; The Greater London Record Office (now renamed the London Metropolitan Archive); Westminster Archives, Victoria Library, London; The General Register Office, London; Somerset House, London; The Search Rooms of the Population Census, Portugal Street (later, Chancery Lane), London; East Sussex County Record Office, Lewes, Sussex;

Kent County Archives, Maidstone, Kent; Buckinghamshire Record Office and County Library, Aylesbury, Bucks; Hendon Reference Library, London; and The Archives of **The Illustrated London News**. Thanks are also due to John Harwood, Librarian of the Missionary Institute London, for numerous references and research indications. Help was also received from the staffs of Westminster Abbey and Southwark Cathedral in London.

Maggie Price Taylor

Maggie Price Taylor began to research the Shorter family in America in 1998. She had retired the previous year, after 39 years of federal service. She is the descendant of Nathan Shorter (born c.1840) enslaved by the Shorter family in Alabama. Throughout 1999-2000 she carried out family research in Washington, DC, where she lives, and in Georgia, Alabama, Maryland and Virginia. The results of this research she shared with Aylward Shorter, and together they wrote the second part of this book.

In the United States, we wish to thank the staffs of The National Archives and Records Administration, Washington, DC; The State of Alabama, Department of Archives and History, Montgomery; The State of Georgia, Department of Archives and History, Atlanta; The Maryland State Archives, Annapolis, MD; The Library of Congress, Washington, DC; The Daughters of the American Revolution, Genealogical Library, Washington, DC; The Martin Luther King Library, Washington, DC; The Library of Virginia, Richmond, VA; The Temple Family History Center, Kensington, MD; The Carnegie Library, Alabama; The Andrew College Library, Cuthbert, Randolph Co., GA and the Atlanta Historical Society Library.

More specifically, we are grateful for advice and assistance provided by Reginald Washington, Archivist/Consultant National Archives and Records Administration, Washington,

DC; Dale L. Couch, Senior Archivist, State of Georgia Department of Archives and History, Atlanta; Willie Maryland and Frazine K. Taylor, State of Alabama, Department of Archives and History, Montgomery, Alabama; Elizabeth Hatfield, Volunteer Genealogy Library Aide, Carnegie Library, Midway, Alabama; Floyd W. Weatherbee, Jr., Genealogy/ Military Specialist, Montgomery, AL; and Jane Gibson Nardy, Certified Genealogical Records Specialist, Atlanta, who completed a comprehensive search for Shorter family records.

We deeply appreciate information and research assistance from major family contributors, especially Randall P. Shorter Sr., Jessie Shorter Lemon; the late Ola Mae Shorter Harden and family; Annie Laura Brown Carter; Earlene Johnson; Margie Shorter; Elvira Taylor Shorter, Bobby T. Jenkins, Sr. and family; Eva Pearman Reddick; Constance Taylor Davis, who traveled to courthouses in Randolph and Clay counties, Georgia, and to Barbour and Clayton counties in Alabama, to research extant Shorter family records; and Delores F. Price, who provided research assistance at the State of Georgia Department of Archives and History, Atlanta. Last but not least, many thanks to Kathleen Mottley, who graciously provided oral family traditions and a tour of the Shorter Cemetery, Eufaula, Barbour Co., AL.

Aylward Shorter,   Maggie Price Taylor,
Nairobi, Kenya.   Washington, DC, U.S.A.

PART ONE

THE SHORTER FAMILY IN ENGLAND

1298-2001

by

Aylward Shorter

CHAPTER ONE

THE NAME SHORTER

Shorter is a derivation of **Schurterre**, the name of a 14th century family of English Wealden glassmakers who held land in and around the village of Chiddingfold, Surrey.[1]The name appears in several forms, as **le Shurtare, le Shurtere, le Shorter, Shertere** and **Shortere**. From the beginning of the 15th century the name was standardized as **Shorter**, but occasional variant spellings are found in English parish registers up to the end of the 18th century. These include **Sorter, Shoorter, Shortter, Shortor, Shortar** and even **Shawter**.

Authorities on English surnames generally interpret the name **Shorter** as being the comparative of **short**, i.e."smaller in stature".[2] The name would therefore be analogous to other comparative surname forms such as **Younger, Elder, Senior** or **Major**. A distinction is drawn between **Shorter** and **Shorters** which is said to derive from **shorthose**.[3] While it is

---

[1] Addison, Sir William, **Understanding English Surnames**, London, Batsford, 1978, pp.33, 157; Kenyon, G.H., **The Glass Industry of the Weald**, Leicester University Press, 1967, pp.29, 31-32, 115-117.

[2] A leading authority is Reaney, P. H., **A Dictionary of English Surnames**, Routledge, London, 1991, 3rd edition, sub **Shorter**, "smaller".

[3] Reaney **op.cit**, sub **Shorters**.

probably true that from an early date the name **Shorter** acquired this obvious comparative meaning, there is evidence that the name had quite a different origin.

This is suggested by **Schurterre** itself, which is an autocthonous English name.[6] Kenyon, the authority on glassmaking in the Weald, suggests that a certain **John ate Schurte**, who held land in Dunsfold in 1298, may have belonged to the same family.[7] The name **ate Schurte** is not explained by Kenyon, but it is a familiar prepositional and topographical form. Elsewhere Kenyon refers to a property owned by another Chiddingfold glassmaker called **atte Bridge** or **at le Bridge**, and to a witness named in a deed as John **atte Purie**, (**purie** meaning possibly "broth" or "pottage").[8] It appears that **ate Schurte** is a similar type of name. What, then, is the meaning of **Schurte** ?

Schurte is Middle English for "shirt" or "tunic", deriving from the Old Norse **skyrta**; and other forms of the word are

---

[6] The form **Schurterre** is, however, ignored by Reaney **op.cit.** as well as by other authors, cf. e.g. Bardsley, C. W., **English Surnames: Their Sources and Significations**, Newton Abbot, 1873, p.432. Michiel Maertens, a Flemish philologist whom I consulted through the kind offices of Rev. Pol Vonck, affirms that **Schurterre** is an autochthonous English name, which is not found in Flanders. Letter Maertens/Vonck 28.1.91.

[7] Kenyon **op.cit**, p.115. Kenyon obtained this information from the unpublished **History of Chiddingfold**, by the Rev. T. S. Cooper.

[8] Kenyon **op.cit.** pp.117, 145. for **atte Bridge**, and p.31 (quoting Guildford Muniment Room 105/1/117) for **atte Purie**. Cf. also **Stratford atte Bow**, later called **Stratford le Bow**, Ekwall, Eilert, **The Concise Oxford Dictionary of English Place-Names**, Clarendon, Oxford, 1990, 4th edition, sub **Bow**. The name **Stratford atte Bow** was made famous by Geoffrey Chaucer, cf. **The Canterbury Tales**, ed. Nevill Coghill, The Folio Society, London, 1956, p.20. For the meaning of **purie** cf. **O.E.D.**, sub **purie**, obsolete 1500.

schurt, schirte, schert and **shert**.[9] It is distinct from **schort**, meaning "short". This derives from the Anglo-Saxon **sceort** or **scort**, and possesses no form spelt with a "**u**".[10]. Kenyon records that John Schurterre of Chiddingfold, possibly the glassmaker, was a brewer there in 1382. If brewing, like glassmaking, was a tradition of the Schurterres, then it could be that **Schurte** is the name of an ale-house, tavern or inn, similar to The Tabard (another form of tunic), the inn at Southwark made famous by Geoffrey Chaucer.[11] This is only conjecture, but it could explain the name **ate Schurte**, which ostensibly means "at the shirt".[12]

If these suppositions are correct, then **Schurterre, Shurtare, Shertere, le Shorter** would have been substantives, rather than comparatives. Many English names which are not comparatives possess an **-er** ending. One of these is **Parker**, deriving from **Park**, and Kenyon records that the Schurterres were "Parkers" of Shillinglee Park, formerly called Shorterhurst, and now known as Surreylands.[13] **Schurterre** would have derived from **Schurte** in a similar way.[14] It is easy

---

[9] Stratmann, Francis H., **A Middle English Dictionary**, Clarendon, Oxford, 1891, sub **schurt**. The modern English word "skirt" also derives from **skyrta**.

[10] cf.Stratmann **op.cit.** sub **schort**, and Clark Hall, John R.,**A Concise Anglo-Saxon Dictionary**, Cambridge University Press, 1960, sub **scort**; cf. **ibid.** sub **scyrte**, the Anglo-Saxon form of **schurte**, meaning "shirt" and "skirt".

[11] Chaucer **op.cit.** p.17, "at The Tabard".

[12] According to Stratmann and Clark Hall **op.cit.**, the preposition **at** or **aet** could mean "with" in certain contexts. John **ate schurte** might then conceivably mean "John with the shirt".

[13] Kenyon **op.cit.** p.116, quoting Cooper.

[14] At the Queen's College Oxford, undergraduates were formerly known as "Tabarders", from the tabard they wore. A "shirter" might be the wearer of a shirt, if not the one who lived at the sign of the shirt.

to imagine how this unusual, and perhaps unwelcome, substantive gave way to the more intelligible comparative of **schorte**, meaning "smaller", and that is what seems to have happened.[15] Of the two, similar sounding names, **Shorter** was ultimately preferred to **Schurterre** and its immediate variants. Probably, this is as much light as can be shed at present on the origin and meaning of the name **Shorter**.

---

[15] At the risk of confusing matters further, it might be noted in passing that the comparative form of the Anglo-Saxon **scort** or **sceort** was **scytra** or **scyrtra**, not unlike **scyrte**, meaning "skirt" or "shirt". cf. Clark Hall, **op.cit.** sub **scytra** and Sweet, Henry, **The Student's Dictionary of Anglo-Saxon**, Clarendon, Oxford 1896 (1928 edition) sub **scort** for **scyrtra**.

CHAPTER TWO

GLASSMAKERS OF THE WEALD AND YEOMEN OF THE CROWN

The Origins of English Glassmaking

The Schurterre family is familiar to those interested in the history of English glassmaking. Medieval glassmaking was concentrated in north Germany, France, Bohemia and Italy. In the 14th century it began in England, in Surrey, where timber from the Weald was used in the forest glass-furnaces. It seems probable that the industry was introduced into England from Normandy.[16]

Glassmakers operated in and around the village of Chiddingfold, which enjoyed a reputation abroad, as well as in England itself.[17] Glass of an inferior quality was made in the north of England, but the glassmaking industry of the Weald, which included both glassware and window glass, was ended abruptly in the 17th century, when Parliament decided that the use of timber from the Weald for the furnaces was wasteful.[18]

---

[16] Kenyon **op.cit.**, p.12.

[17] Kenyon **op.cit.**, p.84.

[18] Addison **op.cit.**, p.33; Kenyon **op.cit.**, p.29.

8 The Shorter Family

The parish registers of Chiddingfold begin in 1563, but although the Shorters had held land in the parish since 1367, and had been associated with the Chiddingfold area since 1298, there are very few references to Shorters in the extant registers.[19] The Shorters or Schurterres of Chiddingfold, Surrey, were the earliest known members of the family. They were also the first English glass-makers of which we can be certain. The scanty genealogical evidence we possess, before the commencement of the parish registers, has been collected by G. H. Kenyon, the historian of Wealden glassmaking. It would seem that the high point of Chiddingfold's medieval prosperity was the second half of the fourteenth century, when the village received a royal charter.[20]

The Schurterres were a yeoman family that held land in Chiddingfold for at least 267 years and were the earliest indisputable glassmakers in the area. John ate Schurte, possibly the earliest known member of the family, held land in Dunsfold in 1298.[21] William le Shurtare was assessed at Witley for the fifteenth and the tenth of 1332.[22] Richard le Shurtere was a member of one of the Chiddingfold tithings at a view of frankpledge in 1343.[23] In 1367 John Alemayne granted John Schurterre the twenty year lease of a tenement at Hazlebridge

---

[19] Kenyon, **op.cit.**.

[20] White, W.R.H., **Chiddingfold St. Mary - A Guide for Visitors**, Chiddingfold 1983.

[21] Kenyon **op.cit.**, p.115.

[22] **Surrey Taxation Returns**, Part 1, p.9, cited by Kenyon **op.cit.**, p.116.

[23] Loseley MSS, p.197, quoted by Kenyon **op.cit.**, p.115. Frankpledge was a system according to which groups of landless householders were bound over to keep the peace, under surety from the hundred (the unit of local government).

Hill (afterwards known as Almeyns), a thousand yards southwest of Chiddingfold Church.[24] It consisted of two gardens with a meadow adjoining. John Schurterre was described in the deed as a "glasier" and Hazlebridge Hill and its surrounding woodlands are known to have been a center of glassmaking in the 14th century.

John Alemayne's name suggests that he came from Germany. It is not known if he was a glassmaker, but he was certainly a glass merchant who supplied glass for the windows of two royal chapels, in the reign of King Edward III, St. George's, Windsor and St. Stephen's, Westminster in 1351-1352.[25] John Schurterre may have been the maker of this glass. His association with Alemayne does not necessarily suggest a German origin for the Schurterre family. As Kenyon remarks, the origin of the Schurterres is not known, but they held land at Chiddingfold in 1367 and were the first Wealden glassmakers of whom we can be certain.[26] John Schurterre died in the reign of King Richard II, c.1369, and we find his widow, Joan, bringing a glazier from Staffordshire in April 1380 to work and share her glass furnace in Kirdford, until her son John should come of age.[27] Five years later John Schurterre junior was in business. An indenture dated August 11th 1385 records an agreement, to which "John Shertere" was a party, with the

---

[24] Guildford Muniment Room, 105/1/72, quoted by Kenyon **op.cit.**, p.29.

[25] Kenyon **op.cit.** pp.28-30, quoting the Exchequer K. R. Rolls. St. George's was an earlier building replaced by the present chapel. St. Stephen's was secularized at the Reformation and became the meeting-place of the House of Commons from 1550.

[26] Two hundred years later in 1567 John le Carre brought glassmakers from Flanders and French glassmakers from Lorraine and Normandy to Britain. The Schurterres were "a native land-owning family", Kenyon **op.cit**, pp.36-37, 108, 115, 145.

[27] Kenyon **op.cit**, p.31, prints the text of the indenture from the Sadler Deeds in the Guildford Muniment Room (105/1/117).

bailiff of Atherington, the English procurator of the Bene-dictine Abbey of Seez in Normandy, for the use of 150 acres of woodland at Strudgwick and Hog Wood, as fuel to make a glass furnace.[28] The terms of the contract forbade the cutting of underwood in June and July, the months of maximum sap flow.

In 1400, at the beginning of Henry IV's reign, Peter Shortere, nephew of John junior, received £6 for supplying five "lodes" of glass to the royal palace at Westminster.[29] A load was two hundred cases or cradles of glass, weighing in all 1,200 lbs.[30] In 1475 there is documentary evidence of a marriage between Richard Shorter and Elizabeth, daughter of John Paytowe (Peytowe).[31] The Peytowes were another well-known family of glassmakers. In 1495 Thomas Shorter conveyed land, called "Estlond", to a member of another glassmaking family, Henry Ropley "glassecaryour".[32] Almeyns remained in the possession of the Schurterre/Shorter family until at least 1610, shortly before glassmaking ceased in the Weald during the reign of King James I.

The Chiddingfold registers record the christenings of John and Mercy, children of William Shorter and Elizabeth née Priest or Preist, at Chiddingfold in 1610 and 1611. However,

---

[28] Guildford Muniment Room, 105/1/119, text printed by Kenyon **op.cit.**, pp.31-32.

[29] **Journal of the British Society of Master Glass Painters**, vol.3, p.25, quoted by Kenyon **op.cit.**, p.29.; John's nephew, Peter Shortere, was also mentioned in a 1391 deed, Guildford Muniment Room 105/1/121, and Kenyon reasonably assumes that he is the glass supplier of 1400, Kenyon **op.cit., p.116.**

[30] Kenyon **op.cit.**, p.29. The amount was nearly the equivalent as that supplied by Alemayne to Westminster and Windsor in 1351.

[31] Guildford Muniment Room, 105/2/9, quoted by Kenyon **op.cit.**, p.117.

[32] Guildford Muniment Room 105/1/140, quoted by Kenyon **op.cit.**, p.29.

baby John died within two weeks of christening and was buried on December 10th 1610 [33]. Their daughter Mercy, is mistakenly named "Mary" in the International Genealogical Index.[34] These were the first and last Shorter family events recorded in the Chiddingfold registers, though the name Shorter appears in the registers of some neighbouring villages about the same time.

For two centuries and a half, therefore, the Schurterre/ Shorter family was associated with glassmaking in the Weald, and provided actual glassmakers over three generations. As Kenyon remarks, there may have been many other unrecorded glassmakers in the family.[35] Glassmaking, however, was not a full-time occupation. A John Schurterre is recorded as being a brewer in Chiddingfold in 1382, and this may have been the glassmaker, John junior.[36]

There are two further references to the Shorters of the Surrey Weald, dating from the 15th century. One is in a Close Roll of November 1481, in the reign of King Edward IV. Close Rolls or "Letters Close" were documents closed by the Great Seal, containing instructions to royal officers in the King's name. This particular letter concerned the gift of Knolles Manor, in the parish of Cranleigh, in the County of Surrey, to Robert Harding and others, held by demise of John Forster and Robert Shorter "gentilmen".[37] The town of Cranleigh is not far from

---

[33] Chiddingfold Registers seen on microfiche and in transcript at Surrey Record Office, Kingston on 21st July 1998.

[34] Study of the actual registers on microfiche revealed the error. The I.G.I. has, in fact, both a "Mary" and a "Mercy", baptized on 15th March 1611. "Mary" is a misreading and a duplication.

[35] Kenyon **op.cit.**, p.83.

[36] Loseley MSS.204, quoted by Kenyon **op.cit.**, p.116.

[37] **Calendar of Close Rolls**, P.R.O., Kraus Reprint, Munich 1954, Edward IV, Edward V, Richard III 1476-1485, no.805.

Chiddingfold, and the rank of gentleman suggests that members of the Shorter family were already beginning to better themselves.

In contrast to Close Rolls, the Patent Rolls or "Letters Patent" were public testimonials. One of these, dating from 1488, in the reign of King Henry VII, grants a pardon of outlawry to Thomas Shorter of Bletchingly, a "chapman".[38] Bletchingly lies further east from Chiddingfold and Cranleigh, on the other side of Redhill, and a chapman was a traveling salesman or pedlar. Thomas Shorter had failed to appear before the justices of the King's Bench to answer Hugh Brown, citizen and mercer of London, touching a debt of £20. 19s. 9d., and for this he required the royal pardon. A mercer was a dealer in fabrics and textiles, and, no doubt, Hugh Brown was one of Thomas Shorter's suppliers. There are numerous 16th century references to the Shorter family in the parish registers of Bletchingly.[39]

We can summarize the information as follows: we hear first of a John Schurterre (i) at Chiddingfold, who died in c.1369; of his son, John Schurterre or "Shertere" (ii), who was born c.1365, and of the latter's nephew, Peter Shortere, who flourished in 1400 and who could have been born in c.1380. The next information comes from the end of the fifteenth century, with the marriage at Chiddingfold of Richard Shorter in 1475 to Elizabeth Peytowe. We do not know if Richard was a descendant of Peter Shortere, but there would have been an intervening generation, if he was.

---

[38] **Calendar of Patent Rolls**, P.R.O., H.M.S.O., London 1914, Henry VII, Vol. I, 1485-1494, p.188. The pardon is dated: "Westminster June 11th 1488".

[39] cf. International Genealogical Index for Surrey.

The Shorters and the Royal Court

Two trends are noteworthy in the history of the Chiddingfold Shorters. One is the growing number of dealings which they had with the court. At this time, when window glass was first being introduced into buildings, the Shorters, as a leading family of glass-makers, had attracted royal notice. The other trend is that the Shorters began to lose interest in glass-making and to move nearer to Staines and London. At the end of the fifteenth century, in 1481, during the reign of King Edward IV, a Robert Shorter "gentilman" surrendered a royal manor, "held by demise", at Cranleigh, a small village in the vicinity of Chiddingfold. This had presumably been an instance of royal favour. In 1488 Thomas Shorter of Bletchingley received a favour from King Henry VII in the shape of a royal pardon for contempt of court. He was a retailer of fabrics and textiles and had been in debt to a London supplier.

Bletchingley lies to the north-east of Chiddingfold, a half-way house to Staines and London. The parish registers of Bletchingley contain numerous references to Shorters in the sixteenth century, and Thomas Shorter of Bletchingley may have been the Thomas Shorter who sold a family property, called Eastlond, in Chiddingfold in 1495 to a glass-maker called Henry Ropley.[40] Although the Shorters retained a meadow in Chiddingfold called Shorterhurst, it is doubtful if it was a glass-house site.[41] In the reign of Elizabeth I, eleven glass-furnaces were suppressed in the Chiddingfold area, and in 1615 the use of wood for fuel in glass-making was prohibited by King James I.[42] By that time the Shorters had abandoned glass-making at Chiddingfold. In 1609 they still owned their

---

[40] Kenyon, **op.cit.**, p.29

[41] Kenyon, **op.cit**, p. 158

[42] White, **op.cit**.

original Chiddingfold property, known as Almeyns, but this was disposed of shortly afterwards.

Soon after the Schurterres appeared in Surrey, a member of the family turned up in Wiltshire. At the end of Edward I's reign judicial measures were taken to deal with roving bandits, guilty of "trailbaston", or the carrying of clubs. In October 1306, William le Shorter was listed as a juror in the hundred of New Salisbury, in connection with trials for trailbaston.[43] There can be no doubt that this William was a member of the Chiddingfold family. His name, le Shorter, is similar to the form of the name in use at Chiddingfold in the first half of the 14th century, and, as far as we know, there were no other people of this name living outside the Chiddingfold area at the time. The Wiltshire William le Shorter may even be the "William le Shurtar" of 1332 mentioned above.

At the end of the following century, in 1483, we find John Shorter, "Yeoman of the Crown", a royal servant at Clarendon Park. Clarendon is now the name of a large mansion standing in a park of three hundred acres at Alderbury, not far from Salisbury.[44] To the north west of the present house are the ruins of Clarendon Palace. This was a residence of the Plantagenet kings, made famous by Henry II's enactment there in 1163 of the Constitutions of Clarendon. During the 15th century Wars of the Roses it seems to have been seldom used by the royal family, and it was eventually disposed of by the Tudors. In the reign of the Yorkist King Edward IV, however, the palace was still maintained, and the park was developed as a rabbit or **cony** warren.[45] Landowners commonly bred rabbits

---

[43] **Wiltshire Archaeological and Natural History Society**, Records Branch 33, 1978, "Gaol Delivery and Trailbaston", p.168; the "Roger le Shorter", mentioned by Reaney, **op.cit.**, sub **Shorter**, was not found.

[44] Walters, L.D'O., **A Complete Guide to Wiltshire**, London, 1920, p.156.

[45] **Cony** was a common medieval term for **rabbit** and for rabbit's fur.

in burrows on an enclosed piece of ground called a warren. Not only was rabbit meat an important ingredient in medieval cooking, but rabbit fur was in great demand for winter clothing and fur trimming.

A Close Roll of Richard III, dated February 8th 1483, refers to the appointment by Edward IV in the previous year of John Shorter, "Yeoman of the Crown", to be launderer at Clarendon, and to be paid in part from the revenues of the royal rabbit warren.

> To the Sherrif of Wilts for the time being. Order to pay John Shorter, Yeoman of the Crown, out of the revenues of that county, the sums undermentioned for his life, and the arrears since 15th November last; on which date, by letters patent, the King conferred on him the office of launderer (**landarius**) of the Park of Claringdon, to be occupied by himself or sufficient deputy with wages of 3d. a day and 13s. 4d. (one mark) for his winter robe; and 10s. at Easter for his summer robe annually, to be derived from the revenues of Wiltshire and the rabbit warren of Claringdon Park, such as John Cousin in the account of Ralph Cheyne, Sherrif of Wilts in 51 Edward III and Walter Worth in the account of John Moigne Sherrif in 18 Richard II received, as appears on record in the exchequer, with all profits, regards and emoluments to the same office annexed.[46]

John Shorter did not lose office when the Tudors came to power. In 1485, King Henry VII, the first Tudor King, confirmed him in office for life in almost identical terms. The Patent Roll, dated September 25th 1485, states that he is to be paid "out of the issues of the County of Wilts and the farm of

---

[46] **Calendar of Close Rolls**, P.R.O., Kraus Reprint, Munich 1954, Edward IV, Edward V, Richard III, 1476-1485, no.879, p.262.

the conies of the said park".[47]   Again, in 1490, King Henry VII granted the office of launderer, in survivorship, to the "King's servant, John Shorter, and Henry Uvedale, one of the King's sewers".[48]

During the 16th century members of the Shorter family appear in and around London: at Staines, Middlesex and in London parishes, notably the parish of St.Bartholomew Exchange. The first historian of the Staines Shorters, Gordon Willoughby James Gyll, a Victorian antiquarian, believed that they were connected to the royal launderer, but offered no evidence for his assertion.[49] It is possible that the royal launderer is the missing link between the Chiddingfold Shorters and the Staines Shorters.

A "Yeoman of the Crown" was a minor royal official, and the title survives today in the "Yeomen of the Guard" and the "Yeomen Warders" of the Tower of London, the corps founded by King Henry VIII. It should not be assumed that, because of his office, the royal launderer resided in Wiltshire, although his revenue came from there. Nor should it be assumed that the William le Shorter who had been listed as a juror in Wiltshire nearly two hundred years earlier had anything to do with the appointment. The royal launderer was empowered to fulfill his office by "sufficient deputy".[50] In any case, since the beginning of the fifteenth century the palace of Clarendon Park had been virtually abandoned by the court. The post of royal launderer at

---

[47] **Calendar of Patent Rolls**, P.R.O., H.M.S.O., London, Henry VII, Vol. I, 1485-1494, p.44. Membrane 4, (22).

[48] **Ibid.**, p.315, June 18th 1490, Membrane 30 (6).

[49] Gyll, Gordon Willoughby James, **A History of the Parish of Wraysbury, Ankerwycke Priory and Magna Charta Island**, London 1862, p.275.

[50] Calendar of Close Rolls, **loc.cit..**

Clarendon Park was therefore a sinecure in more ways than one. It may have been merely a nominal form of royal patronage, a means of rewarding a subject who had obtained the King's favor.

Such patronage would not have been obtained through residence in Wiltshire, in the vicinity of the empty palace. It could only have been obtained through proximity to the actual court, and the court was to be found, increasingly in the fifteenth and sixteenth centuries, at residences up river from London: Richmond, Sheen, Windsor and eventually Hampton Court. The town of Staines and its neighbor, the town of Colnbrook, were strategically placed on the rivers Thames and Colne, in the vicinity of these royal residences. Both Staines and Colnbrook were regarded as royalist enclaves, and were recipients of royal favors and charters. The Shorter family probably moved to Staines and Colnbrook because they enjoyed, or expected to enjoy, royal favor. Equally, they were obliged to leave these places and go to London, when they threw in their lot with Parliament at the outbreak of the English Civil War.

John Shorter, the royal launderer, may have been the first member of the family to reside at Staines. Richard Shorter of Chiddingfold, Robert Shorter of Cranleigh, Thomas Shorter of Bletchingley and John Shorter, the royal launderer, were contemporaries. We do not know their genealogical relationship, but it is possible that they were brothers, or at least cousins. Each in his own way contributed to the decline of the family in Chiddingfold and/or to the rise of the Shorters in other places, chiefly through royal favor and patronage. When the seventeenth century opens, the Shorters at Chiddingfold itself are a mere remnant of a once flourishing land-owning and glass-making family. However, the appointment of John Shorter, Yeoman of the Crown, as royal launderer in 1482 would seem to be the culmination of a process of royal patronage begun by the Chiddingfold Shorters.

18 The Shorter Family

By the end of the 17th century, the Shorter family were well established in West Sussex, and branches of the family appeared in Buckinghamshire, Oxfordshire, East Sussex and Kent (Canterbury); in the 18th century, in West Kent, East Anglia and subsequently, the Midlands. The remainder of this story concerns the Staines branch of the Shorter family and their descendants in London and Mountfield (East Sussex).

CHAPTER THREE

BAKERS AND CHAPEL WARDENS

The Shorter Family in Staines

The town of Staines has been prominent in national affairs for much of England's history. This was mainly due to its proximity to the seat of government at London, sixteen miles away, and to its closeness to the royal seat at Windsor. Also in the vicinity is Runnymede where Magna Carta was signed by King John. Staines was strategically placed on a crossing of the river Thames. From the 12th to the 18th century it possessed the first bridge up river from London, and over that bridge lay the main road to the south west, the Roman road to Silchester. It is not surprising that Staines is mentioned in Shakespeare's histories or that Staines bridge was frequently the first casualty in a civil war.[51]

Soldiers were frequently billeted in Staines, and in 1642, when the Parliamentarians fortified London, the Royalist army occupied the town, and the bridge was partially dismantled.

---

[51] An example is: **Henry V**, Act 2, Scene 3, in which Mistress Quickly says to her husband, Pistol: "Prithee, honey, sweet husband, let me bring thee to Staines". She was offering to escort him to London's furthest boundary and put him on the road to Southampton where the king was embarking his army for France.

Staines thrived as a supply area for London, providing agricultural and market garden produce.[52] Although London was nearby, the roads were not always usable. In 1623, there were complaints that the posts from London took ten hours to reach Staines, and Samuel Pepys became lost at night in the forest near Staines on August 19th 1665.[53] The river, however, provided easier and cheaper transport to London, and all the water of the Thames, from Greenwich to Staines, lay under the jurisdiction of the Lord Mayor and Aldermen of London. The importance of the river to the inhabitants of Staines may help to explain the later involvement of the Staines branch of the Shorter family with the Thames, with boat building and with river transport.

Our chief source for the Shorter family in Staines, and in the neighbouring town of Colnbrook, is Gordon Willoughby James Gyll, a Victorian antiquarian who was interested in the history of Wraysbury and its neighboring parishes.[54] However, Gyll is not always reliable, nor is he consistent in revealing his sources.[55] A valuable corrective is provided by the Shorter Pedigree contained in the 1664 Visitation of London (which actually dates from 1674), and its published variants and additions.[56] This pedigree is chiefly concerned with the descent

---

[52] Cf. Smithers, M. M., **Staines an Illustrated Record**, Shepperton Surrey, 1982; and Pugh, R.B.(ed.), **Victoria History of the Counties of England**, Middlesex, vol.3, 1962, pp.13-14.

[53] **Ibid.**, p.14.; **The Diary of Samuel Pepys**, abridgement of the 1825 edition, Collins, London, no date, p.257.

[54] Gyll, G. W. J, **A History of the Parish of Wraysbury, Ankerwycke Priory and Magna Charta Island**, London, 1862.

[55] An example of Gyll's unreliability is his statement (Gyll **op.cit.** p.274) that John Shorter (2) of Colnbrook was born in 1604, while in the genealogical table (p.275) he gives the same John (2)'s birth date as 1614.

[56] MS of the **Heralds' Visitation of London 1664**, College of Arms, p.135; **London Visitation Pedigrees 1664**, Harleian Society, vol.92, p.124; **Peter**

of Sir John Shorter (4) and his brother Charles (1), and the versions are not complete. While they include the senior male branches of the family, they omit females and junior lines. Another source is provided by the parish registers of Staines and Horton.[57] Finally, there are the records contained in the Colnbrook Town Book, as well as other occasional documents.[58]

The Staines parish registers begin in the early years of King Henry VIII's reign, and they reveal the Shorter family already established in the town. The birth of Thomas Shorter is recorded on August 18th 1529, Thomas son of John Shorter on July 3rd 1541, William son of William Shorter on August 28th 1542, and other children of John Shorter born in 1543 and 1546. The marriage of Thomas Shorter to Mistress Coteno is recorded on June 24th 1530.[59] We do not know for certain where the Staines Shorters came from. Gyll assumes they were connected with John Shorter, the royal launderer, but offers no evidence.[60] The Surrey glassmakers, as we have seen, had contacts with the royal household up river from Staines, and, as we suggested in Chapter Two, members of the family may have come to Staines in expectation of further royal patronage.

Le Neve's Pedigrees of Knights - 1718, Harleian Society, vol.8 (Harleian MS.5801), pp.301-302.

[57] Registers of St.Mary's Staines, Middlesex, Greater London Record Office, X90/105; Transcript of Horton Parish Registers, Buckinghamshire, Society of Genealogists (BU R24).

[58] **Colnbrook Town Book**, Buckinghamshire County Archives, 15/82/1. References to other documents will be given when they are cited.

[59] Cf. Staines registers. "Mistress" is the author's reading of an abbreviation which occurs in the marriage list.

[60] Gyll **op.cit.**, p.275.

22 The Shorter Family

The Staines parish registers open in a fine, rounded script, but the writing deteriorates towards the end of Henry VIII's reign. After his death in 1547, the registers become fragmentary and illegible, but they pick up again towards the end of the reign of Queen Elizabeth I. Without doubt, the religious upheavals of the Reformation period are responsible for this hiatus in the record. Lapses in the 17th century registers are responsible for further gaps in our knowledge. A clear pattern of relationships, however, begins to emerge around 1600 with John Shorter (1) and his family, but the links between these Elizabethan and Jacobean Shorters and their Henrician forbears can only be guessed. As will appear, the Shorters seem to have emerged from the Reformation era as Protestants with a tendency towards Puritanism.

John Shorter (1), who died in 1614, was born c.1550 during this disturbed Reformation period, either in the reign of King Edward VI or Queen Mary I. His baptismal entry has not been identified. There was, however, as we have seen, an earlier Henrician John Shorter, whom we shall call "John Shorter (i)", to whom a son, Thomas, was born in 1541 and other children in 1543 and 1546.[61] It is likely that he also had a son who was his namesake, and it is chronologically possible and genealogically likely that John (1), born c.1550, was this son. The registers also record the baptism of a William (ii), son of William (i), in 1542. William (i) may have been the brother of John (i). If John Shorter, the royal launderer, was the first member of the family to reside at Staines, then it is also chronologically possible that he was the father of John (i) (born c.1510), as well as of William (i) (born c.1505), and possibly of Thomas (born c.1529).

---

[61] Both these were sons named Henry, the first probably having died in infancy. Small Roman numerals "John (i)" are used to distinguish the Shorter lines which were not descended from John (1).

John Shorter (1) (c.1550-1614) married a wife named Elizabeth. He is also known to have been a baker by trade.[62] The
manuscript of the 1664 London Visitation, in the College of
Arms, calls him "Gentleman", but this may have been a
retrospective honor in virtue of his grandson's knighthood.[63]
No doubt, running a bakery at Staines was a profitable
business, given the amount of traffic which passed through the
town. John (1) died in 1614, and the business passed to his
second son, John (2). John (1)'s eldest son William (1) moved
to Colnbrook after two sons were born to him in Staines.
Probably, he is the William whose wife was called Jane, and
who had sons born to him in March 1625 and November 1627,
named Edward and William (2) respectively. He is described as
"son and heir" in the Heralds' Visitation, but only William (2)
is noted among his children.[64] Probably, William (1) was
already dead at the time of the Visitation entry (1674), and
William (2) was the eldest surviving son. Nothing further is
known about William (1) and his family. The old registers of
the Free Chapel of St.Mary, Colnbrook have all disappeared,
and there is no trace of William (1) in the registers of the
neighboring parish of Horton.[65]

John (1) had two further sons, Henry (1) who will be discus-
sed later in this chapter and Nicholas. Nicholas Shorter married
Elizabeth Ward at Stoke Poges, Buckinghamshire, in 1603, and
died there in 1629.[66] Finally, John (1) had a daughter named

---

[62] **Heralds' Visitation of London 1664; London Visitation Pedigrees; Le
Neve**.

[63] Cf. **Heralds' Visitation of London 1664**, p.135.

[64] **Ibid.**, p.135.

[65] Gyll , **op.cit.**, p.290.

[66] Cf. Gyll, **op.cit.**, p.275; Boyd's Marriage Index, Society of Genealogists.
The Stoke Poges parish registers only begin in 1653.

Elizabeth (1) who married William Walton of Staines, a cordwainer, by licence on March 26th 1614.[67]

John Shorter (2) was probably born c.1580. He married Susan, the second daughter of Richard Forbis (alias Forbench, Forbanch or Forebank) of Send, Surrey, and had a family of five sons and two daughters. Elizabeth (2) was probably the eldest, born in 1605, and had already come of age when her father made his will in 1634.[68] From her brother John (4)'s will in 1688 we learn that her married name was Bull. The will mentions her children, but not Elizabeth (2) herself, which suggests that she was already dead by 1688.[69]

John (2)'s eldest son was Richard (1), baptized on May 18th 1606.[70] He is mentioned first in John (2)'s will. After Richard, there is a gap of eighteen years. Children may have been born to John (2) and Susan, during that time, but their absence from his 1634 will suggests that they did not survive. The baptismal and burial registers are again difficult to read at this point. John (2)'s second son, John (4), was baptized on September 19th 1624.[71] A third son, Andrew, was baptized on August 20th 1626 and buried on July 23rd 1627.[72] William, the fourth son,

---

[67] **London Visitation Pedigrees**, Harl. vol.92, p.124; Boyd's Marriage Index, Society of Genealogists.

[68] The Staines registers mention an Elizabeth, daughter of John Shorter, baptized May 31st 1605; P.C.C., Seager 45, 1634.

[69] P.C.C., Exton 129, 1688; she is clearly not the Elizabeth Shorter who married Richard Bull at St. Marylebone in 1683.

[70] Staines Registers, G.L.R.O., X90/105; and **Heralds' Visitation of London 1664**.

[71] Staines Registers, G.L.R.O., X90/105; and 1664 London Visitation.

[72] Staines Registers, G.L.R.O., X90/105.

was baptized in November 1627.[73] William is mentioned in the 1634 will, but not in the 1664 London Visitation, which means that he almost certainly died at an early age. Had he been alive, he would have been mentioned, since he was older than Charles (1). A second daughter, Susanna (1), was born to John (2) around 1628.[74] She is mentioned as being under age in the 1634 will. She may have been married to Thomas Kent, whom John (4) calls "my brother" in his will of 1688 and is presumed to be alive at that time.[75] Finally, Charles (1), the fifth son, was born in c.1629.[76]

King Charles I had already been on the throne for nine years when John (2) made his will on May 8th 1634, "trusting to be saved by the precious death and bloodshedding of Jesus Christ, my only Saviour and alone Redeemer". He bequeathed £10 to Richard and 71 s. to Elizabeth. To John, William, Susanna and Charles he left £10 each when they should come of age. The rest of his goods and chattels he bequeathed to his "loving wife" Susanna, "requesting of her to have a special care in the bringing up of my children in the fear of the Lord".

The Shorters of Colnbrook and Horton

Like his elder brother John (2), Henry Shorter (1) was probably born at Staines in the reign of Elizabeth I, moving in later

---

[73] "November" is conjectural, due to the illegibility of the Staines Registers at this point, G.L.R.O.

[74] The Staines Registers are illegible for the most part at this point, and her birth/baptism has not been traced.

[75] P.C.C. Exton 129, 1688.

[76] He is the last born of John (2)'s children to be mentioned in the 1634 will, P.C.C. Seager 45. His age is not given in the 1664 London Visitation, and his baptism cannot be traced in the Staines registers.

life to Colnbrook town. The town is situated in the Chiltern Hundreds, to the north east of Staines, just inside the border of Buckinghamshire, seventeen miles from London. The town stood across four channels of the river Colne, and, like Staines, also played a considerable role in English history.[77] The conspirators against King Henry IV met at Colnbrook in 1400. A petition for peace was presented to King Charles I there, after the battle of Edgehill in 1642, and after the battle of Brentford, Prince Rupert plundered the town and imprisoned all known Parliamentarians.

What was unusual for a town of some importance, like Colnbrook, was the fact that it did not have a fully fledged parish. Its church was St. Mary's Chapel, a perpetual curacy of the archdeaconry of Buckingham. The chapel was rebuilt in the 1790s and was finally replaced by the new church of St.Thomas when the parish was set up in 1852. All the old registers before that date have disappeared. Colnbrook town, however, received a royal charter from King Henry VIII in 1543, and a second charter from King Charles I in 1635.

The southern part of Colnbrook township lay in the parish of Horton. This was a pleasant rural area where the Digby family were part owners of the manor. John Milton's father rented a house in Horton in 1632, and the poet lived there for six years. It is said that his inspiration for **L'Allegro** and **Il Penseroso** came from scenery in the Horton neighborhood.[78] The Colne Bridge Mills at Horton were used for paper making, and rags collected in London for the process brought the plague to the area in 1626, killing 34 people.[79]

---

[77] Cf. Gyll, **op.cit.**, pp.211, 284, 290-291, 298; Page, William (ed.) **Victoria History of the Counties of England**, Buckinghamshire, vol.3, 1925, pp.246, 248, 281-282.

[78] Page, **op.cit.**, p.281.

[79] Page, **op.cit.**, p.282.

Henry Shorter (1) owned land in Horton and in 1613, together with Sir Robert Digby and others he was involved in a land transaction.[80] He was also a functionary of Colnbrook Town. The Colnbrook Chapel Wardens were elected democratically and exercised various civic functions. This was especially the case during the English Civil War when the town corporation ceased to function. Henry (1)'s name appears several times in the Colnbrook Town Book. On April 12th 1615 he was elected Chapel Warden, "with the consent of the inhabitants of Colnbrook".[81] During that year his name appears in connection with the accounts, and finally at Easter 1616 his signature is found in the Town Book, attesting the election of new Chapel Wardens. On October 25th 1616, the Horton parish registers record his burial.[82] According to Gyll, Henry (1)'s wife was called Margaret, but in the Horton registers her burial on September 6th 1629 is simply recorded as that of "Widow Shorter".[83] Henry (1)'s eldest son Henry (2) was probably born before his father settled in Colnbrook Town, and we know for certain that his wife's name was Margaret. It is likely that she was the Margaret Collins married to Henry Shorter at St. Dunstan's in the West in 1629. This marriage took place during the incumbency of the poet John Donne, who was Dean of St.Paul's and who, at the same time, diligently performed the duties of Rector of St. Dunstan's. Incidentally, in the year of Henry (2) and Margaret's wedding, Isaac Walton was a

---

[80] P.R.O., CP25/2 275/11 Jas 1/Trin.

[81] **Colnbrook Town Book**, Buckinghamshire County Archives, 15/82/1.

[82] **Ibid.**; Transcript of Horton Registers, Society of Genealogists, BU R24.

[83] Gyll, **op.cit.**, p.275; Horton Registers **loc.cit.** Gyll may have been muddling the names of the wives of Henry (1) and Henry (2).

sidesman at this church.[84] Henry (2) and Margaret had two daughters, Barbarie baptized on April 20th 1632, and Elizabeth baptized on April 20th 1637.[85]

Henry (1)'s second son, John (3), was baptized at Horton on July 15th 1604.[86] His name appears in the Colnbrook Town Book in 1626, as elected to be collector of the Horton tithe.[87] A third son, Richard (2) was baptized on October 3rd 1609. Finally, Henry (1) had a daughter named Joanna. Her birth has not been traced, but, since she married for the second time in 1632, she was probably older than John (3) and Richard (2), and was probably born before the family came to Horton. Her first marriage was to Edward Tyrrel of St.Dunstan's, her second (in 1632) to Nathaniel Whetham.[88]

Nathaniel Whetham was remembered by a Shorter nephew, John (5), as "my loving uncle".[89] He played an important role in Oliver Cromwell's army, being appointed firstly Governor of Portsmouth, and then one of the Commissioners for Scotland.[90] After the abdication of Richard Cromwell as Protector, Whetham was appointed Colonel of Foot in the

---

[84] The church is also notorious as being the one in which Samuel Pepys was threatened by a girl wielding a hat pin after he had made advances to her on August 18th 1666.

[85] Horton Registers, **loc.cit.**

[86] Horton Registers, **loc.cit.**

[87] **Colnbrook Town Book**, Buckinghamshire County Archives, 15/82/1.

[88] Gyll, **op.cit.**, p.275.

[89] P.C.C. Parr 120, 1667.

[90] Firth, Charles, and Davis, Godfrey, **The Regimental History of Cromwell's Army**, Oxford 1940 (1991 ed.), vol.1, p.251; vol.2, pp.584-585.

Commonwealth army on February 10th 1660. He garrisoned Chichester and Thorncomb and entered into communication with General Monk. He seems to have opposed the continuance of military rule and to have played a small part in the events that led to the Restoration of King Charles II in the same year.[91]

The name Shorter disappears from the Colnbrook records after 1634. In that year John (3) conveyed his land and property in Horton to Robert Biddle. It consisted of one messuage or dwelling, a garden, an orchard and two acres of farmland.[92] In the same year his uncle John (2) the baker, died at Staines. It seems that the Shorters regrouped at Staines before moving to London, since Richard (2) appears in the Staines registers shortly afterwards. A son (John) born to his wife Dorothy on May 20th 1638 was buried on October 8th of the same year.[93] Twenty years later, as we shall see, Richard (2) and Dorothy were living at Blackfriars in London, while Richard (1), John (4) and Charles (1) of Staines were all living in the several parishes of Southwark. It will be argued in Chapter Thirteen (Part Two) that John (3) of Colnbrook, who sold all his property and disappeared in 1634, may have been the John Shorter who sailed to Virginia in 1635.

John Shorter (iii) ("Jhon [sic], son of Jhon [sic] Shorter Senior" - i.e. John Shorter (ii)), was christened at Staines on 26th February 1602 [94]. A daughter called Martha was christened on 2nd October 1603 and a son called Humphra on

---

[91] Firth and Davis, **op.cit.**, vol.2, p.560.

[92] P.R.O., CP25/2 398/10 Chas I/Mich.

[93] Staines registers, G.L.R.O., X90/105.

[94] Staines registers, G.L.R.O., X90/105. The Greater London Record Office is now renamed the London Metropolitan Archive, but the microfilm reference is unchanged.

14th December 1610. [95]. Finally, another son, Richard, was christened on 22nd January 1613. John (ii) was probably the son of William (ii). It will be argued in Chapter Seven that John (iii) was possibly John Shorter, the Waterman, who also lived in Southwark. The Waterman's son Thomas was regarded as a kinsman of Sir John Shorter (4)'s granddaughter Catherine, Lady Walpole, although he did not belong to the immediate family of the Lord Mayor.

There can be little doubt that the removal of the Shorter family from Staines to London was caused by the outbreak of the English Civil War. With their Puritan sympathies and parliamentary connections, it would not have been safe for them to remain in the royalist climate of Staines and Colnbrook. However, there were some later family links with Staines. In 1653, under Oliver Cromwell's Protectorate, the Staines parish registers record that one Thomas Shorter was clerk of the parish and involved in poor relief. Finally John (8), the son of Charles (1) moved back to Staines with his wife Elizabeth at the beginning of the 18th century. It was there that their three children were born and Elizabeth herself was buried.[96] We now follow the fortunes of the Shorter family in London.

---

[95] I am grateful to the archivist of the London Metropolitan Archive for helping me to decipher the Jacobean writing of this entry, on 26th May 2000.

[96] Cf. Staines Registers, G.L.R.O., X90/105.

CHAPTER FOUR

NORWAY MERCHANT AND RULER OF LONDON

Early Life of Sir John Shorter in London

Most, if not all, the Shorters of Staines and Colnbrook moved to London when the English Civil War broke out. By 1674 the three surviving sons of John (2) were installed in three Southwark parishes: Richard (1) in the parish of St. George the Martyr, John (4) in Christchurch parish, and Charles (1) in the parish of St. Saviour (formerly St. Mary Overie), later to become Southwark Cathedral.[97]

Three years later, **The Little London Directory** gives John's residence as Bankside, and that of Charles as "Queen Hive".[98] The Parish of St. George the Martyr is first mentioned in the 12th century. During Richard Shorter (1)'s residence there, the body of Oliver Cromwell was received at the church in 1658, and taken thence to Somerset House for its lying-in-state. Richard (1)'s first son was baptized there in 1645.[99]

---

[97] **Heralds' Visitation of London 1664** (1674), p.135.

[98] **Little London Directory of 1677**, London 1878, **sub** Shorter.

[99] Registers of St. George the Martyr, G.L.R.O. (X92/30), February 4th 1644/5.

At the time of his death in 1688 John (4) held property in several parts of London, in the city, in Westminster and in Southwark.[100] Bankside in Southwark was a narrow street along the river Thames, lined with wharves and warehouses. It was also the site of London's oldest theatres, the Rose Theatre demolished at the beginning of the 17th century, and Shakespeare's Globe Theatre. This was closed by the Puritans in 1642, at about the time the Shorter family moved into Southwark, and was demolished two years later. Their place was largely taken by gardens and brewhouses. John Shorter (4)'s business partner, Josiah Child, was, among other things, a brewer, and John (4) himself mentions a brewhouse and coalyard, among his property in Christchurch parish.[101] According to Woodhead, John (4)'s Bankside property included "a great dock", and his will mentions a house in Christchurch, as well as other edifices and yards.[102] The parish of Christchurch did not come into existence until 1671, some thirty years after the Shorters moved to Southwark, the church being built on part of the so-called Paris Garden Manor. In spite of this change of parish, John (4) and his son John (9) were both buried at St. Saviour's.[103]

"Queen Hive" refers to Queen Hithe, a wharf off Upper Thames Street on the north bank of the river. Presumably this was the business address of Charles Shorter (1), since he and his family continued to be associated with St. Saviour's

---

[100] cf. His will, P.C.C., Exton 129, 1688.

[101] P.C.C. Exton, 129, 1688.

[102] Woodhead, J.R., **The Rulers of London 1660-1689**, London and Middlesex Archaeological Society, 1965, p.149; P.C.C. Exton 129.

[103] For John (4) cf. discussion below about his tomb; for John (9), cf. will of John (11), P.C.C., Edmunds, 746.

parish.[104] It should also be mentioned that no fewer than seven prisons were situated in Southwark, the most famous being the Clink and the Marshalsea prisons, both used mainly for debtors.

At the age of seventeen, John (4) was apprenticed to James Shirley of the Goldsmiths' Company in 1641, and, after becoming a fully-fledged goldsmith in 1668, he was eventually elected Prime Warden of the Goldsmiths in 1676.[105] His first claim to fame, however, was as Captain of the London Trained Bands.[106] The London Trained Bands were the elite of the local militia, affiliated to the Honorable Artillery Company. During the English Civil War they were greatly increased in strength and saw service in engagements outside London, at the relief of Gloucester and the battle of Newbury. The young John (4) was eighteen years old when the Civil War broke out, and his promotion to Captain suggests that he distinguished himself as a soldier.[107] Afterwards, as Lord Mayor, he was made Colonel of the Yellow Regiment in 1687.[108] This honor may also have been due to his military reputation in the Trained Bands.

A portrait of John (4) by an unknown painter shows him with fine features, a pointed beard, a high lace collar and lace cuffs,

---

[104] Charles (1)'s will confirms the fact, P.C.C., Pyne 40, 1697.

[105] Woodhead, **op.cit.**, p.149; Baddeley, John James, **The Aldermen of Cripplegate Ward from A.D.1276 to A.D.1900**, London 1900, p.79; Heal, Ambrose, **The London Goldsmiths 1200-1800**, Cambridge University Press 1935, p.242.

[106] Harleian, vol.92; Le Neve, **op.cit.**, p.301; **Notes and Queries**, 6th s., X, p.72.

[107] Numerous authorities, following, the **Heralds' Visitation of London 1664** and its published versions in Harleian vol.92 and Le Neve, **op.cit.**, which state that he was 49 years old in 1674, calculate his year of birth as 1625. The Staines registers, however, show clearly that he was born in 1624.

[108] Woodhead, **op.cit.**, p.149.

in the style of the 1630s-1640s.[109] A later portrait shows John (4) as a rather coarse, long-haired Puritan, wearing a cloak and white neckerchief.[110]

Supplier of Timber to the Navy

After the English Civil War, John (4) built up a fortune from the timber trade in partnership with Josiah Child, a banker and one of the biggest merchants in the country.[111] John (4) was called variously a "Norway merchant" and a "Danish timber merchant".[112] His son John (9) to whom he bequeathed his yards "as long as he shall use and assign the said yards the trade of Norway merchant", owned ships running to Norway, Sweden and Denmark.[113] One of the principal heirlooms bequeathed by John (4)'s brother Charles (1) to his son, John (8), was his "Norway silver tankard".[114] No doubt, John (4) did business with the Baltic countries as well as with Norway, but he seems to have preferred the title "Norway merchant". As we shall see in Chapter Fourteen, Part Two, Sir John Shorter (4) and his son John Shorter (9) of Bybrook, crossed the Atlantic several times to New England and Virginia, to explore new American sources of timber.

---

[109] Original in the collection of Lady Thornton.

[110] Print in the Sutherland Collection of the Ashmolean Museum, Oxford, from an original at Strawberry Hill, now in the possession of Earl Waldegrave.

[111] **Notes and Queries**, 7th s. IV, p.142, 181; Bryant, Arthur, **Samuel Pepys: The Man in the Making**, London 1967, p.209.

[112] **Notes and Queries**, 2nd s. XII, p.14; Gyll, **op.cit.**, p.274.

[113] P.C.C. Exton 129, 1688; **Notes and Queries**, 7th s. IV, p.142.

[114] P.C.C., Pyne 40, 1697.

In 1665 he and Child, who also provisioned the fleet, contracted with the Navy for masts, yards and bowsprits.[115] Three years earlier, however, there was an abortive contract mentioned by Samuel Pepys, Clerk of the Acts at the Navy Board. Pepys, defending his massive contract with Sir William Warren for Scandinavian timber in 1663, wrote in a letter to Commissioner Peter Pett in June 1665:

> That to this hour I never heard you, either publicly or privately, oppose this contract or offer any better or other, saving one with Mr. Shorter, which he upon treaty did voluntary decline...[116]

The "Mr. Shorter" of Pepys's letter is almost certainly John (4). Although his brother Charles (1) was also in the timber trade, he seems to have operated on a smaller scale.

In 1663, the year of Pepys's aborted contract, John (4) entered the ranks of the gentry, being granted armorial bearings by the College of Arms on November 20th, as follows: "John Shorter of London, merchant" - Arms: **Per saltire or and sable a bordure counterchanged**. Crest: **A griphon's head sable gorged with a collar and between the wings or**.[117] This simple but attractive heraldic "ordinary", the **saltire**, was later superseded by a more elaborate coat, but the griphon crest remained the same. It seems to have been inspired by an earlier grant to "Shorter of Kent" in 1614 of arms as follows: **Azure a griphon passant or between three estoiles argent**. Crest: **A griphon's head and neck or between wings azure semee of stars**

---

[115] **Notes and Queries**, 7th s. IV, p.181.

[116] Bryant **op.cit.**, p.191.

[117] Patent dated November 20th 1663 to John Shorter of London, merchant. Cf. Letter of Archibald Russell, Lancaster Herald, to the author 20.4.48.

argent.[118] The only Shorters present in Kent at the beginning of the 17th century appear to be those of Canterbury, and, as far as can be ascertained, they were unrelated to the Staines Shorters.[119]

A few years earlier, John (4) married Isabella, the daughter of John Birkett of Crosthwaite, Borrowdale in Cumbria.[120] We do not know how he met his bride, nor has the date of his marriage been traced. However, a son was born to them, John (9) in 1660, the year of King Charles II's Restoration.[121] In June 1674 a second son, Thomas (1), was born to them. The Christchurch baptismal register was badly damaged by fire and only a central fragment of each page survives. However, the month and year of Thomas (1)'s birth can be identified.[122] There were no other children of the marriage.

By the time of Thomas (1)'s birth John (4) was a prosperous and well known London merchant. In the following year, 1675, he was named Sheriff of London and Middlesex, together with

---

[118] November 1614 Arms and Crest assigned by Patent to "Shorter of Kent". The author has inspected the register at the College of Arms, and the document offers no further information concerning the identity of the recipient.

[119] However, their coat of arms is substantially similar to that of **Shorte** or **Shorter** of Staffordshire. cf. Harl. vol. 17, p.237: **Azure a griffin rampant between three estoiles argent. Crest: A griffin's head and neck argent between two wings displayed azure**.

[120] This is the probable interpretation of "Croistath in Burroughdale in Com.Cumberland", given by the **Heralds' Visitation of London 1664**.

[121] The birthplace and exact date of birth have not been traced. The calculation is based on the **Heralds' Visitation of London 1664**, in which John (9)'s age in 1674 is given as 14.

[122] The International Genealogical Index gives the parents as "John and Jezabella"; cf. Christchurch Southwark Registers, G.L.R.O., X 15/146.

Thomas Gold.[123]   The sheriffs attended the Lord Mayor, had certain legal duties and acted as links between the city and the House of Commons. John (4) was knighted by King Charles II at Guildhall on October 29th 1675, and in the following year was elected Alderman of Cripplegate Ward on July 4th.[124]

In October 1676 Sir John (4) became President of the Bridewell and Bethlehem Hospitals, and retained these posts until his death. Bridewell stood on the site of a former royal palace beside the Fleet river. It was a prison, a hospital and a workhouse, intended for vagrants, homeless children, petty offenders and disorderly women. When Sir John (4) assumed his duties, it had been recently rebuilt after the Great Fire, and, unlike other places of this kind, had teaching and medical staff. A regular feature of the institution were the twice-weekly public flogging sessions, in which the punishment was brought to an end by the president of the court, knocking the table with a hammer.[125] Bethlehem Royal Hospital, or "Bedlam" as it was popularly called, was a lunatic asylum, and had just been tranferred in 1676 to a magnificent new building, intended by Robert Hooke, its architect, to resemble the Tuileries in Paris. Sir John (4) was the first president of the new establishment. The chained patients were placed in cells along the galleries, like caged animals in a menagerie. Bedlam was one of the sights of London and donations from the public contributed to its running costs.[126]

Five years later, in 1681, Sir John (4) was nominated as a Whig candidate for the office of Lord Mayor, in opposition to

---

[123] Baddeley, **op.cit.**, p.79; Woodhead, **op.cit.**, p.149.

[124] Baddeley **op.cit.**, p.79.

[125] cf. Weinreb, Ben and Hibbert, Christopher, **The London Encyclopaedia**, London 1983, **sub** "Bridewell", pp.86-87.

[126] **Ibid.**, **sub** "Bethlehem Royal Hospital", p.60.

the court favorite, Sir John Moore. Moore polled 1,831 votes and Sir John (4), 1,591.[127] In December 1682, however, Sir John (4) fell foul of Charles II for attending an unauthorized assembly of Dissenters, or conventicle, at Pinmakers' Hall, and the Court of Aldermen was ordered to remove him from his Aldermanry. This was effected by a **Quo Warranto** judgment in October 1663.[128]

Lord Mayor of London

King Charles II died in 1685, to be succeeded by his brother, James II. With the accession of James, Sir John (4)'s fortunes changed. The new king was a Roman Catholic, who was determined to promote his Church by every means at his disposal. In his campaign against the established Church he courted the support of Dissenters, such as Sir John Shorter (4). It is also possible that he was acquainted with him as a supplier of timber to the navy, when he was Lord High Admiral. In any case, having superseded the City Charter by Royal Commission, he restored Sir John (4) to his Aldermanry on August 6th 1687, and to his rank of precedence. By the same usurped authority, the King appointed Sir John Shorter (4) to be Lord Mayor of London on October 29th in the same year.[129]

The royal patent of appointment bestowed an exceptional favor on the new Lord Mayor. He was allowed to decide on his own form of service in the Mayoral Chapel and to have whomsoever he pleased to preach before him.[130] It seems,

---

[127] Baddeley, **op.cit.**, p.79.

[128] Baddeley, **op.cit.**, p.79; **Notes and Queries**, 7th s. vol. IV, p.61.

[129] Baddeley, **op.cit.**, pp.79-80; Woodhead, **op.cit.**, p.149; Beaven, J., **The Aldermen of the City of London**, London 1913, vol.2, p.191.

[130] **Notes and Queries**, **Ibid.**; Baddeley, **loc.cit.**.

however, that Sir John (4) acted circumspectly and did not avail himself of this privilege. He did not, in fact, appoint an official chaplain, or hold any religious service in the Guildhall chapel. It is known, however, that John Bunyan, the author of **Pilgrim's Progress** and one of the founding fathers of the Baptists, was a member of Sir John (4)'s household for a time, and that Bunyan had a chapel in Southwark. The Southwark antiquarian, Thompson, described the relationship:

> Sir John Shorter, Lord Mayor of London, who lies buried in our Lady Chapel, is said to have so valued the ministrations of Bunyan, and bestowed so much friendship on him, that he was looked upon as his Lordship's chaplain (unofficially of course) in the year 1688 when both passed to their celestial city, let us hope.[131]

This is perhaps the place to ask what Sir John (4)'s religious convictions were. Gyll's statement that he was "a supposed Papist" may be discounted without any need for discussion.[132] Narcissus Luttrell, who is our authority for much of the information concerning Sir John (4)'s inauguration, calls him "a great Presbyterian", while the diarist, John Evelyn, referred to the new Lord Mayor in characteristically supercilious terms, as "an Anabaptist, a very odd, ignorant person, a mechanic, I think".[133] By "mechanic", Evelyn probably meant "artisan". This diversity of denominations attributed to Sir John (4), coupled with his apparent readiness to kiss the Catholic king's hands and accept the mayoralty, may suggest a certain

---

[131] Thompson, Canon, **The History and Antiquities of Southwark Cathedral**, London 1910, p.229. Sir John (4) died four days after Bunyan, cf. **Notes and Queries**, 7th s. vol. IV, p.61.

[132] Gyll **op.cit.**, p.274.

[133] Baddeley **op.cit.**, p.79, quoting Luttrell, N., **Diary**, vol.I, p.417; Evelyn, John, **Diary**, ed. Bray W., London 1879, vol. 3, p.41. (The editor mistakenly identifies the Lord Mayor in question as Sir John Peake).

elasticity of conscience. However, this suggestion does not seem to be supported by the evidence. In his will, which was drawn up in August 1688, he expressed anxiety about the religious upbringing of his younger son Thomas. He was "to be brought up in the fear of God and instructed in the Protestant religion".[134] It seems, moreover, that he was not so much an out and out Non-Conformist, as an occasional conformist, who publicly took the Sacrament according to the usages of the Church of England.[135] There is no doubt, however, that he had Puritan leanings at a time when the various Non-Conformist denominations were in a largely embryonic stage of development. He is known to have taken regular advice from the Puritan party leaders, and to have invited dissenting ministers of various denominations to Grocers' Hall, which then served as the Lord Mayor's official residence.

During Sir John (4)'s mayoralty the trial and acquittal of the seven bishops took place in London, and, like other dissenters, he probably supported them against James II's Declaration of Indulgence.[136] What then did the King gain from befriending Sir John Shorter (4) ? If he was seeking support for the toleration of Catholics, there is no doubt that he was disappointed. However, he was able to make Sir John (4)'s inauguration in 1687 the first public engagement of the newly appointed papal nuncio, and the Lord Mayor himself may have considered this a small price to pay for his rehabilitation and promotion.

Sir John Shorter (4)'s inauguration as Lord Mayor on October 27th 1687 was a splendid occasion, financed for the most part by the Goldsmiths' Company. The road was newly graveled all the way from Charing Cross to the City for the King's procession. The pageant included verses by Matthew

---

[134] P.C.C., Exton 129, 1688.

[135] **Notes and Queries**, 7th s. vol. IV, p.101.

[136] **Notes and Queries**, 7th s., vol. IV, p.101.

Taubman, the poet laureate, and a first tableau, depicting Truth, Justice, Temperance, Fortitude and Mercy. The second tableau represented the patron saint of the Goldsmiths, St.Dunstan pulling the devil's nose with a pair of red-hot pincers. The third tableau was the contribution of the Company of Watermen and Lightermen. It was a model ship, a merchant adventurer to Norway and Denmark, named "The Unity of London". It was 145 feet in length and 45 feet high, and appropriately laden with timber. It also sported 22 guns and possessed a crew, consisting of captain, mate, boatswain, mariners and trumpeters.[137]

The banquet at Guildhall which followed the pageant, was attended by King James II, in person and the whole court. The guests included Catherine of Braganza, the Queen Dowager, and Prince George of Denmark and his wife, the future Queen Anne. Queen Mary of Modena, had been expected but was unable to attend because of a sudden indisposition.[138] Also in attendance was the papal nuncio, Count Ferdinand d'Adda, Bishop of Amasia and later Cardinal, for whom the occasion was his first public recognition. The climax of the celebrations came when the Captain of the pageant ship, dressed in Indian silk and a rich, fur cap, made a lengthy address to His Majesty.[139]

The invitation of the papal envoy was not calculated to make Sir John (4) popular, and John Evelyn evidently thought that the gesture would have the effect of harming the King's cause.

---

[137] **Notes and Queries**, 2nd s., vol. IV, pp.142 ff.; Humpherus, Henry, **History of the Origin and Progress of the Company of Watermen and Lightermen of the River Thames with Numerous Historical Notes, 1514-1859**, London 1874, vol.1, pp.358-9.

[138] **London Gazette**, October 30th 1687; **Notes and Queries**, 7th s. vol. IV, pp.142 ff.

[139] Humpherus, **op.cit.**, vol.1, pp.358-359.

A strange turn of affairs, that those who scandalised the Church of England as favourers of Popery, should publiquely invite an emissary from Rome, one who represented the very person of their Antichrist.[140]

James II, however, was delighted, being "well satisfied with the whole entertainment", and granted a new coat of arms to Sir John (4) as a token of appreciation.[141] The royal patent was dated October 14th 1687. While the crest remained as before: **A griphon's head sable gorged with a collar or between two wings of the same**, the arms were entirely different and included no less than a ducal coronet. They were: **Sable a lion rampant or (ducally) crowned argent between three battle-axes silver, the staves gold.**[142] The arms were to be borne by Sir John (4)'s descendants and those of his brother Charles (1).

The prestigious new coat of arms was also connected with Sir John (4)'s acquisition of a country-seat in Kent, called Bybrook. On becoming a member of the gentry, it was necessary to acquire a "seat", but there is no evidence that Sir John (4) had any previous family connections with the county, or that he spent any time at Bybrook. Edward Hasted, the antiquarian states that Sir John (4) bought Bybrook in 1688.[143] The new coat of arms is evidence that it had already been purchased by October 1687, because the shield incorporated the arms of a previous owner of Bybrook, Sir William Hall: **sable, three battle-axes or**. The inspiration for placing a lion between the battle-axes may have come from the arms of "Shorter of

---

[140] Evelyn, **loc.cit.**

[141] **Notes and Queries**, 2nd s. vol. XI, pp.152, 217; Baddeley **op.cit.** p.80, quoting Luttrell, N., **Diary**, vol. I, p.417.

[142] College of Arms, **Register of Nobility and Gentry**, vol.3, p.329.

[143] Hasted, Edward, **A History and Topographical Survey of the County of Kent**, 2nd edition, Canterbury 1797, vol.7, p.549.

Kent", already mentioned, with their **griphon passant between three estoiles**.[144]

Apart from the trial of the seven bishops, the only notable event of Sir John (4)'s mayoralty was the spectacular accident which ended it prematurely on September 4th 1688. Gyll saw the hand of God in this occurrence, punishing one who, if not the pawn of the Popish King, had recognized the Pope's ambassador.

> This interposition of Divine providence has occurred to several mayors, and in our time a Lord Chancellor has died suddenly, **viz.** Lord Campbell in June, 1861; and this is generally thought to be without precedent, in the plenitude of power, whence arises a reflection on the vanity of ambition, for where and on what occasion could a trite morality receive a fresher point?[145]

No doubt there were contemporaries of Sir John Shorter (4) who shared this opinion. The accident occurred on August 27th 1688, two months before the end of the Lord Mayor's term of office, and nearly four months before James II's ignominious flight from the Kingdom. Perhaps the interposition of Providence worked to preserve Sir John (4)'s reputation as James II's inglorious reign reached its climax.

On August 27th 1688 he went to Smithfield to open the annual St. Bartholomew's Fair. On his return, it was customary for the Lord Mayor to call on the Keeper of Newgate and partake of "a cool tankard of wine, nutmeg and sugar". Major Richardson and the Rev. Samuel Smith met Sir John (4) under Newgate, and handed up the tankard of spiced sack.[146] Sir

---

[144] More will be said about Bybrook in Chapter Six below.

[145] Gyll ,**op.cit.**, p.274.

[146] **Notes and Queries**, 7th s., vol. IV, p.142, speaks of the accident taking place under "Rahere's arch". Rahere was Henry I's court jester, who became

John (4) was mounted on a somewhat skittish horse, which reared and threw its rider to the ground. According to the Ellis correspondence, the horse started at the sight of the "large glittering tankard". Luttrell, however, suggests that the silver lid of the tankard snapped shut with so much force that it frightened the horse.[147]

Sir John (4) was taken up alive but unconscious. He was carried first of all into the Keeper's house at Newgate and from there to his home in Bankside. He regained consciousness and dictated his will on August 31st, describing himself as being "sick and weak in body, but of sound and perfect mind and memory, all praise be given to God". On the same day, a special court was held in the justice hall of the Old Bailey to consider "my Lord Maior's sickness and the small hopes of his recovery". Four senior aldermen were chosen to go to the King, in the event of Sir John (4)'s death, and to seek the appointment of a new Lord Mayor. The latter was, no doubt, further saddened by the death of his friend, John Bunyan, which occurred on that day.

Sir John (4) lingered for twelve days with a severe fever, eventually dying at 11 o'clock in the morning of September 4th. While he lay dying, news was brought to him of two offices in his gift which had fallen vacant and which were worth £3,000 to him. On the day of his death the aldermen and Town Clerk

---

an Augustinian and was the founder of the Church and Hospital of St. Bartholomew the Great, Smithfield. The accident did not take place under the archway that leads to the church. Moreover, Newgate, recently rebuilt after the Great Fire, could not be described as "Rahere's arch".

[147] **Notes and Queries**, 6th s. vol. X, p.73, (Ellis letter of August 30th 1688); **Notes and Queries**, 7th s. vol. IV, p.181; Baddeley, **op.cit.**, p.80, quoting Luttrell N., **Diary**, p.458.

went to Windsor to inform the King, who appointed Sir John Eyles to succeed him on September 5th.[148]

To his son, John (9) the Lord Mayor left the bulk of his possessions, and requested him to deal "fairly and kindly" with his mother and brother. Specified properties were bequeathed to Dame Isabella in her own name, and afterwards to his son Thomas (1), and then, for want of issue, to John (9), his son John (11), to Charles (1) and his heirs. The Lord Mayor's grandson, John (11) was to receive another set of houses and properties. Smaller bequests of £100 each were made to the daughters of Charles (1), Hannah (1) and Margaret, to his "brother". Charles (1) was to receive £200, and Catherine, his granddaughter, £400. Thomas Kent ("my brother") and his wife, and the children of his sister, Elizabeth (2) Bull, were to receive £10 apiece. Finally, land was bequeathed to the parish of Christchurch and money was to be distributed to the poor by his son John (9).[149] This copyhold was known afterwards as "Sir John Shorter's Charity".[150] The extent and complexity of this will testifies to the Lord Mayor's considerable wealth.

Sir John Shorter (4) was laid to rest in the Lady Chapel of St. Saviour's Southwark. Since 1626 this small chapel had become known as "the Bishop's Chapel", because it contained the ornate, canopied tomb of the revered Anglican divine, Lancelot Andrewes, Bishop of Winchester. Sir John (4)'s memorial was placed on the north wall, eastward from the altar. Here Dame Isabella Shorter was later buried in 1703, and the inscription

---

[148] Baddeley, **op.cit.**, p.80-81; Kirk, J., **Biographies of English Catholics 1700-1800**, London 1909, **sub** "Shorter" p.210. Kirk muddles Sir John (4) with John (9).

[149] P.C.C., Exton 129, 1688.

[150] **Notes and Queries**, 7th s. vol. III, pp.443-444.

recorded her age as 72 years.[151] In August 1830 this small chapel, which had been disfigured by many alterations, was demolished and several monuments were moved from it into the main church, including that of Bishop Andrewes, which was re-erected in the south choir aisle. Since every letter of the inscription on Sir John (4) and Dame Isabella's memorial stone had been obliterated, it was not saved, but perished along with the chapel itself.[152]

The ill-fated Lord Mayor left two other memorials in the city he ruled. One was "Shorter's Court" in Throgmorton Street, mentioned in Stowe's 18th century survey; but this has not survived.[153] The other is "Shorter Street" which can still be found, off Cable Street, near the Tower of London.

---

[151] Allen, Thomas, **History of London**, Cowie and Strange, London 1828, vol.4, p.501.

[152] Thompson, Canon, **History and Antiquities of Southwark Cathedral**, London 1910, p.156; Taylor, W., **Annals of St. Mary Overy**, London 1833, p.101; Dollman, Francis T., **The Priory Church of St. Mary Overie Southwark**, London 1881, p.19; Stow, John, **A Survey of the Cities of London and Westminster and the Borough of Southwark**, edited by John Strype, London 1755, vol.2, p.14-15.

[153] Stow, op.cit, p.832.

CHAPTER FIVE

BROTHERS OF THE LORD MAYOR

Richard (1)

Sir John (4)'s elder brother, Richard (1), was eighteen years older than himself, and the absence of his name from the Lord Mayor's will suggests that he was already dead in 1688. The 1674 Visitation names his wife as Mary Whiting from Stanwell, a village north of Staines, situated today on the southern perimeter of Heathrow Airport.[154]

Richard (1) was residing in St. George's parish, Southwark, in 1674.[155] The parish registers record the baptism of his son, John, on February 4th 1645, but they become fragmentary in 1651, and there is a complete gap between 1653 and 1657.[156] On February 12th 1648, the burial of Jeremy, son of Richard Shorter is recorded.[157] The Heralds' Visitation mentions a single "son and heir" of Richard (1), Charles (3), aged 21, born

---

[154] **Heralds' Visitation of London 1664**, (1674). The visitation seems to be ignorant of her father's Christian name.

[155] **Ibid.**

[156] G.L.R.O., X92/30, Registers of St. George the Martyr, Southwark.

[157] **Ibid.**

therefore **circa** 1653.[158] This means that Richard (1)'s firstborn son was also dead by that time. We do not know of any other children.

So far, no further light has been shed on Richard (1), and it is not known what profession he followed. We know a little more about his son, Charles (3). He was licensed on August 4th 1674, to be married in St. George's Southwark to Elizabeth Kempsall of Staines, who was aged about 17 at the time. The license describes the bridegroom as "Charles Shorter, Gentleman", which indicates that he was already basking in the reflected gentility of his uncle, the future Lord Mayor. The marriage license gives his place of residence as New Inn, which may indicate that he was connected with the legal profession.[159] Their first child was baptized at Staines on June 13th 1675.[160] Probably they are the same Charles and Elizabeth to whom a child was born in 1676 and baptized at St. Mary Adchurch on March 13th.[161]

Charles (1)

Charles (1) was closer in age and interests to his brother, Sir John (4). Consequently, much more is known about him. We learn from the Heralds' Visitation in 1674 that he was married

---

[158] **Heralds' London Visitation 1664** (1674). Charles (3)'s marriage license also dated 1674, gives his age as being "about 24", **Harl.** vol. 23, p.231. The heralds' informant, presumably Sir John (4) or Charles (1), were probably guessing their nephew's age, which, as the marriage license shows, was not exactly known to Charles (3) himself.

[159] **Harleian Society, London Marriage Licences**, vol.23, p.231.

[160] Registers of St. Mary's Staines, G.L.R.O.

[161] International Genealogical Index for London/Middlesex.

to Susan, the daughter of Peter Theobald of Canterbury, and that he had by her five sons and two daughters.[162] Only the eldest son can be found in the baptismal register of St.Saviour's Southwark, but there is mention of a third daughter, Susanna (2), who is not named in the Visitation, and who may have died in infancy. Charles (1)'s will, drawn up in 1693, omits any mention of his sons Charles (2) and Peter.[163] However, it mentions another daughter, Margaret, who must have been born soon after the 1674 Visitation took place. The latter lists sons and daughters separately, but it is possible to establish the order of birth of the daughters with the help of marriage licenses. The result is as follows. The eldest son, John (8), was born in 1658 and his baptism took place on March 18th at St. Saviour's, Southwark.[164] Charles (1) was aged about 28 at the time, and is described as "Timber Merchant". John (8) entered the legal profession as a clerk in Doctors' Commons. This was a college of advocates and doctors of Civil Law, which handled ecclesiastical cases, particularly marriage licenses. In the reign of King Charles II, between 1674 and 1678, John (8)'s name regularly appears on allegations for marriage licenses in the parish of St. Saviour's, Southwark. He is variously described as "John Shorter of Doctors' Commons, London, Gent.", or as "John Shorter of St. Saviour's Southwark,

---

[162] **Heralds' Visitation of London 1664** (1674). Notes taken by the author from family papers belonging to Henry (3), when they were briefly on loan to him in the 1940s, contain the name of a sixth son, Samuel. However, this name is not in the Visitation or printed pedigrees; nor is it in the parish registers.

[163] P.C.C., Pyne 40, 1697.

[164] Parish Registers of St. Saviour's Southwark, G.L.R.O., X39/4b.

Gent."[165] The college was situated near St. Paul's Cathedral and functioned up to 1867.[166]

In spite of his professional involvement with marriage law, John (8)'s own marriage was less regular. On July 22nd 1688, he married Elizabeth Collett at St. James, Dukes's Place, near Aldgate, a parish that was infamous for irregular marriages in the 17th century. Between 1644 and 1691, 40,000 couples were married there without license, banns or parental consent. The church was demolished in 1874 and the Sir John Cass School now covers the site.[167] John (8) received the bulk of his father's property when Charles (1) died in 1696.[168] He and Elizabeth moved back to Staines, where two daughters were born to them there: Susanna Maria, born on September 30th 1705 and baptized two days later, and Sophia Maria born on April 13th 1707, baptized on May 9th. A son was born to them on July 27th 1712. A comment beside the entry in the parish register can be deciphered as follows: "and the same day it was baptized and died at home".[169] Elizabeth, described in the registers as "Madame Shorter", was buried in 1729, but there is no record of John (8)'s death.[170]

---

[165] cf. **Harleian Society**, vol.34, London Marriage Licenses 1669-1679, London 1892, pp.126, 143, 144, 146, 167. 174, 215.

[166] Squibb, G.D., **Doctors' Commons - A History of the College of Advocates and Doctors of Law**, Clarendon, Oxford, 1977.

[167] Weinreb and Hibbert, **op.cit.**, p.712.; **Boyd's Marriage Index**, Society of Genealogists, gives the year of the marriage as 1686, but the **International Genealogical Index** gives the 1688 date; cf. also Family Papers in the author's possession, and **Harleian Society** vol.92, p.124, which describes John (8) as "living 1688", presumably because he was married in that year.

[168] P.C.C., Pyne 40, 1697.

[169] Staines Registers, G.L.R.O., X 90/105; Gyll, **op.cit.** p.186.

[170] Gyll , **op.cit.**, p.186.

Charles (1)'s eldest daughter, Mary (1), was born **circa** 1659.[171] She married Thomas Clarke, a dyer of Christchurch, Southwark, at St. Dunstan's in the East on February 16th 1680.[172] Thomas was about 32 when they married, but died before **circa** 1690. We learn from Charles (1)'s will that Mary's second husband was John Walker.[173] Charles (1)'s second son, Charles (2) was born **circa** 1660, but his absence from his father's will suggests that he was already dead. His second daughter, Susanna (2), was baptized at St. Saviour's Southwark on April 10th 1662.[174] Again, there is no reference to her in her father's will. Peter was born **circa** 1663, and is also absent from the will. It is possible that these three children all died in London's Great Plague of 1665.

Charles (1)'s fourth son, William (4), was born **circa** 1665 and survived the plague to become a distiller in Christchurch, Southwark. On January 3rd 1690 he got married there to Mrs. Mary Pope, a widow aged 39 and fourteen years his senior.[175] William (4) was alive when his father made his will in 1693. **The Gentleman's Magazine** of November 19th 1734 records the death of a "near relative of Sir Robert Walpole's Lady", one "Shorter Esq."[176] This can be no other than William (4) who was buried at St. Mary le Bow in that year, and who fits the

---

[171] **Harleian Society**, London Marriage Licenses, vol.24 p.21.

[172] **Harleian Society**, vol.30, p.21.

[173] P.C.C., Pyne 40, 1697.

[174] cf. St. Saviour's Registers, G.L.R.O., X39/1b.

[175] **Harleian Society**, vol.31, p.51.

[176] Musgrave, William, **Obituary Prior to 1800**, London 1901, **sub** Shorter.

description of "a near relative" of Catherine.[177] He was first cousin to her father, John (9).

Caleb was born **circa** 1667 and married Dorothy Mills at St. James, Duke's Place on February 2nd 1688, barely six months before his eldest brother's irregular wedding in the same church.[178] He was alive when his father made his will in 1693. Charles (1) was evidently worried about him and left the sum of £50 specifically to provide him with employment.[179] Joshua was probably born **circa** 1669. He is mentioned in the 1674 London Visitation and in his father's will.[180] We do not know if he married or the nature of his profession.

Charles (1)'s third daughter, Hannah (1), was born **circa** 1771 and married Daniel Poule or Powle at St. Dunstan's in the East on January 3rd 1690 at the age of around 19. Her husband was a dyer, about four years older than herself.[181] Finally, Charles (1)'s fourth daughter, Margaret, was born **circa** 1674. She is not mentioned in the 1674 Heralds' Visitation and she appears as a minor in her father's 1693 will, provision being made for her marriage.[182] She may have been the Margaret Shorter who married Thomas Coleman at Ealing in 1700.[183]

---

[177] cf. Boyd's London Burials, Society of Genealogists.

[178] International Genealogical Index.

[179] P.C.C., Pyne 40, 1697.

[180] **Heralds' Visitation of London 1664**, (1674), p.135; P.C.C., Pyne 40, 1697.

[181] **Harleian Society**, vol.24, p.168. Charles (1) calls his son-in-law "James" in his will, but it is presumably the same man. P.C.C., Pyne 40, 1697.

[182] P.C.C. Pyne 40, 1697.

[183] Boyd's Marriage Index, Society of Genealogists.

In 1659, soon after their marriage, Charles (1)'s wife, Susanna, brought him land in St. Mary's parish Bermondsey.[184] Charles (1) was also involved in a lawsuit with James Attlee in 1673.[185] The plaintiff was a Southwark plumber, who claimed that Charles (1) was surety for an unrecovered debt. Charles (1) denied any involvement and the case was dismissed. Charles (1)'s will of September 20th 1693 reveals that he was much less wealthy than his brother, the Lord Mayor. He left £400 to Margaret; £230 to Joshua and £50 to Caleb. Joshua and Caleb received property at Rotherhithe, but his wharf and other property went to John Kirk and William Raymond, who were probably in business with him. The other bequests are almost an inventory of his household possessions. John (8) received his "Norway silver tankard" and his "three books of the martyrs". Mary (1) was given a "silver candle cup and cover". William (4) was to get his other silver tankard; and Joshua, a silver plate and "sweetmeat spoons". Caleb received a cup and spoons; Hannah (1), a silver porringer and spoons and Margaret, a silver salt. Daniel ("James") Powle was to get his livery gown; John Walker, his beaver hat; Joshua, his "best hanging coat". The testator's books were to be divided among William, Joshua and Caleb. All the other household goods and linen were to be divided between Margaret and Joshua. After some other bequests to "my brothers" Thomas Turner and Thomas Kent, the remainder of the property went to John (8).[186]

Apart from the children of John (8), other Shorter grandchildren of Charles (1) have not been traced. William (4)'s wife,

---

[184] G.L.R.O., 0/86/1-3, indenture of 1659.

[185] P.R.O., C3, 221/2.

[186] As has already been suggested in Chapter 3, Thomas Kent was probably the husband of Charles (1)'s sister, Susanna (1). Nothing is known of Thomas Turner.

marrying at 39, would have borne him few, if any, children. The names, Caleb and Dorothy Shorter, are nothing if not distinctive, but they do not appear in London parish registers. Finally, there is no record of Joshua marrying, and he may have died soon after his father. We now return to the descendants of Sir John Shorter (4).

CHAPTER SIX

JOHN SHORTER OF BYBROOK

Bybrook House

On his daughter's monument in Westminster Abbey, John (9) is described as "John Shorter Esq. of Bybrook in Kent". The property had been purchased shortly before the Lord Mayor's death, and, although it is unlikely that his son spent very much time there, he was the first member of the family to have an opportunity of doing so. At the time of the purchase, Bybrook was a mansion and hamlet situated between Kennington and Ashford on the Canterbury road. Today it is part of the outskirts of Ashford, close to the M20 motorway.

The name Shorter occurs in Canterbury parish registers from the early seventeenth century, and it begins to appear also at the end of the century in the registers of Hothfield and Bexley. The latter is situated on the Kent-Surrey border, south of London, and during the 18th century Shorters began to spread out to parishes in the area: Bromley, Crayford and Milton by Gravesend. From Hothfield in the south they spread to parishes nearer to Bybrook: Great Chart and Westwell, and possibly Woodchurch and Kenardington. This movement of Shorters to parishes in the relative vicinity of Bybook does not seem to be connected with the Lord Mayor's purchase, nor is it likely that the purchase itself was connected with the earlier presence of Shorters in Kent. The recorded links between Shorters in Kent and East Sussex, together with other genealogical indications, suggest that the family in Hothfield originated in Salehurst, East Sussex. If this is the case, then it is unlikely that they had any immediate connection with the London family that purchased Bybrook.

The name Bybrook refers to a tributary of the river Stour - "the mansion by the brook".[187] As Hasted remarks, it was "an ancient seat" which had belonged to the Godwin family and which came into the possession of the Belknap family at the end of King Edward III's reign. Sir Robert Belknap, Chief Justice of the common pleas, was impeached by the Commons for treason after the Peasants' Revolt in 1387. He was banished to Ireland and his estates became forfeited to the Crown. In 1389 King Richard II granted the property to William Ellys, one of the Conservators of the Peace for Kent, and it then passed into the hands of a series of families: Shelley, Tilden, Best, Hall and Nott. The heirs of Charles Nott sold it to Sir John Shorter (4).[188]

When Hasted saw Bybrook, almost half a century after it had passed out of the hands of the Shorter family, it was a ruin.[189]

> The antient mansion of Bibrooke has been uninha-
> bited and in ruins for several years; but the front of it,
> which has a stately appearance, is still remaining entire.
> A low mean building has been erected against the south

---

[187] Furley, Robert, **The Annals of Kennington in Kent**, Ashford 1877.

[188] Hasted, **op.cit.**, vol.7, pp.548-550; Furley **op.cit.**, p.14; **Calendar of Patent Rolls**, P.R.O., London H.M.S.O., 1902, vol.4, Richard II 1388-1392, pp.93-94.

[189] Hasted, **loc.cit.**, p.550.

side of it, which is made use of as the farmhouse belonging to the estate.[190]

In the 19th century Furley recorded that the ruin was subsequently converted into a farmhouse and that it still possessed one of the finest chimneys in the district. A nearby watermill also belonged to the estate.[191] Bybrook House, as it is called today, stands in its own grounds. The core of the building is a modest, Elizabethan timber-frame house, considerably enlarged by modern additions. The brick exterior is much restored, with modern porch and mullioned windows at the front in Tudor style, and there are two sets of double chimneys. At one side of the house, the original brick exterior is much less pretentious and bears traces of successive alterations. There are stone sections in the fabric and a quantity of stone in the garden and surrounding walls. These may be relics of the imposing facade observed by Hasted two hundred years ago.[192]

John (9)'s London house was in Norfolk Street, off the Strand now covered by Arundel Great Court, opposite the Aldwych.[193] The street had been built in 1682, the year after John (9)'s marriage, on part of the former Arundel House, and during his residence there his neighbors included Peter the Great of Russia; William Penn, the founder of Pennsylvania; Sir Roger de Coverley; and William Mountford, the actor.[194]

---

[190] **Ibid.**

[191] Furley, **op.cit.**, pp.14-15.

[192] The author visited the house on July 22nd 1991, through the kindness of a member of the Saunders family, who are the present owners.

[193] Gyll, **op.cit.**, p.275.

[194] Cunningham, Peter, **A Handbook of London Past and Present**, London 1850, p.369.

John (9) was nearly assassinated in mistake for the latter by the notorious Lord Mohun in 1692. Gyll tells the story as follows:

> .   John Shorter, father of Lady Walpole, was walking down Norfolk Street, Strand, just before Mountford was stabbed, and Lord Mohun mistaking him for that unfortunate son of Thespis, came up, and embracing him, said, "Dear Mountford", but Mr. Shorter undeceived him and walked home. He had scarcely reached his own house in Norfolk Street when he heard the noise and scuffle in the street which was occasioned by Mountford's murder. The exclamation of Lord Mohun was supposed to have been the signal for the assassins to attack their prey, and it was fortunate for Mr. Shorter that he was not their victim.[195]

Lord Mohun was indicted for Mountford's murder, but was acquitted; and seven years later, was acquitted of a second murder.

Timber Merchant

John (9) was living in Christchurch Parish, Southwark at the time of his marriage in 1681, and he continued to operate his father's timber business there, after the Lord Mayor's death in 1688.[196] As we shall see in Part Two, Chapter Fourteen, John (9) crossed the Atlantic to America a number of times, either with his father, or - after his father's death - on his own. John (9)'s grandson, Horace Walpole, mentioned him several times in his correspondence.

---

[195] Gyll, **op.cit.**, p.275.

[196] **Harleian Society**, vol.24, p.156.

My grandfather, my mother's father, was a Danish timber-merchant, an honest, sensible Whig, and I am very proud of him.[197]

My mother's father was a timber merchant. I have many reasons for thinking myself a worse man and none for thinking myself better; consequently, I shall never blush at anything he did.[198]

Evidently, John (9) supported the House of Orange and the deposition of his father's benefactor, King James II. His Whig allegiance, however, was not subjected to the ultimate test, since he died during the reign of Queen Anne, and, therefore, before the advent of the House of Hanover and the long Whig supremacy. Nevertheless, his political opinions, as well as his wealth, must have been a factor in securing the marriage of his daughter to Sir Robert Walpole.

John (9)'s own marriage was a socially advantageous one. In July 1681 he married Elizabeth Philipps, daughter of Sir Erasmus Philipps, Baronet, of Picton Castle, Pembrokeshire.[199] The marriage license, which was dated July 11th, states that he was 22 years old at the time, and his bride about 19. The wedding took place in the Savoy Chapel, since the parish church had long been demolished and work did not begin on James Gibbs' new church until 1714.[200] As we have seen, John

---

[197] Lewis, W.S., (ed.), **The Correspondence of Horace Walpole**, Oxford 1983, vol. 29, p.232.

[198] Lewis, **op.cit.**, vol.40, p.24.

[199] Registers of St. Mary-le-Strand, Westminster Archives. The day of the month is not given, but the license was dated July 11th 1681, **Harleian Society**, vol.24, p.156.

[200] **Harleian Society**, vol.24, p.156; Weinreb and Hibbert, **op.cit.**, p.741.

(9) and Elizabeth came to reside in the parish after their marriage.

The Philipps family, which is that of the present Viscount St. David's, is an illustrious one.[201] Horace Walpole cherished a pedigree of his grandmother's family which included Cadwallader; a bastard of King Henry VIII; the Plantagenets and the poet John Dryden. He wrote:

> I have a pedigree of my mother, drawn up by the late Sir John Philipps, my cousin, and father of the present Lord Milford, in which it is clear that we are descended from Cadwallader.[202]

> On my mother's side [my pedigree] has mounted the Lord knows whither, by the Philipps to Henry VIII, and has sucked in Dryden for a great-uncle; and by Lady Philipps' mother, Darcy, to Edward III and then I stop for brevity's sake - especially as Edward III is a second Adam; who almost is not descended from Edward ? [203]

John (9) and Elizabeth had three sons and two daughters. None of their baptisms have been traced in the registers of either Christchurch, Southwark, or St. Mary-le-Strand. It is likely that they were all born by **circa** 1689 at Christchurch, and that the move to Norfolk Street took place between 1689

---

[201] cf.**Burke's Peerage**, London 1727, p.2007, where the Philipps lineage is traced to Tadifor ap Colwyn.

[202] Lewis, **op.cit.**, vol.33, p.454. A copy of this pedigree hangs still at Strawberry Hill, where the author saw it in 1995.

[203] Paget Toynbee, (ed.), **The Letters of Horace Walpole**, Oxford 1905, vol.9, p.207.

and 1692. As has been noted already, the Christchurch parish registers are badly burnt and mostly indecipherable.[204]

Catherine Shorter

Catherine was born **circa** 1682 and married Sir Robert Walpole, popularly regarded as Britain's first prime minister, at the Knightsbridge Chapel on July 30th 1700. There was a certain amount of haste and secrecy about the marriage, but she brought her husband a dowry that was enormous by the standards of the day, £20,000.[205] Lady Catherine was an extravagant woman of fashion, and it was said that she wasted large sums of money. The dowry was mostly spent on the wedding, on the christening of her firstborn, Edward, and on jewelry.[206] Walpole's biographer, Coxe, describes her as "a woman of exquisite beauty and accomplished manners".[207] Her portrait by Michael Dahl, in the Marquis of Cholmondeley's collection at Houghton Hall, shows a dark haired woman of beautiful complexion, with full lips and somewhat soulful eyes. Her head is slightly inclined, and her forearms lightly folded. She wears a blue and white dress.[208] Another portrait at

---

[204] This is presumably the reason why the baptisms have not been traced, and not, as was suggested in Shorter, Aylward, "Horace Walpole's Catholic Uncle", **Catholic Ancestor**, vol.3, no.6, Nov. 1991, p.225, because John (9) had an aversion to infant baptism.

[205] **Dictionary of National Biography**, Smith and Elder, London 1909, vol.20, p.637, **sub** "Walpole".

[206] **Ibid.**

[207] **Ibid.** quoting Coxe.

[208] A color reproduction of the painting may be found in Jones, Christopher, **Number Ten Downing Street - The Story of a House**, B.B.C., London 1985, p.39. The author saw this portrait at Houghton Hall in June 1998.

Houghton Hall shows her in red, with the young Horace Walpole as a child.[209] It is attributed to C. Gervas. Numerous other portraits, miniatures and engravings of her exist, but probably the most striking portrait of all hangs in the Pump Room at Bath. It is by either William Hoare or Arthur Pond and shows Catherine, wearing a large hat with a feather, a satin dress and a long pearl necklace of four strands.[210] Although she seldom visited Houghton Hall, Norfolk, a relief of her bust appears in the marble cove of the Stone Hall.

Lady Catherine spent much of her time at her husband's house in Chelsea, and it was presumably there that she entertained Voltaire to dinner in either 1727 or 1728.[211] In 1735, however, she became the first mistress of Number 10, Downing Street, when they moved to the newly altered house which has remained the official residence of British prime ministers ever since. Lady Catherine ruled on the second floor, where her boudoir is now the white dining-room.[212] Her dining-room is now the blue drawing-room, and it was there that she entertained Queen Caroline, the consort of King George II, in 1736. The Queen sat at table with Lady Catherine, while Sir Robert stood behind the Queen's chair.[213]

Because of Sir Robert Walpole's infidelities, there was much gossip concerning the parenthood of Horace, his son. The latter, however, was never in any doubt about the identity of his mother, and was extremely attached to her, as his letters testify. The authorities today accept that Sir Robert and Lady Catherine

---

[209] The author saw this portrait also at Houghton Hall in June 1998.

[210] The author saw this portrait at Bath on June 8th 1995.

[211] Lewis, **op,cit.**, vol.41, p.149, Horace Walpole to Voltaire 21.6.1768.

[212] Jones, **op.cit.**, pp.43, 46.

[213] cf. Jones, **op.cit.**, p.49.

were the parents of Robert, Edward, Horace, Mary and
Katherine.[214]   More information about Lady Catherine will be
given in Chapter Eight below.

John (9)'s Descendants

John (9)'s son and heir was John (11), born **circa** 1684.
Charlotte was born **circa** 1687; Arthur, **circa** 1688; and
Erasmus **circa** 1689, these three being minors when their father
died in 1707. Chapter Eight of this book will be devoted to
John (11) and his brothers. In July 1716, Charlotte married
Francis Seymour Conway of Ragley, County Warwick, who
was later created Baron Conway and Killultagh in County
Antrim (1679-1732). No doubt the Walpole connection had
much to do with this advantageous alliance. Her eldest son,
Francis Seymour Conway (1719-1794) became Earl, and later
1st Marquis, of Hertford, and her second son, Field-Marshall
Henry Seymour Conway (1721-1795) was a noted friend and
correspondent of his cousin, Horace Walpole. There was also a
daughter, Anne Seymour Conway. Baron Conway died in
1732, and his widow, Lady Charlotte, died on February 12th
1733 and was buried at Arrow on February 23rd.[215] Charlotte's
portrait by Sir Godfrey Kneller reveals that she was not as dark
as her sister, Catherine. She is shown to have light brown hair,
brown eyes and a somewhat sallow complexion. She is wearing

---

[214] cf. **D.N.B., loc.cit.**; and cf. Jones **op.cit.**, p.49 for the colorful rumor that
Horace was Lady Catherine's son by Frederick Lewis, Prince of Wales.

[215] cf. **D.N.B.**, **sub** "Conway", vol.4, p.976; and Hugh 8th Marquis of
Hertford, **Ragley Hall** (Guide), Derby, 1989. Presumably, Charlotte was
laid to rest in the vault of Arrow Parish Church. Her name, however, does
not appear on the brass plaque on the north wall of the chancel, which lists
mainly the names of males buried in the vault. The author visited Arrow
Church and Ragley Hall on July 23rd 1992.

a blue satin dress and her right hand holds a white flower in her lap.[214]

The late Princess Diana of Wales (died 1997) was descended from both Catherine Shorter and Charlotte Shorter. Her father, the 8th Earl Spencer, was the great grandson of Adelaide Horatia, herself the great great granddaughter of Charlotte Shorter. Adelaide Horatia was also granddaughter of Anne Waldegrave, whose mother was a great granddaughter of Catherine Shorter. Prince William of Wales, heir to the British throne, is thus a descendant of these two Shorter women.

John (9) made his will on September 30th 1702.[215] He asked to be buried "in a private manner, without unnecessary shew and attendance", and he left £100 each to his wife, to John (11), to his brother-in-law Sir John Philipps, Bart., and to his brother Thomas (1). £2,000 were to go to Charlotte on marriage or majority, with an annual allowance of £60 in the meantime. £1,500 were to be held in trust for each of his two, other sons, Arthur and Erasmus, which they were to receive on attainment of majority, though a codicil raised Arthur's sum to £2,000. Their maintenance in the meantime was to be paid from the interest on the trust money. John (11) received the remaining property and Thomas (1) and Sir John Philipps were appointed executors.

Complying with the terms of this will was complicated by a number of factors. Thomas (1) died intestate before John (9), and the latter died in foreign parts, in February 1707.[216] Moreover, John (11), his residuary legatee, was also out of the

---

[214] The portrait by Kneller hangs in the Ante Room of Ragley Hall, and is reproduced in Hugh 8th Marquis **op.cit** on p.7. The same author mistakenly states (p.14) that she was the daughter of the Lord Mayor.

[215] P.C.C., Poley, 45, 1707.

[216] The probate is annotated "pts", which signifies a death abroad.

country at the time of his father's death. We know from John (11)'s will that his father was buried at St. Saviour's, Southwark, so it seems likely that John (9) died on board one of his ships, rather than in Scandinavia.[219] The will was proved by Sir John Philipps on February 15th 1707, and again by John (11) on June 10th, after his return to England.

On April 25th 1710, Sir John Phillips brought a case against John (11), Charlotte, Arthur and Erasmus, which was heard before the Master of the Rolls.[220] Sir Robert Walpole had been acting as guardian of the young Shorters, since Picton Castle in Pembrokeshire was too remote from London. However, Philipps was suing to recover debts from the estate of Thomas (1) - in vain, as it turned out. John (9)'s widow, Elizabeth died on July 27th 1728 in the first year of King George II.[221] We shall now go back to the first half of the 17th century, to consider another branch of the Shorter family.

---

[219] P.C.C., Edmunds 746, 1746.

[220] Philipps versus Shorter, 25th April 1710, G.L.R.O. 0/335/1.

[221] **Historical Register Chronicle**, London 1728, p.41, "Died Mrs. Shorter, Mother of John Shorter Esq., one of the Commissioners of the Stamp Duties, and of Sir Robert Walpole's Lady"; cf. also Boyer, **Political State of Great Britain**, vol.36, 1728, p.93.

CHAPTER SEVEN

JOHN SHORTER WATERMAN

The Waterman

When the sons of John Shorter (2) moved to Southwark shortly before the English Civil War, they found another branch of their family already installed there in St. Saviour's parish, the family of "John Shorter, Waterman", as he is invariably described in the parish registers. The presence of two families called "Shorter" in Southwark already infers a link, especially as they both seem to have moved there at about the same time. A link is further suggested by the mention of "John Shorter, Waterman" in Sir John Shorter (4)'s will.[222] In it the Lord Mayor disposed of some houses and tenements which had belonged to "John Shorter, Waterman", bequeathing them to his grandson, John (11).[223]

The term "waterman" was applied to all who conveyed passengers on the river, as opposed to "lightermen" who conveyed goods. Watermen and Lightermen together formed a worshipful company which had received a charter from King

---

[222] P.C.C., Exton 129, 1688.

[223] We do not know the circumstances in which the property was acquired, but it was "lately bought", cf. **Ibid.**

Henry VIII, under which they were ruled by a court of eight watermen, known as "Overseers and Rulers", appointed by the Lord Mayor. In 1641 they received a further concession: the eight were to be chosen by twenty "assistants" elected from among their number.[224] The earliest record of such an election dates from 1659, but "John Shorter, Waterman" is not among those listed. He may, however, have been elected before 1659, or the term "waterman" may refer to simple membership of the worshipful company, rather than to an official status within it. The watermen were much involved, as we have seen, in the pageant of Sir John (4)'s inauguration as Lord Mayor, and their contribution shows that they took a favorable view of the appointment of a ship-owning timber-merchant to that office. Watermen were in constant danger of impressment for the Navy, and they looked to the Lord Mayor, who held jurisdiction over the River Thames, for protection and support. In fact, Sir John (4) took an interest in their affairs and intervened in February 1688 to ensure a fair election of their "assistants".[225]

"John Shorter, Waterman" was already established in Southwark by 1638, when a daughter, Sarah, was born to him there on October 26th.[226] Who was he and where did he come from? A likely hypothesis is that he and John (iii) are one and the same, and that he moved - probably via Staines - to Southwark shortly before the other branch of the family.[227] It is not impossible that John (iii) should have discovered a career on the Thames, at almost the same time that his distant cousin,

---

[224] Humpherus, **op.cit.**, vol.1, p.277.

[225] Humpherus, **op.cit.**, vol.1, pp.358-359.

[226] Parish registers of St. Saviour's Southwark, G.L.R.O., R278/4.

[227] See the discussion on John (iii) and John (3) in Chapter Three. The hypothesis is that John (iii) was John Shorter Waterman and that John (3) sailed to Virginia in 1635.

John (4), was entering the timber trade on the same river.[228] Conclusive evidence has not yet been found for this identification. We know that another cousin, a grandson of Henry (1) of Colnbrook was present in London in the reign of King Charles II. This was "John Shorter, Leatherseller" or John (5), who referred to his "loving uncle Nathaniel Wetham" in his will of 1667.[229] John (5) is almost certainly the son of Richard (2) who left Horton at the same time as his brother, John (3) and cousin John (iii), in **circa** 1634. John (5) was probably born to Richard (2) and his wife Dorothy at Staines, following the death of an earlier infant called John in 1638, but the state of the Staines parish registers does not permit us to confirm this.[230] John (5)'s marriage license states that he was about 29 years old in 1666.[231] If he were born in, say, 1639, his exact age at marriage would have been 27.

Horton Shorters in London

Richard (2) and Dorothy settled in Blackfriars and had three daughters (born probably in the 1640s) who are mentioned in John (5)'s will: Sarah whose married name was Williams, Elizabeth who married James Painter and Hannah whose husband was Nathaniel Ashwell.[232] Richard (2) was an officer of the Court of the Upper Bench, as the King's Bench was

---

[228] John (iii) and John (4) were fourth cousins.

[229] P.C.C., Parr 120, 1667.

[230] A "John" born to a "Richard", baptized in 1645 at St. George the Martyr, Southwark, would be too old for John (5) who was "about 29" when he married, cf. **Harleian Society**, vol.23, p.119. We have already assumed that this was a child of Richard (1).

[231] **Harleian Society**, vol.23, p.119.

[232] P.C.C., Parr 120, 1667.

called under Oliver Cromwell's Protectorate. In 1653 he was defendant to a bill of complaint in Chancery for the unlawful apprehension of Richard Farmer. It was successfully argued by the prisoner's wife, Margaret Farmer, that her husband was a prisoner of the Upper Bench entitled to parole.[233] Five years later, in 1658, Richard (2), Dorothy and their children were involved in more complex litigation, brought before the Lords Commissioners for the Custody of the Great Seal of England, by one Mrs. Mary Burtchall. The proceedings refer to an earlier judgment of 1646, which suggests that Richard (2) and Dorothy were already in London at that time. The plaintiff, as executrix of his will, claimed goods and money which had belonged to her brother Edward Ellsings, a lodger in the house of the Shorter family at Blackfriars. She also claimed ill treatment at the hands of Richard (2) and his wife. The defendants successfully established that Ellsings was in debt to his landlord, that he had died in the Shorter home, and that Richard (2) had even paid his funeral expenses. The goods claimed by the plaintiff were either the original property of the Shorters or claimed by them in lieu of rent. In fact, Richard (2) argued, Mrs. Burtchall owed the Shorter family money, rather than **vice versa**. The complaint was lodged on May 1st 1658 and the answers on May 15th and 18th.

John Shorter (5), Leatherseller, was living in the parish of St. Clement Danes, the Strand, on June 29th 1666, when he was granted a license to marry Elizabeth, daughter of William Adderley of St. Margaret's Westminster.[234] Within eighteen months, both husband and wife were tragically dead. John died in June 1667, his wife in November of the same year. They left no issue. Perhaps they were belated victims of the Great Plague in a parish which had not felt the sterilizing effect of the Great Fire. The only beneficiaries in John (5)'s will were his wife, his

---

[233] P.R.O., Chancery Proceedings, C6/126/46; C6/31/6.

[234] **Harleian Society**, vol.23, p.119.

sisters and his uncle, Nathaniel Whetham.[235] Elizabeth left her property to her sisters-in-law and to the Adderley family.[236]

Descendants of the Waterman

We do not know the name of John Shorter (3) Waterman's wife, but the baptismal registers of St. Saviour's Southwark record the birth of six of his children. Sarah (1), born in 1638, has already been mentioned. Most fathers of families at the time gave at least one son their own Christian name, but no son of John (3) is so named in the register. Another John Shorter (7) does, however, appear as married to "Phoebe", and as having a child named John (10), baptized on December 30th 1667.[237] It is probable that John (7), husband of Phoebe, is the eldest son of John (iii), born either before or after Sarah (1).

The St. Saviour's register tells us that John (7) was "clerk to Dr. McQuarrie of Axe Yard". In the baptismal entry of his second son Thomas (3) on December 21st 1670, John (7) is described as "porter". Axe Yard has been made famous by Samuel Pepys who lived there from 1658 to 1660, and it has been described as situated

> on the west side of King Street, just where the dense congeries of alleys and lanes that lay between the [Whitehall] Palace and Westminster shaded away into that corner of the Park which is today the Horse Guards Parade.[238]

---

[235] P.C.C., Parr 120, 1667.

[236] P.C.C., Carr 120, 1667.

[237] G.L.R.O., X39/1b, R/133. John (10), at age 18, may be too young to be the John Shorter who married Alice Ashton at St. George's Southwark on September 18th 1685, G.L.R.O., X/92/30.

[238] Bryant, **op. cit.**, p. 38.

Although John (7) worked in Axe Yard, he continued to live in Southwark until **circa** 1680. On May 5th of that year, a child born to John (7) and Phoebe was baptized with name of Stephen (1) at St. Benet's Paul's Wharf, and on November 12th 1683, a daughter called Joan. John (7) was buried at the same parish in 1689.[239]

The Waterman's second son Richard (3) was baptized at St. Saviour's on July 8th 1650; Anne, his second daughter, on March 6th 1654; Alice on March 25th 1657; Thomas (2) on June 6th 1660; and Mary (2) on January 6th 1662.[1] Like his brothers, Richard (3) apparently moved north of the river. Most probably, he is the Richard, married to Elizabeth, to whom children were born in the parish of St. Botolph's Bishopsgate and later in St. Dunstan's Stepney. Esther was baptized at Bishopsgate on August 15th 1680. A son, Richard, who was baptized on August 27th 1682, presumably died in infancy, since the next son born to Richard (3) and Elizabeth on September 9th 1683 was also called Richard (4).[1] The next three children born to Richard (3) and Elizabeth were baptized in St. Dunstan's Stepney: John on August 20th 1688; Mary on December 22nd 1689 and George (1) on October 25th 1694.[1] We learn from the Stepney Baptismal Register that Richard (3) was a weaver who lived in Phoenix Street.

George (1), was the only one of Richard (3)'s sons who remained in the area, and who carried on his father's weaving trade. Mary (4), his elder daughter, was baptized at St. John's Hackney on May 12th 1717.[240] Elizabeth (7), Richard (5) and Thomas (5) were all baptized at St. Dunstan's Stepney, on

---

[239] Guildhall Library, Registers of St. Benet's Paul's Wharf; International Genealogical Index; Boyd's London Burials.

[240] G.L.R.O., Baptismal Index of St. John's Hackney.

October 1st 1722, March 19th 1724 and May 27th 1727 respectively.[241]

The Waterman's third son, Thomas (2), is to be identified with Thomas Shorter who died on February 3rd 1718 and was buried at St. Margaret's Westminster.[242] This Thomas was "chamber-keeper" or "office-keeper" at Whitehall for the Secretary State for the Northern Province, Sir Joseph Addison. Such a position was presumably part of the patronage of Sir Robert Walpole, bestowed on him as a relative of Lady Catherine.[243] A chamber-keeper acted as receptionist who controlled access to the secretary of state's office. Thomas (2)'s wife was named Dorothy and they had two children: Thomas (4) and Ellina, both baptized at St. Margaret's Westminster, on June 27th 1686, and October 13th 1687 respectively.

John Shorter (iii) Waterman probably died **circa** 1680, and the disposal of his houses by the Lord Mayor in 1688 suggests that he was then no longer alive. A John Shorter died in the Marshalsea Prison in November 1678, and was buried at St.

---

[241] G.L.R.O., Registers of St. Dunstan's Stepney; International Genealogical Index. The line continued with Thomas (5) marrying Charity and having two sons: William, baptized at Hackney on May 27th 1772 and George, baptized there on June 17th 1774. William had a son, George, baptized at Stepney on October 21st 1795.

[242] Boyd's London Burials; **Historical Register Chronicle**, 1718, p.6.

[243] There is no other Thomas among Lady Walpole's Shorter relatives who can be identified as Addison's chamber-keeper; cf. **Historical Register Chronicle**, London 1718, p.6: "Died February 3rd 1718, Mr. Shorter Chamber-Keeper of the Secretary of State's Office in Whitehall" and **Magnae Britanniae Notitia**, ed. Chamberlayne J., London, 25th edition, 1718, p.31. "Thomas Shorter: Office-Keeper of Secretary of State, Rt. Hon. Joseph Addison for the Northern Province". A James Shorter is listed as another chamber-keeper in the office of the stamp-duties, and a Robert Shawter was a messenger in the Excise Office, **Ibid.** 1716 24th ed., p.528 and 1723, 26th ed., p.527. John Shorter (11) was, of course, a Commissioner for Stamp Duties.

George's Southwark.[244] This might be the waterman, but inmates of the Marshalsea came from other parishes besides Southwark.[245] In the next chapter we return to Lady Catherine Walpole and her brothers.

---

[244] G.L.R.O., X92/30.

[245] The word "lately", applied by the Lord Mayor in his will to his purchase of the waterman's property, might suggest that 1678 is too early a date for the latter's death, cf. P.C.C., Exton 129, 1688.

CHAPTER EIGHT

HORACE WALPOLE'S CATHOLIC UNCLE

John (11)

When Catherine Shorter married Sir Robert Walpole in 1700 her brother John (11) was aged about 16 or 17. The connection with the Walpoles, and specifically with Sir Robert, whose ascendancy in British politics was to endure for forty years, offered new opportunities to Lady Catherine's family. Statesmen in the 18th century built up a political base through patronage, and it was inevitable that John Shorter (11) should forsake his father's timber business for government office. Moreover, the Walpole marriage entailed a thoroughgoing Whig allegiance and brought the Shorters into contact with the Hanoverian court itself. John (11) was accordingly given a university education. He was admitted as a Fellow-Commoner at Clare College, Cambridge, on July 2nd 1703, and matriculated in the same year.[246] However, there is no record of his having taken a degree. As we have seen above, he was traveling abroad when his father died in 1707, and he may have been making the grand tour as a finishing touch to his education.

---

[246] **Alumni Cantabrigiensis**, Part 1 to 1715, Cambridge 1927, **sub** Shorter.

Besides settling his father's estate, John (11)'s first responsibility was to secure the marriage of his sister Charlotte in 1716. His brother Arthur was in weak health, but his younger brother Erasmus joined Queen Anne's army in 1708, and his commission was confirmed in 1715, after George I came to the throne.[247] No doubt John (11) had to wait until the beginning of Walpole's ascendancy in 1720, in the wake of the so-called South Sea Bubble, to secure a truly lucrative place in government. In 1725, he was appointed one of the Commissioners for the Stamp Duties, at a salary of £400 **per annum**.[248] Stamp duty was a common revenue device for taxing commercial and legal documents, newspapers, cards and dice, and when it was extended to the American colonies by the Stamp Act of 1764, became a contributory cause of the American Revolution. John (11) was one of five commissioners, the principal being Sir Brocas Gardiner Bart., to whom he was eventually promoted second.[249]

John (11)'s London house was in Cleveland Row, at the Green Park end of Pall Mall, close to St. James's Palace, and conveniently situated for court functions. As we have seen, his mother died in 1728, and two years later, early in 1730, John (11) was received into the Catholic Church, probably in one of the capital's Catholic embassy chapels. In the following year, Dr. Robert Witham, the President of Douay College, wrote to Bishop Gifford's procurator in Rome that the new convert's imprudence had cost him a place at court and had jeopardized the whole Catholic community.

---

[247] Dalton, Charles, **English Army Lists and Commission Registers - 1661-1714**, London 1960, vol.5, 1702-1707, p.35 and fn.8.

[248] Chamberlayne, J. (ed.), **Magnae Britanniae Notitia**, London 1725, 27th edition, p.170. He is mistakenly entered as "John Short", but the correct form "Shorter" occurs in all subsequent editions up to 1737.

[249] cf. Chamberlayne, **op.cit.**, 36th ed., 1735, p.89.

The last letters from England acquaint me that one Mr. Shorter, brother-in-law of the great Sir Rob[ert] Walpole, who was converted about a twelvemonth ago, and by his conversion lost a place at Court of £800 sterling a year, has lately had the indiscreet zeal to tell George's son, called Prince of Wales, to his face, that he had no right to that Title of Prince of Wales, which belonged to another. This has so exasperated the Court, that the Catholicks apprehend it may be of ill consequence to them all at the opening of this Parliament, by Acts for enforcing laws and oaths against them as of Abjuration or the like, such as their conscience and Loyalty can never take, unless a few misled persons.[250]

The letter reflects the pessimism and apprehension of the Catholic exiles, rather than the reality of the situation in England, because, in spite of his imprudence, John (11) retained his post as Commissioner for the Stamp Duties until 1737, the year of Lady Catherine's death. If any appointment was forfeited, it must have been one that was in the offing, because he does not appear in the lists of the royal household. In his will, he refers to his servant, William Stott, twice risking his life for him, and no doubt, as the threat of a second Jacobite invasion drew nearer, he was living dangerously in Cleveland Row.[251]

---

[250] Williams, J.A., **Catholic Recusancy in Wiltshire, 1660-1791**, Catholic Record Society, 1968, pp.62, also p.13; cf. also Westminster Cathedral Archives, var.ix, 132, postscript to letter of January 24th 1731; and Kirk, J., **Biographies of English Catholics, 1700-1800**, London 1909, p.210 which confuses John (11) with his father, John (9).

[251] P.C.C., Edmunds 746, 1746.

The Jacobite Shorters

It is interesting to speculate about John (11)'s conversion. It took place when Walpole's hold on government was already beginning to fail, and it must have been viewed by the families of his two sisters as a betrayal and a want of gratitude towards his Whig benefactors. Perhaps, he had flirted with the Jacobites in Paris or Rome, during his travels abroad, or perhaps there was a lingering loyalty to his grandfather's friend, the unfortunate James II, as well as a disenchantment with the Hanoverians. The remark he is alleged to have made to Frederick, Prince of Wales, certainly implies Jacobite loyalties. His brother, Arthur, is known to have shared his Jacobitism even more passionately.[252] Erasmus, however, continued in the army, serving both King George I and King George II. He may even have fought against the Old Pretender in 1715, but retired a year or two before the '45.[253] Without any doubt, this divided loyalty was the cause of the animosity which reigned between John (11) and Arthur on the one hand, and their brother Erasmus, on the other. It also explains why Erasmus was Horace Walpole's favorite Shorter uncle, and why he scorned John (11) and Arthur.

Lady Catherine Walpole died at Chelsea on August 20th 1737. Although she was afraid of ghosts, she apparently had no fear of death.[254] Her son Horace Walpole wrote somewhat condescendingly: "I believe few women could behave so well". She spoke of death "with less indifference than one speaks of a

---

[252] Conway to Walpole, 29th August, 1746, Lewis **op.cit.**, vol.37, pp.255-256.

[253] cf. Dalton **op.cit.**, p.35.

[254] Conyers Middleton to Horace Walpole August 25th 1737, Lewis **op.cit.**, vol.15, pp.4-6.

cold".[255] Lady Catherine was interred in Westminster Abbey in the south aisle of King Henry VII's Chapel.[256] Her tomb is set against the back of the choir stalls, near the tomb of Mary Queen of Scots, and the Countess of Lennox. Horace Walpole was determined to give his mother a fitting memorial or "cenotaph", as he called it, and it was no accident that Henry VII's Chapel was chosen as the setting, since the Walpoles already had an interest in the building. It had recently become the Chapel of the new Order of the Bath, established by King George I in 1725, at the behest of Sir Robert Walpole, and, together with the rest of the Abbey, was being restored according to the plans of Wren and Hawksmoor.[257] Having paid £40 for the grave itself, Horace Walpole commissioned a marble statue by the Italian sculptor, Filipo Valle. It was based on an antique original, in the Villa Mattei in Rome, of Livia Drusilla, wife of the Emperor Augustus.[258] The statue arrived in 1743 and was set up on a pedestal designed by John Michael

---

[255] Lewis **op.cit.**, vol.40, p.24.

[256] Five members of other branches of the Shorter family are buried in Westminster Abbey. Three of them belonged to the parish of St. Margaret's Westminster: Solomon buried in the cloisters on January 29th 1678; Sarah, his daughter, buried in the cloisters on September 15th 1663; and Thomas, his son, a member of the Westminster Abbey Choir, buried at the south end of the East cloister on March 19th 1673. Mrs. Anne Tanner, nee Shorter, was buried in the south cloister on August 3rd 1727; and Susanna, daughter of John Shorter of Witney, Oxon, wife of the Abbey Precentor, Dr. William Whitfield Dakins, was buried in the south cloister on December 11th 1834. cf.**Harleian Society**, vol.10, p.193, n.1, and refs. **sub** "Shorter".

[257] Swan, Conrad, **The Chapel of the Order of the Bath**, London, 1978.

[258] Paget Toynbee, **op.cit.**, vol.1, xli; Lewis **op.cit.**, vol.22, pp.27, 98n.;vol.40, p.24. The author visited the Villa Mattei, now the Villa Celimontana, on May 27th 1991. The private collection it once housed has been dispersed to public museums, and the statue of Livia has not yet been traced.

Rysbrack, the Dutch sculptor who came to England in 1720.[259] Rysbrack's first design was considerably more grandiose, with a pediment and apse behind the statue. One is grateful for the simple plinth which was eventually adopted.

Thomas Allen, the 19th century historian of London, describes it as a "tall, but graceful, musing statue". He continues:

> If we except the numberless folds of the garment, and perhaps the forefinger of her right hand, which appears to be just entering her ear, this is a most exquisite monument.[260]

The epitaph composed by Horace Walpole is as follows:

> To the memory of Catherine, Lady Walpole, eldest daughter of John Shorter Esq. of Bybrook in Kent, and first wife of Sir Robert Walpole, afterwards Earl of Orford, Horace, her youngest son, consecrates this monument. She had beauty and wit without vice or vanity, and cultivated the arts without affectation. She was devout, though without bigotry to any sect; and was without prejudice to any party, though the wife of a minister, whose power she esteemed but when she could employ it to benefit the miserable, or to reward the meritorious. She loved a private life, though born to shine in public, and was an ornament to courts, untainted by them. She died August 20th 1737.

---

[259] Lewis **op.cit.**, vol.40, p.24; Esdaile, Katharine A., **English Church Monuments**, Batsford, London, 1946, p.64.

[260] Allen, Thomas, **History of London**, Cowie and Strange, London 1828, vol.4, pp.103-104.

It was about this time that John (11) left office and withdrew to Bybrook.[261] At Little Chart, not far from Bybrook, there was an outpost of Catholicism at the Darrell family's mansion of Calehill, and there was even an offshoot of this group at Ashford.[262] It is not impossible that John (11) had something to do with the recusants of Kent. There is even a local tradition of a priest hole at Bybrook House.[263] John (11)'s brother, Arthur, was an invalid who spent nearly all his time at Bath, taking the waters. As Jacobites, it was no doubt more prudent for both brothers to seek retirement at some distance from the capital, as the prospect of a second Jacobite invasion threatened to become a reality. John (11) was already in his early fifties, and had drawn up his will in 1734. Its opening sentence has a Catholic flavor, with its reference to the merits of Christ's passion and the remission of sins.

> First and foremost I commend my soul into the hands of almighty God, my Master, hoping through the meritorious death and passion of my Lord and Saviour, Jesus Christ, to receive remission and pardon of all my sins, and my body I leave to the earth to receive a decent and Christian burial.[264]

He asked to be buried in the parish church at Kennington, if he died at Bybrook. If he died in London, he wanted to be buried as near as possible to the grave of his father John (9) at St. Saviour's Southwark. His funeral was to be private, with a

---

[261] Shorter, Aylward, "Horace Walpole's Catholic Uncle", in **Catholic Ancestor**, vol.3, no.6, November 1991, pp.225-229, summarizes John (11)'s life.

[262] Whatmore, J.E., **Recusancy in Kent**, mimeographed 1973, p.57, cf. Downside Abbey Monastery Library, 55714, Box 99/C23C.

[263] Communication from an informant at Bybrook garden center on July 22nd 1991. The author was unable to verify the rumor.

[264] P.C.C., Edmunds 746, 1746.

hearse and two coaches only, and a single pair of horses to each vehicle. To Catherine, then still alive, he bequeathed his picture and all the family pictures, together with his old chinaware. His house in Cleveland Row he left to his servant William Stott, together with his plate and household furniture, but not the linen or pictures. This bequest was "out of a grateful regard for his long and faithful services to me and for risqueing [sic] his life twice for me". There was a small bequest to his maidservant Anne Chancellor, but all other property was to go to Arthur, John (11) having no wife or children. Erasmus was not even mentioned.

The Jacobite uprising was in full swing, and Bonny Prince Charlie was still in England when John (11) died at Bybrook in 1746. He was buried in the churchyard of St. Mary's Kennington on February 11th.[265] His nephew, Henry Seymour Conway, wrote to his cousin, Horace Walpole:

> Poor uncle John! I am not sorry he's dead as you may imagine, so shall say no melancholy things about it. I delight in your interview with Erasmus and what a number of doleful dirges you are to expect from Arthur![266]

Arthur proved the will, as sole executor, on March 20th, but by the time he came again to London in August, the Battle of Culloden had been fought, the Young Pretender was a fugitive, and Jacobite hopes had been dashed. Arthur's Whig nephews indulged all their spite, and Conway wrote to Walpole:

---

[265] Kent County Archives, original Register of St. Mary's Kennington, P207/1/20: "John Shorter, Esq., buried." The author visited Kennington on July 22nd 1991, and received a letter from Rev. Colin G. Preece, Vicar of St. Mary's, dated September 19th 1991. There are several 18th century tombs with indecipherable inscriptions, but none can be identified, as there is no accurate plan of the churchyard which goes back to the 18th century. There is no Shorter monument in the church.

[266] Conway to Walpole, March 3rd 1746, Lewis, **op.cit.**, vol.37, p.256.

But you can't imagine how much you surprise me by telling me Arthur is in town. I had no notion that anything but the Pretender's being crowned there could bring him so far, and then he would only be dragged up to expire in peace after seeing that glorious day. Poor man, what can you do with him, with all his miseries and all his complaints?[267]

The following month he wrote again:

But of all strange things, what you tell me of Arthur's being without miseries is the most strange; when I saw him he was made up of stone, gravel, gout, rheumatism, ruptures etc. with more whinings and pinings and greater disorders of mind and body. Pray give my duty to him as a part of what, in his state of whining, used to be near and dear. I want to know how it fares with his Jacobitism, and how he bears the misfortunes of his friends.[268]

John (11) proved to be the last Shorter to live at Bybrook. Arthur took no interest in it, but continued to live at Bath, where he died and was buried in Bath Abbey on February 14th 1750.[269] His will begins:

I desire that my body may be devoutly interred in the Abbey Church of Bath in the same grave with Sir Erasmus Phillips Baronet.[270]

---

[267] Conway to Walpole, August 29th 1746, Lewis **op.cit.**, vol.37, p.255-256.

[268] Conway to Walpole, September 15th 1746, Lewis **op.cit.**, vol.37, p.256.

[269] **Registers of Bath Abbey, Harleian Society**, vol. 28, p.439.

[270] P.C.C., Busby 786, 1751.

Arthur had a strong attachment to his grandfather, the baronet, and had a portrait painted of him in 1733.[271] Presumably his last request was granted.[272] Like his brothers, Arthur had no wife or children. Apart from small annuities to a clergyman, to his maidservant and two godsons, he left all his property to his surgeon, John Donn or Dunn,

> In gratitude for his kind and assiduous care and attendance on me through a long series of illnesses and for his many services to me in my own affairs.[273]

Captain Erasmus Shorter

Once again, Erasmus Shorter was cut out of the inheritance, and this time Bybrook passed into the hands of Mr. John Dunn, Arthur's executor. Erasmus, however, had enjoyed a distinguished military career as a cavalry officer in the Hanoverian army. In 1708, at the age of about 19, he had been made Cornet to Major Herbert Lawrence of the Queen's Own Regiment of Dragoons, 3rd Hussars. In 1709 he transferred to the Duke of Schomberg's Regiment of Horse. In June 1715 his commission as Lieutenant in Major-General Sybourg's

---

[271] **Notes and Queries**, 3rd Series, vol.1, p.118.

[272] In the event of Sir Erasmus's tomb being removed, Arthur asked to be buried near the grave of Mrs. Stewart. I am indebted to my nephew, Mr. Damian Hutt, for his research into Arthur Shorter's burial place. He tells me Sir Erasmus Phillips's tomb is located under the pews in the south nave, and is numbered 26 in the Abbey Wardens' list. When the pews were installed in 1872, Charles Russell recorded the details of the ledger stones and additional burials. Number 26 is unaccountably missing from the record. A plaque to Sir Erasmus Phillips is to be seen at the east end of the north wall of the Abbey, but it does not mention Arthur Shorter. There is no mention of a Mrs. Stewart in the Wardens' list.

[273] P.C.C. Busby 786, 1751.

Regiment of Horse, 7th Dragoon Guards, was renewed by King George I, and on July 22nd he replaced Ensign Smith of Cobham's Dragoons. In 1740 he was still serving as a cavalry officer and had attained the rank of Captain.[274]

Captain Erasmus Shorter owned a house at Park Place, St. James's, but died in lodgings in Chancery Lane on November 23rd 1753, and was buried at St. James's Piccadilly.[275] According to his nephew Horace Walpole, "his death and the circumstances have made extreme noise". This was because his Swiss servant was suspected, not only of embezzling some of his master's effects, but even of hastening his death. He was arrested on the following day, but Horace interceded for him and charges were dropped.[276] Since Erasmus died intestate, and without close relatives, a statutory notice was placed in **The Daily Advertiser** of December 17th 1753, as follows:

> If any gentleman has any knowledge of the will of the late Capt. Erasmus Shorter of Park Place St. James's, he is hereby humbly desired to give what intelligence thereof he can, to Mr. A. B. at the White Horse Tavern in Holborn, over against Chancery Lane.[277]

No will was found and the Walpoles and Conways became heirs-at-law to Erasmus's fortune of £30,000. Horace and his brother, Edward, together with Francis Earl of Hertford, Henry

---

[274] Dalton, **op.cit.**, vol.5, p.35 and fn.8; Dalton, Charles, **George the First's Army, 1714-1727**, London 1912, vol.2, p.188.

[275] Paget Toynbee, **op.cit.**, vol.1, xli; Boyd's London Burials, Society of Genealogists; Lewis **op.cit.**, vol.14, p.25, vol.37; p.372.

[276] Paget Toynbee, **op.cit.**, vol.3, p.202; Lewis **op.cit.**, vol.13, p.25 and fn.vol.37, p.372.

[277] Lewis, **op.cit.**, vol.37, p.372, fn.2.

Seymour Conway and Anne Seymour Conway, received £6,000 apiece.[278]   In this way, the direct line of the Lord Mayor's descendants died out, and the Shorter fortune was dispersed.

---

[278] Lewis, **op.cit.**, vol.4, p.359 n.; vol.9, pp.156, 161; vol.13, p.25 and n., 26 n.; vol.14, p.25; Paget Toynbee, **op.cit.**, vol.1, p.xli.

CHAPTER NINE

RICHARD SHORTER OF MOUNTFIELD

Mountfield Village

The name Shorter first appears in the records of Mountfield village, East Sussex, in 1719. On September 14th of that year, Richard Shorter married Grace Bunce in the village church of All Saints. Both are described as being "of this parish". The rest of Part One of this book concerns the Shorters of Mountfield and their descendants, and it is appropriate to say something first about the village and its location.

Mountfield village is situated on the London to Hastings road, directly north of Battle, Sussex, in the forested hill country of the High Weald.[279] The river Rother flows in a deep valley through this country towards Rye, its main affluent being the river Brede, which is fed by several source brooks in the Mountfield area. About two thirds of the village is woodland, but the remaining third is open farmland of indifferent quality, with a subsoil of sand and gravel. Much of this land is under permanent grass. The 12th century church of All Saints, with its Norman chancel arch and ancient Norman

---

[279] This description relies on **Victoria History of the Counties of England, A History of Sussex**, vol.9, "The Rape of Hastings", O.U.P., London 1937, pp.226, 234-236; Goodsall, Robert H., **The Eastern Rother**, Rochester Press, London 1981 (reprinted), pp.3-4, 146; also on the author's own observation during a visit to Mountfield on June 27th 1991.

font, stands on a hill overlooking the wooded slopes and farm clearings of the village.

When Richard and Grace were married in the church, Mountfield probably had a population of around four hundred, and the owners of the manor were the Nicholl family.[280] A hundred years later, William Cobbett rode through the area to Battle in January 1822 and left a vivid description.

> The rest of the way to Battle presents alternately clay and sandstone. Of course, the coppices and oak woods are very frequent. There is now and then a hop-garden spot, and now and then an orchard of apples or cherries, but these are poor indeed when compared with what you see about Canterbury or Maidstone....
>
> I cannot quit Battle without observing that the country is very pretty all about it. All hill or valley. A very great deal of woodland in which the underwood is generally very fine, though the oaks are not so fine and a good deal covered with moss.[281]

Mountfield was an area of ancient and extensive iron production. Other activities included charcoal burning, the cutting of hop-poles and the mining of a bed of gypsum for plaster or cement. In 1719 the open field system was probably still practiced, since the reform of agriculture only began to affect East Sussex in the latter half of the 18th century. Most of the inhabitants would have been engaged in small-scale farming and livestock raising.

---

[280] The population in 1801 was 564. A hundred years later it was 562, 102 people having emigrated to America. cf. **Victoria History of the Counties of England, A History of Sussex**, vol.2, London 1907, p.223, fn.23.; vol.9, 1937, pp.234-236.

[281] Cobbett, William, **Rural Rides**, London 1893, 2 vols, pp.71, 78.

From Mountfield the undulating woodland gradually flattens out towards the Kentish border, as the rivers Brede and Tillingham join the Rother and flow through low-lying floodland to the sea. Beyond the estuary, and below sea-level, lies the strange world of Walland and Romney Marshes. Almost the last village on the relatively high ground between the rivers is Peasmarsh, similar in population size, acreage and soil consistency, to Mountfield. Its parish church, dedicated to Saints Peter and Paul, stands on high ground in a spacious churchyard. From the center of Peasmarsh village, the road runs towards the Kentish border and on to Romney Marsh.

Three years after their marriage at Mountfield we find Richard and Grace at Peasmarsh, and it was there that Richard died in 1728. His widow returned to Mountfield, and the burial of two of her surviving children in the same year is the last mention of the Shorter family in the Mountfield and Peasmarsh registers for over forty years. On September 1st 1771 William Shorter (5) was baptized at Peasmarsh, and on July 2nd 1791 he was living at Mountfield when he married Elizabeth Shoesmith in the neighboring village of Brightling.[282] William (5) (1771-1833) is the "patriarch" of the Shorters of Mountfield.

The Identity of Richard

There are two basic problems to be confronted in the story of the Mountfield Shorters: the origin and identity of Richard and the forty year gap in the parish record. In 1719 branches of the Shorter family had been established since the 16th century in

---

[282] Transcripts of the parish registers of Mountfield, Peasmarsh and Brightling, East Sussex Record Office, Lewes; cf. also International Genealogical Index for Sussex. The Mountfield burial register states that William (5) was 62 years old when he died on April 3rd 1833, thus confirming 1771 as the year of his birth.

Salehurst and Hastings; and, for scarcely more than a decade, in the parish of Bodiam, adjacent to Salehurst on the Kentish border. About the same time, Shorters - also possibly from Salehurst - were beginning to establish themselves across the Kentish border in Hothfield, Woodchurch and Great Chart. A local parish would be the first place in which to look for Richard's origins. However, an exhaustive search in the parish registers of East Sussex and West Kent has failed to come up with any record of Richard's birth. In itself, this may not be surprising. Parish records are not always complete and some are damaged or indecipherable. It is not impossible therefore, that Richard was born locally.

Against this must be set the unusual choice of the name Richard in an age when the same Christian names were handed down from generation to generation. Before 1719 there is no record of any member of the Shorter family in East Sussex being called Richard. The first Shorter to be given the name Richard in West Kent was probably named after a relative by marriage. This occurred at Great Chart three years before the wedding of Richard and Grace at Mountfield.[283] The absence, for more than a century, of any Shorter in the area called Richard, contrasts with the London branch of the family in which, as we have seen, Richard was a common name. Another remarkable fact is that the Mountfield Shorters reproduced the pattern of male Christian names found among the Shorters of Staines and London, **viz.** John, William, Thomas, Richard and, less commonly, Henry. This pattern is not complete in Sussex or Kent. For example, in Salehurst, Bodiam and West Kent only the names John and Thomas occur. While in Hastings, these are joined by William.

If Richard's origin is to be sought outside the Sussex-Kent border area, then we must look for guidance to the family traditions of the Mountfield Shorters. The first tradition explicitly

---

[283] He may have been named after Richard Bourne, who married his second cousin, Elizabeth Shorter.

links them with the London family of the Lord Mayor. The story of the latter's spectacular accident, as well as the alienation of the family fortunes to the Walpoles and Seymours, were handed down across the generations.[284] Henry (3) (1847-1915) was especially jealous of this family connection. His signet ring bore the Lord Mayor's griphon crest, as did his servants' livery buttons.[285] He also made use of the whole Shorter coat of arms (with lion and battle axes) on correspondence cards.[286] When Clement King Shorter, editor of the **Illustrated London News** at the turn of the 19th/20th centuries, published an article about Sir John (4), implying a family relationship, Henry (3) was outraged and is reported to have said of the editor: "He is not a member of our family !"[287] For upwardly mobile Sussex farmers to claim an illustrious London family connection may be a sign of snobbery, but it is less easy to explain the self confidence which led them to deny this privilege to others. One feels they must have been very sure of their claim. It is also noteworthy that the Mountfield Shorters described their rank on early marriage certificates as "Gentleman" or "Gentleman Farmer". This was even true of

---

[284] As a child, both stories were related to the author by his grandfather Wilfred Wynn Shorter (1875-1952), and he was able to scrutinize Henry (3)'s family papers and pedigrees, lent by his cousins, the daughters of Elizabeth Louise (1871-1949).

[285] The author inherited the signet ring from Wilfred in 1952, and gave it to his brother Crispin, on entering the seminary in 1955. Wilfred kept several examples of the livery buttons, after Henry (3)'s death. One is still in the author's possession.

[286] One such card is in the author's possession.

[287] Clement King Shorter belonged to a Norfolk branch of the family. Besides being editor of the **Illustrated London News**, he edited, at different times, several other periodicals of a similar format. The author recollects seeing the article among Henry (3)'s papers in the 1940s. The librarians of the **I.L.N.** kindly attempted to trace it for me via the picture index (the only existing index of these periodicals), but without success. The author heard of Henry (3)'s outrage from his grandfather, Wilfred.

Robert (1822-1862) who had been in service.[288] Finally, pride of family was, no doubt, involved in the two Shorter intermarriages: Henry Shorter (3) (1847-1915) to his first cousin, Eleanor Shorter (1847-1929) in 1870; and George Shorter (1862-) to his second cousin Elizabeth Louise Shorter (1871-1949) in 1898.

It is possible that Richard Shorter of Mountfield had a London origin. If this was the case, the records offer only one possible candidate, Richard (4), grandson of John Shorter Waterman. The Waterman's descendants are the only known surviving line of the Staines-London Shorters in England. Born in 1683, Richard (4*) would have been aged 36 when he married Grace Bunce in 1719, and 45 when he died in 1728.[289] As we have seen, it was not unheard of for men at that time to marry in their thirties. For example, William (4) married at the age of 35, and John (8) at 30. Moreover, if Richard (4*) was a stranger from London, it would have taken time for him to settle in Sussex and to win the confidence of his bride's family, though they may well have been flattered by the attentions of a well-connected, if poor, Londoner. This identification remains the only hypothesis, in default of further evidence.

Evidently, Richard (4) did not choose his father's profession as a weaver in Stepney, but left his younger brother, George, to follow in Richard (3)'s footsteps. His disappearance from the London record suggests that he moved elsewhere. Life in the eastern suburbs of 18th century London was far from easy. Living conditions could be unhealthy, and a young man's future was only assured by apprenticeship to a trade. Richard (4*) chose his wife from a village on the London-Hastings road. He may have traveled down that road, trying to make a living. The

---

[288] cf. G.R.O. Marriage Certificate of Henry Shorter (3) and Eleanor Shorter, 1870.

[289] The asterisk signifies that the identification is a hypothesis, requiring further proof.

Sussex Weald was not, at that time, a place in which to settle and become a successful farmer, but, as we have seen, it offered opportunities for casual work of different kinds. Richard (4*) did not stay long in Mountfield after his marriage. He spent four years of his married life there and the remaining five years at Peasmarsh. After his death, his widow returned at once to Mountfield. This does not suggest that he had any permanent holding at either Mountfield or Peasmarsh, and there are no settlement orders or other documents which refer to him.[290] There were, however, representatives of the Bunce family in Peasmarsh, and it looks as if Richard (4*)'s chief security in the area was his wife's family.[291]

On January 3rd 1720 Elizabeth, daughter of Richard (4*) and Grace was baptized at Mountfield.[292] On February 27th 1723 another daughter, Ann, was baptized at Peasmarsh. Then, on January 12th, their son Richard (6) was baptized also at Peasmarsh.[293] Two years later, on March 5th 1728, Richard (4*) was buried at Peasmarsh.[294] Then, in quick and tragic succession, the small children, Elizabeth aged eight and Richard (6) aged two, died and were buried at Mountfield, on

---

[290] Research at the East Sussex Archives in Lewes has not revealed any records. David Martin, the local historian of the area, knows of only two references to 18th century holdings by Shorters in the area. These were at Warbleton, probably by members of the Salehurst family. Letter to the author, June 27th 1991.

[291] East Sussex Record Office, Lewes, Transcript of Peasmarsh Parish Registers, e.g. burial of Anne Bunce, October 30th 1720.

[292] East Sussex Record Office, Lewes, Transcript of Mountfield parish registers.

[293] East Sussex Record Office, Lewes, Transcript of Peasmarsh parish registers.

[294] East Sussex Record Office, Lewes, Peasmarsh parish register (original): "Richard Shorter was buried".

September 1st and October 3rd 1728.[295] The widowed Grace was left with a single daughter, the five year old Ann. The next family event recorded at Peasmarsh was the baptism of William (5), the son of John (13) and his wife Elizabeth on September 1st 1771.

The Shorters in Romney Marsh

Our second problem concerns the identity of John (13) and his relationship to Richard (4*). In attempting to solve this riddle, the second tradition of the Mountfield Shorters proves helpful. This is the collective memory of a sojourn in Romney Marsh. Wilfred (1875-1952) spoke frequently about this tradition and was fascinated by the marsh's strange terrain. One of his favorite authors was Richard Harris Barham, a 19th century vicar of the Romney Marsh parish of Snargate (1817-1821). In his **Ingoldsby Legends**, Barham celebrated the strangeness of the marshes, as well as the ghost stories and smuggling legends associated with them.[296]

In the 18th century, members of the Shorter family are found in only one Romney Marsh parish, that of Ivychurch.[297] The first to be mentioned are John Shorter ("of this parish") who married Elizabeth Hopper on May 23rd 1762, and the children born to them there.[298] A quarter of a century later, "John

---

[295] East Sussex Record Office, Lewes, Transcript of Mountfield Parish Registers.

[296] Ingoldsby, Thomas, **The Ingoldsby Legends**, London, J. M. Dent, 1898 (reprinted 1930).

[297] Shorters are also found in the parish of Lydd, south of Old Romney. This is not strictly Romney Marsh. The parish area consists largely of Denge Marsh and the desolate projection of Dungeness, with its stony beaches. These Shorters were probably related to those of Woodchurch.

[298] Kent County Archives, Maidstone, Ivychurch parish registers, P203.

Shorter of Woodchurch parish" married Mary Small of Ivychurch on January 8th 1788, and started another family in the village. These two Shorter families seem to be unrelated, and also to have little in common. John Shorter of Woodchurch is a member of the family established in that parish since the beginning of the 18th century. It included several paupers and baseborn children, and several of its members died in the poorhouse. John, the husband of Elizabeth Hopper, however, cannot be identified as one of the Woodchurch Shorters.

Of the several Shorter couples in East Sussex and West Kent, called "John and Elizabeth", only the Ivychurch pair are contemporary with the parents of William (5) at Peasmarsh. Moreover, the Hopper family is not mentioned in the Ivychurch registers until 1803, whereas it is found in East Sussex in the mid-18th century.[299] The Elizabeth Hopper whom John Shorter married in 1862, may be Elizabeth, daughter of Thomas Hopper, born at Guestling in 1728; or Elizabeth, daughter of Moses and Mary Hopper, born at Ticehurst **circa** 1742.[300] Even more significant, perhaps, is the fact that the Bunce family, so numerous at Mountfield, and mentioned also in Peasmarsh, had its representatives at Ivychurch in the persons of the Reverend William Bunce and his son, the Reverend John Bunce.[301] It looks, therefore, as if the Shorters and Bunces are a common thread, linking the parishes of Mountfield, Peasmarsh and Ivychurch, and that John Shorter of Ivychurch is to be identified with John (13).

---

[299] Edward, son of William and Ann Hopper, was buried at Ivychurch on March 17th 1803, cf. Kent County Archives, Ivychurch parish registers, p. 203.

[300] cf. East Sussex Record Office, Lewes, transcripts of Guestling and Ticehurst parish registers.

[301] Kent County Archives, Maidstone, Ivychurch parish registers, P203.

"The world, according to the best geographers, is divided into Europe, Asia, Africa, America and Romney Marsh", so wrote Richard Harris Barham.[302] It is, indeed, an unearthly place. William Cobbett compared its vast, flat pastures to the American prairies.[303] The alluvial sediment, of which the marsh is composed, sometimes produces high quality pasture land. However, the quality of the soil is variable and the pastures cannot carry the same numbers of sheep in winter, as in summer. Moreover, the population is so small that it is inadequate for other farming systems.[304] Cobbett thought that the area had been depopulated, and no doubt some people moved away when the Martello Towers and the Royal Military Canal were built as defences against the threatened Napoleonic invasion. Nevertheless, the population of the villages was traditionally very small, and the huge churches were not constructed for vanished congregations but, as a heavenly insurance against the sea and other elements.[305]

Ivychurch is situated some twelve miles by road from Peasmarsh. In 1831 it had a population of 198, and a few miserable houses.[306] When John (13) settled there, it could not have been much bigger. Marsh fever was endemic. The village consisted of an "island" in the marshes, and its "monolithic" parish church of St. George was one of the largest and most spacious

---

[302] Ingoldsby, Thomas, **op.cit.**, p.87.

[303] Cobbett, **op.cit.**, pp.22-23.

[304] Holloway, William, **History of Romney Marsh**, London John Russell Smith, 1849; Forbes, Duncan, **The Fifth Continent**, Hythe, Shearwater Press, 1984, p.10-11; Murray, Walter J.C., **Romney Marsh**, London, Robert Hale, 1953 (1982 ed.), pp.118-119, 123, 128, 135.

[305] cf. Goodsall, **op.cit.**, pp.63-64; Forbes, **op.cit.**, p.89.

[306] Holloway, **op.cit.**, p.173.

in the area.[307] John (13) evidently settled there in the first years of the youthful King George III's reign, and celebrated his wedding to Elizabeth Hopper in the monumental church on May 23rd 1762. An Edward Shorter who died at Ivychurch on December 25th 1799, aged 33 years, may have been his son.[308] He would have been born in 1766, but his baptism is not recorded at Ivychurch; and he may have been born at Peasmarsh or elsewhere. Five years later, on September 1st 1771, William (5), son of John (13) and Elizabeth was baptized at Peasmarsh, and the fact that there are no records of children being born to them at Ivychurch between 1762 and 1774 suggests a long absence from Romney Marsh of ten years or more. On March 1st 1774, another son, Stephen, was baptized at Ivychurch. Finally Thomas (6) was baptized on September 29th 1777, but died two years later and was buried at Ivychurch on April 18th 1778. John (13) was buried at Ivychurch on March 10th 1790, after 28 years of married life. He was probably about fifty years old.[309]

That there is a relationship between John (13) and Richard (4*) is suggested by the links with Peasmarsh and Mountfield. Like Richard (4*), John (13) seems to have been an itinerant laborer. His baptismal record has not so far been traced. It is not impossible that he was the son of Richard (4*) born in **circa** 1728, perhaps posthumously. He may even have been a nephew of Richard (4*) - perhaps the son of his brother, John (12), who, like him, disappeared from London's eastern

---

[307] Jacobs, Elsie M., **Across the Marshes**, Brookland, no date, p.37; Bagley, Geoffrey Spink, **Pictorial Guide to Romney Marsh**, Rye Museum Association 1986, pp.34-35.

[308] Kent County Archives, Maidstone, Ivychurch parish registers, P203.

[309] For all these references, cf. Kent County Archives, Maidstone, Ivychurch parish registers, P203. The author visited Ivychurch on July 27th 1992. The Shorter gravestones may be among those of 18th century appearance with indecipherable inscriptions.

suburbs.[310] In default of evidence, the relationship remains a working hypothesis.[311] With the marriage of William (5) in 1791, and his return to Mountfield, we re-enter the realm of historical certainty.

---

[310] An 18th century gravestone close to the south wall of the chancel of Peasmarsh Church may offer a clue. The author saw it on July 27th 1992, and offers this reading of the (almost illegible) inscription: "In Memory of Mr.John Shorter who departed this life on the...day of...17...". John (13) was, as we have seen, buried at Ivychurch. Is this possibly the grave of John (12) ? If so, his burial is not recorded in the Peasmarsh register.

[311] As we have seen, there is no John, let alone a John who married an Elizabeth, in the other parish registers of East Sussex and West Kent, who can be identified with John (13).

CHAPTER TEN

FARMERS OF THE SUSSEX HIGH WEALD

The Shorters at Banks Farm

When William (5) married Elizabeth Shoesmith at Brightling on July 2nd 1791, he was already established at Mountfield.[312] In view of his son John (14)'s twenty year association with The Banks Farm and the neighboring Baldwin's Farm, it is likely that William (5) began as an agricultural laborer there. The Banks is a rambling country mansion to the west of All Saints Church, standing in its own grounds at the end of a long drive. Up to 1943 the estate comprised 142 acres, with a further 101 acres let to a tenant farmer.[313] The land is a pleasant series of wooded ravines and open ridges. The house, which has a gabled front, possesses an original 15th century timber frame and was enlarged in Elizabethan and Jacobean times.[314] Extensive Victorian additions were made in the 1860s and

---

[312] East Sussex Record Office, Lewes, transcript of Brightling parish registers.

[313] East Sussex Record Office, Lewes, **Auctioneers' Brochure**, July 2nd 1943.

[314] The author visited the house on June 27th 1991, and was kindly shown round it by the present owner, Mrs. Helm. The **Auctioneers' Brochure** of 1943 describes it as basically "Jacobean", but there is evidence that it is considerably older.

1870s. When William (5) came to Mountfield, Richard Ruck was the owner, and it was later inherited in the mid-19th century by Sir John Bennett, Lord Mayor of London.[315]

The Banks Farm is adjacent to the mansion, and incorporates the stables. The present farmhouse is a Victorian conversion of a brick oast house. When William (5) came to Mountfield, the tenancy of Banks Farm was held by the Avan family.[316] The other holding, Baldwin's Farm, is situated to the right of The Banks' drive, across an open valley. In 1851, when John (14)'s widow, Lydia, was manager, it had 130 acres and employed five laborers.[317] In 1909, the large scale ordnance survey shows that it had a total of thirteen buildings.[318] Up to 1841, it belonged to George Kenward.[319]

William (5)'s wife, Elizabeth, came from a well-known local family, the Shoesmiths. The first mention of them at Brightling dates from the 1780s, but they were well established at Bodiam, Seddlescombe and Whatlington from an earlier date.[320] She was baptized at Mountfield on October 22nd 1768, the daughter of William and Mary Shoesmith. William (5) and

---

[315] Information from documents in possession of the present owners. Wilfred (1875-1952) had a number of ghost stories about the old house which he related to the author in the 1940s. One concerned a phantom coach and horses which drove through the buildings.

[316] Edward Avan held the farm from 1780 to 1801; Sarah Avan, from 1802 to 1813. A Rev. Carter held it from 1824 to 1827. Documents seen at The Banks on June 27th 1991.

[317] P.R.O., 1851 Census.

[318] **Ordnance Survey**, 25 inch, 1909.

[319] P.R.O. 1841 Census.

[320] East Sussex Record Office, Lewes, cf. transcripts of relevant parish registers.

Elizabeth had a total of ten children. The first was Elizabeth (9), baptized on April 8th 1792.[321] On December 13th 1814, at the age of 22, she married Thomas Kemp at Mountfield. Sophia was baptized on February 8th 1794 and was buried at Mountfield on April 27th 1827, aged 33. Richard (7) was baptized on December 6th 1795. Nothing more is known about him, and he does not figure in any census. He probably died in infancy and the burial was unrecorded.[322] William (6) was born in 1796.[323] On May 26th 1821 he married Anne Pilbin at Mountfield. Little is known about Anne, and her baptismal entry has not been traced. However, the marriage was witnessed by Stephen Pilbin, probably her father, and on February 9th 1827 an Anne Pilbin, aged 56, was buried at Mountfield. This may have been her mother. Anne bore William (6) four children. On August 19th 1821 Sarah was baptized, but died three weeks later and was buried on September 9th.[324] On August 11th 1822 Robert was baptized, about whom more will be said in the next chapter. On April 7th 1826 Sophia was baptized, but died the following month and was buried on May 23rd.[325] Finally, Emily was born in 1825

---

[321] The genealogical information in this chapter is based on the transcripts of Mountfield parish registers at the East Sussex Record Office, Lewes, supplemented by the P.R.O., Census of 1841 HO107/1108, 1851 HO107/1636, 1861 RG9/564 and 1871 RG10/1035.

[322] A Richard Shorter, Higgler, is mentioned in the 1851 Census as living with his family at Flitterbrook, near Mayfield. His age, however is given as 48, which makes him too young to be Richard (6). This Richard is presumably the Richard Shorter who had a freehold house and land at Flitterbrook in 1837, and was a registered elector in the first parliament of Queen Victoria. Cf. **East Sussex List of Registered Electors**, Baxter, Lewes 1837, p.74.

[323] No baptismal entry has been traced for William (6). However, the 1851 census states that he was born at Mountfield and gives his age as 55.

[324] East Sussex Record Office, Lewes, transcripts of Mountfield parish registers.

[325] **Ibid.**

and was baptized on March 3rd. On December 28th 1843, at the age of 18, she married Jethro Jarrett at Mountfield.[326]

At some time between 1825 and 1841 Anne died. We find William (6) in the 1841 census, living as a widower with his teenage daughter, Emily.[327] He is described as an "agricultural labourer". In 1851 he is described as a "farm bailiff", and he has as housekeeper, a widow named Hester Blackford from Burwash. Probably, he was employed as farm bailiff by one of the local Mountfield estates. From 1861 he is no longer mentioned at Mountfield. We know he was present in London at the death of his son, Robert, in 1862.[328] He himself died at Brampton Place Bexley on July 18th 1866.[329]

John (14) was born to William (5) and his wife Elizabeth in 1798, being baptized in Mountfield's Norman font on January 20th. He was 21 years old when he married Lydia Nash at Mountfield on April 10th 1819, and his bride was a year younger. In 1827 he took up the tenancy of The Banks Farm, and he remained its owner occupier until 1841.[330] Ten years later, John (14) appears in the list of registered electors for the

---

[326] **Ibid.**

[327] Presumably, Robert was away at school on the night of the census.

[328] G.R.O. Death Certificate of Robert Shorter, 24th February 1862, Marylebone, Christchurch, no.376.

[329] G.R.O. Death Certificate, July 20th 1866, Dartford, Bexley, no.32. There was another branch of the Shorter family at Bexley, but the name, age and former occupation of "Farm Bailiff", exactly fit those of William (6).

[330] Letter of David Martin, July 27th 1991; also list of tenants seen at The Banks on June 27th 1991.

first parliament of Queen Victoria in 1837.[331] His qualification was as an occupier of land.

John (14)'s eldest child was William (7), born at Mountfield in 1820.[332] Ellen was born in 1822 and baptized on June 30th. Sarah Louisa was baptized on December 21st 1825. Lydia (1) was baptized on December 28th 1828, but died in 1832, aged three years and eight months. She was buried at Mountfield on July 5th. Spencer was baptized on April 1st 1831, but he died the following year, aged seventeen months. He was buried on June 25th 1832. Finally, George (2) was born at Mountfield in 1834.[333]

The 1841 Census found the family still living at The Banks Farm, together with John (14)'s widowed mother, Elizabeth. However, later in the same year John (14) moved from The Banks Farm to Baldwin's Farm which had previously belonged to George Kenward. This purchase of a larger holding is an indication of John (14)'s relative success as a farmer, possibly a result of the 19th century boom in hop growing. However, six years later John (14) was dead at the comparatively early age of 49. His death occurred on October 3rd 1847, and his burial took place at Mountfield on October 9th. He left his farm and £40 **per annum** to his widow, Lydia. After her death everything was to be shared equally among his four surviving children, William, Ellen, Sarah and George. His goods and chattels were valued at less than £800.[334] Lydia died at Salehurst in 1884, at

[331] **East Sussex List of Registered Electors**, Baxter, Lewes, 1837, p.81. John (14) voted for George Darby and Elliott Fuller. George Darby was elected as M.P.

[332] The 1851 Census gives his birth date as 1820. His baptismal entry has not been traced.

[333] 1851 Census; the baptismal entry has not been traced.

[334] Will of John Shorter of Mountfield, farmer, drawn up December 3rd 1846, proved 1854. East Sussex Record Office, Lewes.

the age of 85 years. She was buried at Mountfield on January 23rd.

Farmers and Innkeepers

Just over two years after John (14)'s death, at the time of the 1851 Census, the family was still at Baldwin's Farm, employing five agricultural laborers and three house servants, but by this time William (7) had moved to Hunter's Farm in the neighboring village of Brightling. On June 1st 1844, at Mountfield, he married Eleanor Forsdick from Tunstall in Suffolk.[335]   In the early years of their marriage, William (7) and Eleanor tried their hand at keeping an inn at St. Leonard's-on-Sea. It was called The Fountain Inn and it was there that their eldest child, Eleanor, was born on February 6th 1847.[336]   Two years later they reverted to farming. Hunter's Farm lay in more heavily wooded country to the west of Mountfield village and was only large enough in 1851 to require the services of three laborers. More will be said of Eleanor in the next chapter. Lydia (2) was born to them at Brightling in 1849. Two years later, a third daughter, Mary Ann, was born. She was baptized at Brightling on April 6th 1851. In 1870 she witnessed her elder sister's marriage to Henry (3), her married name being Morris.[337] William (8) was born at Brightling on September 19th 1852, and was baptized there on December 5th of that year. Elizabeth was born at Brightling in 1854.[338] By 1856, William (7) and Eleanor were innkeepers again, this time looking after the Red

---

[335] Eleanor is sometimes rendered "Elenor", or "Ellen"; and Forsdick, "Fosdick".

[336] G.R.O. Birth Certificate, registered March 3rd 1847.

[337] G.R.O., Marriage Certificate registered July 2nd 1870, at Camberwell.

[338] 1861 Census, P.R.O., RG 9/571/93 v.

Lion Inn at Bodiam. On July 28th 1856, George (4) was born to them at Bodiam, and was baptized at Brightling on November 30th.[339] Kate was born at the Red Lion Inn on November 22nd 1857 and was baptized at Brightling on February 21st 1858. She died a year later.[340]   Finally, Georgiana was born at Bodiam on October 20th 1859 and baptized there on October 22nd.[341] William (7) and Eleanor had abandoned innkeeping for farming once more. The baptismal register describes William (7) as "farmer", and Georgiana's birth certificate does the same, giving his address as Knowlehill, Bodiam.

The 1861 Census reveals the family still at Bodiam. William's farm consisted of only 24 acres, and one man and two boys were employed on it. The eight-year old William (8) is described as "farmhand" and "cow boy", while the seven year old Elizabeth was attending the church school.[342] On his daughter Eleanor's marriage certificate, William (7) is described in 1870 as "Gentleman Farmer" and the address given is "Dulwich".[343]. His wife Eleanor (née Forsdick) died, at the age of 72, on May 30th 1896. At that time William (7) was still alive, and was described as being of "independent

---

[339] G.R.O. Birth Certificate, registered at Ticehurst, August 2nd 1856; East Sussex record Office, Lewes, transcripts of Brightling parish registers. Eleanor's name appears as "Ellen" in the baptismal register, but not on the birth certificate.

[340] G.R.O. Birth Certificate, registered at Ticehurst December 1st 1857; East Sussex Record Office, Lewes, transcripts of Brightling parish registers; G.R.O. Deaths Index, March 1859, Ticehurst, 2b 69.

[341] G.R.O. Birth Certificate, registered at Ticehurst, October 25th 1859; East Sussex Record Office, transcripts of Bodiam parish registers.

[342] 1861 Census, P.R.O. ,RG 9/571/93 v.

[343] G.R.O. Marriage certificate, registered July 2nd 1870. The 1871 Census shows that the family was no longer living at Bodiam. The Dulwich address has not yet been traced in the census.

means". They lived in Cold Harbour Lane, Carshalton, Surrey.[344] The mention of a "Fosdick Trust", a legacy from Elizabeth Forsdick (or Fosdick), in the will of Eleanor (1847-1929) suggests that the family came into some money.[345]

Emigrant, Gold-digger and Mayor

William (8), the erstwhile "farmhand" and "cow boy" emigrated to America in 1869, at the age of 17. Six years later, in 1875, he returned to Britain to fetch his younger brother, George (4). The brothers lived first in Black River, Michigan, and then settled in Shelton, Washington State. William (8) married Sarah Clearwater (1860-1896) in October 1877. She is buried in Shelton. In December 1898 William married again Margaret Isabell McLarty (1868-1950) in Ontario, Canada. By his first marriage he had three children: Maude Amy (1877-1935), Ella (1880-1904) and Bennett (1888-1890). By his second marriage he had another three children: Jean Elizabeth (1900-1948), Wilfred (1902-1944) and Nellie (1904-1954).

William (8) was a colorful character. He was first of all a farmer in Michigan. After this, he worked as an engineer for Russell A. Alger in the logging industry and followed Alger west. He then became involved in the Klondike Gold Rush in the Yukon in the late 1890s. He served as Mayor of Shelton and kept a furniture store there. An oyster farm that he started became famous, when he exhibited samples at the 1901 Pan American Exposition. He died on April 23rd 1923 at Shelton

---

[344] G.R.O. Death Certificate, registered June 1st 1896. The registration of William (7)'s death has not yet been identified.

[345] Somerset House, Will (Admon.) of Eleanor Shorter, December 27th 1924.

WA, and is buried there. His brother George (4) had a large family.[346]

Baldwin's Farm

We now return to the family of John (14) and his wife Lydia (née Nash), William (7)'s brothers and sisters. Their second child was Ellen, baptized at Mountfield on June 30th 1822. On October 17th 1843, at the age of 21, she married Richard Hook of Catsfield in Mountfield Church. John (14)'s third child, Sarah Louisa, was baptized at Mountfield on December 21st 1825. She witnessed her nephew, William (7)'s marriage to Eleanor Forsdick on June 1st 1844 and her cousin Robert's marriage to Jane Trayes on December 23rd of the same year. Lydia (1) was born to John (14) and Lydia (née Nash) in 1828. She was baptized on December 28th of that year, but died at the age of three years, eight months and was buried at Mountfield on July 5th 1832. Spencer who was baptized on April 1st 1831, died aged 17 months and was buried on June 25th 1832.

Finally, George (2) was born at Mountfield in 1834.[347] By 1859 he had married Sarah Ellen Palmer and their first child, Julia, was baptized at Mountfield on December 27th of that year. Their son, George (3), was baptized on November 9th 1862, and a second daughter, Marian, on June 3rd 1867. In 1861 George (2) was managing his father's farm at Baldwin's, and his widowed mother, Lydia (née Nash) was still living with them.[348] Ten years later, however, Baldwin's was in other hands. When George (3) married his cousin Elizabeth Louise

---

[346] Information concerning William (8) was given to Dr. M. P. Taylor by Patricia Brannon the granddaughter of William (8)'s daughter Jean Elizabeth. Communication of Dr. M. P. Taylor, November 23rd 1999.

[347] Cf. 1851 Census. His baptismal entry has not been traced.

[348] 1861 Census.

Shorter in 1898, he was farming Lydon's Place at Edenbridge in Kent.[349]

Other Descendants of William (5) at Mountfield

We now go even further back to William (5) and Elizabeth (née Shoesmith) and the rest of their family at Mountfield. After John (14), the next child was their fourth son, Thomas (7). He was baptized at Mountfield on July 6th 1800. He was nearing 40 when he married Charlotte Moseley of Mountfield on January 4th 1838.[350] His wife was already expecting a child, who was christened Selina on March 7th 1838. A second daughter was born to them in the following year and was christened Bertha Maria on April 12th.[351] On October 23rd 1842, their son Raymond was baptized and finally another daughter, Adoline Lucy, on January 10th 1846.

In his 30s Thomas (7) was already working as a gamekeeper, probably for one of the Mountfield estates, and he remained a gamekeeper all his life. The successive census entries show him living at different addresses: John's Hop Farm in 1841, Lark Cottage in 1851 and 1861, and Keeper Cottage in 1871. His wife Charlotte died in 1852 and was buried at Mountfield on September 28th.[352] In the 1870s he had a housekeeper

---

[349] G.R.O. Marriage Certificate, registered October 15th 1898. Elizabeth Louise was the author's great aunt Louie. George (2) and Sarah's names can be made out on one of the Shorter gravestones at Mountfield, in an otherwise indecipherable inscription.

[350] Charlotte Moseley was born in Seddlescombe, according to the 1851 Census.

[351] The 1851 Census calls her Martha Maria.

[352] Thomas was later buried in the same grave. The inscription on the gravestone states that she died in 1854 at the age of 44. The burial register, however, states that she died in 1852, at the age of 41. The inscription was

called Mary Crouch. Thomas (7) died in 1872, and was buried at Mountfield on September 3rd.[353] His tomb is in the churchyard, not far from the church's south porch.[354]

William (5)'s fifth son, James, was baptized at Mountfield on Christmas Day 1802. In 1851 we find him at Baldwin's Farm, working as a servant, for John (14)'s widow. Nothing more is known about him, except that he died at East Peckham in Kent and was buried at Mountfield on July 22nd 1871.[355]

Sarah was William (5)'s third daughter. She was born in 1805 and was christened on March 10th. At the age of 26, she married George McKechnie of St.Marylebone, London, at Mountfield on December 27th 1831. Twelve years later she was present in Mountfield to witness her neice Ellen's marriage to Richard Hook. Stephen, William (5)'s sixth son, was baptized at Mountfield on August 23rd 1807. He may have been the Stephen Shorter who married Miriam Henbrey at Bodiam on March 25th 1845, but, apart from this, nothing more has been discovered about him.[356] William (5)'s fourth

---

probably made when Thomas died twenty years later, and the family trusted to memory.

[353] The Mountfield burial register gives his age at death as 74, but according to the baptismal register, he was born in 1800; East Sussex Record Office, Lewes, transcripts of parish registers.

[354] The author visited the church on June 27th 1991 and July 27th 1992. The tombstone is broken, but the inscription on the broken half is legible. It repeats Thomas's age as being 74, and the year of death it gives seems to be 1871.

[355] His age in the Mountfield burial register is given as 67, but the register is often inaccurate at this period. His real age would have been 69. There is no other plausible James Shorter.

[356] East Sussex Record Office, Lewes; transcript of Bodiam parish registers.

daughter and tenth child was Mary. She was baptized on March 15th 1810 and died the same day.

William (5), most of whose life coincided with the long reign of King George III, outlived George IV and saw the accession of William IV before dying in 1833. He was buried at Mountfield on April 3rd. His tomb, which is also that of James Shorter (1802-1871), is not far from the south porch of Mountfield church. The inscription "William Shorter, born 1771" can be discerned.[357] Elizabeth, his widow, lived on at The Banks Farm for another eleven years and was buried at Mountfield on March 1st 1844.[358]

When Thomas (7), the gamekeeper, died in 1872, he was the last member of the Shorter family still living at Mountfield. All the other descendants of William (5) and his wife Elizabeth had moved away from the area. There were several reasons for the exodus. Some family members had been attracted by the new opportunities afforded by London. Others, who remained in agriculture, probably found Mountfield too small. The Shorters were successful farmers, but the size of the farm holdings and the soil quality of the High Weald limited further progress. In the next chapter we follow the fortunes of those members of the family who moved to London in the early years of Queen Victoria's reign.

---

[357] The author visited Mountfield church and examined the Shorter tombs on June 27th 1991, and again on July 27th 1992. The inscription also mentions Anne Shorter who died in 1871. This may have been the wife of James.

[358] 1841 Census; and East Sussex Record Office, Lewes, transcripts of Mountfield parish registers.

CHAPTER ELEVEN

RAILWAYS, HOPS AND HIGH FINANCE

From Mountfield to London

Robert Shorter, the only son of William (6) and Anne, née Pilbin, was 22 years old when he married Jane, the daughter of Edward and Jane Gwinnett Trayes, at Mountfield on December 23rd 1844.[359] Jane Trayes was born at Bishop's Lydeard, a village four miles north west of Taunton, Somerset, in 1818. Her father, Edward, was in service and this may explain his presence at Mountfield at the time of his daughter's marriage. He may have been working in one of the big households of the neighborhood, perhaps the Banks itself. Three years after the wedding Robert is found working in London where his eldest son, Henry (3), was born on August 30th 1847.[360] Three generations of elder sons separate Robert from his putative 18th century London forbears, and the memory of these origins may have been a factor in his return to the metropolis. More immediately, however, early Victorian London was perceived as a place of economic opportunity. Victorian households were in need of servants, and the birth of the railways would soon offer a wide range of employment.

---

[359] East Sussex Record Office, Lewes, transcript of Mountfield parish registers; G.R.O. Marriage Certificate, Battle, December 23rd 1844.

[360] G.R.O. Birth Certificate registered at Christchurch St. Marylebone September 22nd 1847.

The work force came largely from the rural areas of south-eastern England.

Robert Shorter was an enterprising young man . He wasted no time on agricultural pursuits at Mountfield, but moved to Broadley Street in the Christchurch district of Marylebone, London, where he and Jane occupied an apartment in a large tenement.[361] Robert may have been influenced in his choice of Marylebone by his aunt Sarah, whose husband George McKechnie was living there at the time of their marriage. It may even have been George and Sarah who found Robert his first London job. Another influence was, no doubt, his father-in-law Edward Trayes.

On Henry (3)'s birth certificate, Robert's occupation is described as "servant". Almost certainly this means that, from his first coming to London, he was in service with Sir Francis Grant at 73, Sussex Villas. Two years later, on his second son's birth certificate, he is described as "butler", and in the 1851 Census he appears as butler in the Grant household.[362] Sir Francis Grant was a Scottish painter, and elder brother of General Sir James Hope Grant. In 1847, he was 44 years old and had already become one of the leading portrait painters of the day. In 1866 he was elected President of the Royal Academy and was knighted by Queen Victoria. He became a Catholic in 1875 and died in London three years later.

Robert lived in the Grant family home, together with Francis and his wife Isabella, their four daughters and a Prussian governess. During the 1850s, the Grants moved into 27 Sussex Place (otherwise known as Sussex Lodge), a fine house overlooking Regent's Park, which had been built from designs by John Nash. The house was demolished in 1957 and replaced

---

[361] Number 5, Broadley Street. Although they were not living there in 1851, the type of dwelling can be identified in the 1851 Census.

[362] 1851 Census, P.R.O., HO 107/1490, 967r.

by the headquarters of the Royal College of Obstetricians and Gynaecologists.[363]   To occupy the position of butler in such a distinguished household was no mean achievement for a Sussex farmer in his mid-twenties. It was also a considerable step up the social scale. Since a Victorian butler commanded the entire below stairs establishment, of footmen, maids and kitchen staff, Robert must have been a personable young man with the requisite leadership qualities.

In 1849, Jane was living in the lodge of Mount Pleasant, a large establishment in Melton Mowbray, Leicestershire, belonging to the Hill family. The 1851 Census reveals that she was living there with her elder sister, Mary Edwards, whose husband was butler at Mount Pleasant.[364] Evidently, the two butlers' wives had joined forces. It was at Mount Pleasant that Robert and Jane's second son, William (9) was born on December 30th 1848.[365] A third son, Frederick, was born at Mount Pleasant on March 2nd 1851.[366] Finally a daughter, Emma, was born on December 16th 1852. It seems that Jane's labour came on unexpectedly, because the birth certificate records the place of birth as being the Churchyard at Melton Mowbray.[367] Emma would seem to be the lastborn.

At some time in the 1850s Robert left the Grants' employment and became a railway clerk. However, he remained a close friend of the Grant family, because they took

---

[363] Thorne, J.O., and Collocott, T.C., (eds.), **Chambers Biographical Dictionary**, Edinburgh 1974, p.560 **sub** Grant; Weinreb and Hibbert, **op.cit.**, p.849.

[364] 1851 Census, P.R.O., HO 107/2091/298.

[365] G.R.O. Birth Certificate, registered January 31st 1849.

[366] G.R.O. Birth certificate, registered March 18th 1851.

[367] G.R.O. Birth Certificate, registered January 5th 1853.

him in during his final illness in 1862. Robert and Jane bequeathed to their son Henry (3) two fine oil portraits of themselves, which must have been executed by Sir Francis.[368] Robert appears as a young man, with soft eyes and a gentle, almost timid, expression. Jane is considerably more self-possessed, and her expression is somewhat severe.

These were the great years of railway expansion and rail was a prestigious new mode of travel, comparable in our own day to travel by air. In fact, the great railway termini of London were the "airports" of the Victorian age. King's Cross Station had just been built in 1851-1852 and was owned by the Great Northern Railway. St. Pancras Station was built after Robert's death, and until it was completed, the Midland Railway also used King's Cross. The new Paddington Station, designed by Isambard Kingdom Brunel for the Great Western Railway, was also being built in the 1850s, and replaced the wooden structure that Queen Victoria used for her journey from Slough in 1842. Marylebone Station, however, was not put up until the end of the 19th century.[369]

Altogether, more than 130 railway companies were formed in Britain, and their surviving archives are massive.[370] Robert Shorter's brief career as a railway clerk has not yet been traced. It is likely that he was employed in the Railway Clearing

---

[368] The portraits became the property of Elizabeth Louise (1871-1949), in whose possession the author last saw them. Wilfred Wynn (1875-1952) possessed photographs of the portraits, and copies have recently been made by a photographic restorer. Without access to the originals, it is impossible to identify the signature of the artist.

[369] For information concerning the London railway stations, cf. Weinreb and Hibbert, **op.cit.**.

[370] They are lodged at the P.R.O. at Kew. The author has begun to research the early staff registers, particularly those of the Midland, Great Western, and London and North Western Railways. The name Shorter occasionally appears, but no member of the Mountfield family has yet been identified.

House, which had offices in Seymour Street during the 1850s. The Railway Clearing House employed the largest number of clerks and dealt with the co-ordination of passengers, goods and parcels from the various railway companies. Today, in an age of near universal literacy, the word "clerk" is synonymous with "office-worker", that commonest of modern avocations. In mid-Victorian times the word had not yet been devalued, and Robert's job with the railways would probably have raised him in the social estimation. It was certainly preferable to domestic service or trade, and was not entirely at variance with the rank of "gentleman" to which he aspired. The 1861 Census found the family living together at 6, Omega Terrace, Alpha Road, in the St. Paul's district of Marylebone.[371] All the children, who ranged from the age of 13 to 8, were attending school.

Less than a year later, tragedy struck the little family. Robert fell ill with "rheumatic pleurisy" and pneumonia and lingered for eleven days. Sir Francis and Lady Isabella Grant took him into their home in Regent's Park, where he died on February 22nd 1862 at the early age of 39, his father William (6) being present at the deathbed.[372] When Henry (3) got married in 1870, the family was living at Westbury Terrace in Westbourne Square. We shall follow the fortunes of Henry (3) in due course.

Robert's widow, Jane, died at the age of 70, on June 9th 1888. At the time of her death, she was living at 22, Brondesbury Road, Willesden, and her son William (9) was present at her bedside. Her grandson, Wilfred Wynn (1875-1952), then aged 13, remembered the old lady as an irascible martinet. He and his sisters were unmoved by her

---

[371] 1861 Census, P.R.O., RG 9/85, 26 r/v.

[372] G.R.O. Death Certificate, registered February 24th 1862. The William, who was present and who reported the death, was presumably William (6), and not William (9) who was only 13 at the time.

death, and continued playing in the garden, as the coffin was carried out of the house on the day of her funeral.[373]

Nothing further is known about William (9), and his marriage, occupation and death have not been identified. Frederick, like his father, died at a comparatively early age. He lived to be 44, dying of typhoid fever on October 28th 1895. At the time of his death, he was a Jobber on the Stock Exchange, and lived at 14, Station Road, Harlesden. His mother-in-law, Mrs. C. Brown, was present at his death.[374] Nothing further has been discovered about his sister, Emma.

Stock Exchange and Commodity Market

Henry (3) is described as a stock exchange clerk, at the time of his marriage in 1870. By 1875 he had become a stockbroker, but from 1881 onwards his occupation was that of hop agent.[375] It seems, therefore, that Frederick followed his elder brother into the Stock Exchange. The Stock Exchange, properly so-called, dates from 1773. James Peacock's building was put up in 1801, and this was replaced by a larger building, erected by Thomas Allason in 1853. This was the institution which Henry (3) joined. By 1878, there were more than 2,000 brokers, and a new building was begun in 1882, to the designs of J. J. Cole.[376] Shortly before this, Henry (3) joined the commodity market and became a dealer in hops.

---

[373] Reminiscence of Wilfred Wynn (1875-1952), communicated to the author's mother.

[374] G.R.O. Death Certificate, registered October 31st 1895. His marriage has not yet been traced.

[375] The **List of Members of the Stock Exchange Year Ending March 1876**, E. Couchman, London 1875, lists Henry (3) as a broker, with his address as Haddon House, Sutton; but he is no longer listed in 1877.

[376] Weinreb and Hibbert, **op.cit.**, pp.825-826, **sub** Stock Exchange.

As London and the British population grew in the nineteenth century, so did the consumption of beer. Eventually, there were more than a dozen breweries in the London area. With the increased consumption of beer, came an increase in the production of the hops which gave beer its distinctive flavor. Hop-fields expanded in Sussex and Kent, and hundreds of hop-pickers descended on them annually from London. Henry (3) and his family came from the hop-growing areas of south-east England, and through his hop-growing relatives, he no doubt had other contacts. This may explain his move from the stock market to the hop business. As a hop agent, he would have been selling hops on behalf of the producers. Some commodities were marketed in the London Commercial Sale Rooms on Mincing Lane, but most of the hop merchants operated from the Hop Exchange in Southwark Street.[377] It is not known what firm, if any, Henry (3) represented. There was, of course, money in hops. Wilfred (1875-1952) used to recall a couplet scrawled by street urchins on the gate of a fine London house acquired by a hop merchant: "Who'd ha' thought it; hops ha' bought it !"[378] This could have been Henry (3) himself, who became wealthy enough to set up house in north London, and employ his own liveried servants.

It is against this background that Henry (3)'s marriage to his second cousin, Eleanor Shorter, should perhaps be viewed. We have already met Eleanor Shorter in Chapter Ten, the sister of William (8) who emigrated to America. The marriage was an exercise in family solidarity, uniting finance with farming, and it was an exercise that was repeated when Henry (3)'s daughter, Elizabeth Louise, married her first cousin once removed, George (3), in 1898. Henry (3) and Eleanor's marriage was

---

[377] Cf. Post Office London, **Trades Directory**, London 1908, **sub** Hop Merchants. Henry (3) had probably retired by this time.

[378] Communicated to the author in the 1940s.

solemnized in St. Giles's Camberwell on July 2nd 1870, and they moved at once to 4, Upper Vernon Road, Sutton, where their first child, Elizabeth Louise, was born on October 3rd 1871.[379] In 1875 they were living at Garden Lodge in Sutton High Street, when Wilfred Wynn was born on April 26th.[380]

Six years later, Henry (3) and Eleanor were back in Dulwich, living at 57, Park Road, and it was there that two further daughters were born to them: Marion Maud, known as "Maudie", on March 5th 1881, and Ellen Mabel on October 19th 1882.[381] Another six years separates these two from the lastborn, Henry Robert, known as "Robbie". He was born on February 3rd 1888, at 16, Sheriff Road, Kilburn, to which address the family had now moved.[382] When Elizabeth Louise and Wilfred Wynn both married in 1898 and 1899 respectively, the family was living at 23, Walm Lane, Willesden Green.

Elizabeth Louise married her first cousin once removed, George Shorter (3), the son of George (2) and Sarah Ellen (née Palmer), who was then farming at Lydon's Place, Edenbridge, Kent.[383] The marriage took place on October 15th 1898 at St. Andrew's Willesden. She was a widow, and 79 years old, when she died at Chippenham on May 8th 1949.[384]

---

[379] G.R.O. Marriage Certificate, registered July 2nd 1870, Camberwell; also G.L.R.O., Camberwell parish registers, P73/GEO/33, 1868-1870; X/89/42; G.R.O. Birth Certificate, registered November 14th 1871.

[380] G.R.O. Birth Certificate, registered May 20th 1875.

[381] G.R.O. Birth Certificate, registered May 4th 1881; G.R.O. Birth Certificate, registered November 25th 1882.

[382] G.R.O. Birth Certificate, registered March 16th 1888.

[383] G.R.O. Marriage Certificate, registered October 15th 1898. They had three sons: Mervyn, Guy and Wilfred, and three daughters: Marjorie, Molly and Eileen.

[384] G.R.O., Death Certificate, registered May 10th 1949.

Wilfred Wynn married Florence Mary Adams at St. Marylebone Church on February 11th 1899. He was then a clerk on the Stock Exchange, aged 23, and she was a nurse at the Middlesex Hospital, aged 29.[385] Her father, William Herbert Adams, had worked for a time in the Army and Navy Stores, before serving with the 23rd Royal Welsh Fusiliers, in which regiment he was commissioned a Captain. He married Charlotte Drayson in Carshalton on June 27th 1865, and then joined his regiment which had been stationed in India since the Indian Mutiny. For a time he was encamped at the Khyber Pass. The regiment returned to England in about 1870 and was stationed at Aldershot. The family lived there until William Herbert Adams accepted the post of store manager in the Hudson's Bay Company at Winnipeg, Canada, in 1883, being joined there by his eldest son, Ernest, in the following year. In June 1886, he received the commission of Factor in the Hudson's Bay Company, and his remaining seven children joined him in Canada in the same year.

Florence Mary was born on October 7th 1870, after the family returned to England from India, and she was sixteen years old when she accompanied her brothers and sisters to Canada.[386] In 1904, William Herbert Adams retired from the Hudson's Bay Company, and died in London in 1910. His daughter, Florence Mary, had preceded his return by several years, in order to take up nursing.[387] Florence's elder brothers, Ernest Dupin Adams (1868-1961) and Henry Chawner Adams (b.1869) remained in Canada, the former as a rancher and horse

---

[385] G.R.O. Marriage Certificate, registered February 11th 1899.

[386] G.R.O. Birth Index, Kensington, Oct.7th 1870.

[387] The author is indebted to his second cousin, Nancy Milley (née Adams) of Vancouver, for providing him with information on the history of the Adams family. Cf. also G.R.O. Marriage Certificate registered June 27th 1865 and G.R.O. Death Certificate, registered January 22nd 1910.

breeder, the latter as Town Clerk of Battleford Saskatchewan. Her younger brother, Stanley Wells Adams (1871-1954) became an actor, singer and stage director who spent his last years in Beverley Hills, CA.

Marion Maud, died of cancer in Brighton, at the age of 43, on July 30th 1924. She was unmarried and her brother Wilfred Wynn was with her when she died.[388] Ellen Mabel married Cecil Sydney Burkett-Smith, a surveyor, on July 21st 1928. The marriage took place in Hove Parish Church, and the couple went to live in Dorking, Surrey. She died in Portsmouth in 1950.[389]

The saddest blow to befall Henry (3) and Eleanor's family concerned Henry Robert. As a teenager, Robbie became an apprentice seaman in the Merchant Navy, and went to sea in a mercantile training ship named the Madagascar. The ship was in the Atlantic on the afternoon of November 6th 1903, when Robbie, who had gone aloft, accidentally fell from the mast to the deck and was killed. He was less than three months from his sixteenth birthday, and was buried at sea.[390]

Henry (3) and Eleanor retired to Hove, where he died, aged 67, on April 28th 1915, at 13, Wilbury Villas.[391] When his will was proved in September 1915, his effects were valued at £3,425. 12s. 11d. He bequeathed the oil portraits of Robert and Jane to Wilfred Wynn, along with some old china, and two

---

[388] G.R.O. Death Certificate, registered July 31st 1924, Brighton.

[389] G.R.O. Marriage Certificate, registered at Hove July 21st 1928; G.R.O. Deaths Index, March 1950, 6b, 518.

[390] The story was related to the author by Wilfred Wynn; cf. also G.R.O., Marine Register of Deaths, no.95057, return made in October 1906. The accident took place in latitude 18.00 south and longitude 31.50 west, at 3.30 p.m. on November 6th 1903.

[391] G.R.O. Death Certificate, registered April 30th 1915.

bronze and gilt candelabra. His grandfather clock, by Bowra of Sevenoaks, he bequeathed to Elizabeth Louise, together with two bronze figures mounted on black and white marble. Wilfred Wynn, who collected clocks, exchanged the grandfather clock for the oil portraits. A leasehold house, 8, Hilltop Road, Hampstead, was bequeathed to his widow, Eleanor.[392]

Eleanor lived for a time at 83, Montpelier Road, Brighton. She survived her husband by fourteen years, dying at 78, Tisbury Road, Hove, on November 15th 1929. She was 82 years old.[393]   Photographs of Henry (3) reveal a solid businessman, with the Shorter features of prominent nose and large, well-lobed ears. He was bearded in the prevailing fashion set by King Edward VII and King George V. In her photograph, Eleanor appears every inch a Shorter, tall and with the same prominent nose as her husband and cousin.[394]   The marriage of Wilfred Wynn and Florence Mary Adams took place on the threshold of the twentieth century, the subject of the final chapter in the first part of this book.

---

[392] Somerset House, Will of Henry Shorter, drawn up September 27th 1911, probate granted September 27th 1915.

[393] G.R.O. Death certificate, registered November 16th 1924; Somerset House, Will of Eleanor Shorter, drawn up Dec.27th 1924.

[394] Elizabeth Louise, the author's great-aunt "Louie", looked remarkably like her mother.

CHAPTER TWELVE

TWENTIETH/TWENTY-FIRST   CENTURIES

Wilfred Wynn and Florence Mary

Wilfred Wynn and Florence Mary began their married life at 14, Grosvenor Gardens, London NW5. Wilfred commuted daily to the Stock Exchange, then housed in J. J. Cole's building, which had been completed in 1888.[395]Shortly after their marriage, the Boer War broke out on October 11th 1899, and all London was agog with news of the besieged British garrisons. When word came of the relief of Mafeking on May 17th 1900, the young City businessmen celebrated wildly, and Wilfred came home that night on top of a cab.[396] On June 8th 1905, Alan Wynn was born at Grosvenor Gardens.[397] He was their only child, and, from the age of two and a half, suffered from bone trouble. He was obliged to wear iron calipers on his legs until he was twelve years old. By 1911, when Henry (3)

---

[395] Weinreb and Hibbert, **op.cit.**, p.826, **sub** Stock Exchange.

[396] Family oral tradition.

[397] Cf. G.R.O. Births Index, Hendon, 3a, 347, June 1905.

made his will, the family was living at 10, Aylestone Avenue, Brondesbury Park.[398]

The First World War broke out on August 4th 1914, and Wilfred, after first serving in the special constabulary, joined the army. He was commissioned a Second Lieutenant on March 11th 1917, and served in the 8th Garrison Battalion of the Hampshire Regiment.[399] This regiment which became the Royal Hampshire Regiment in 1946, was nicknamed the "Cat and Cabbage", on account of its other ranks' cap badge, which included an Indian royal tiger and the Hampshire or Winchester rose.[400] Wilfred, who eventually attained the rank of Captain, served in France, notably at Abbeville, where his responsibilities included guarding munitions and supervising troop movements by rail. On two occasions the ammunition dump he was guarding was blown up by enemy artillery fire, and in one of these incidents he was buried and had to be dug out.

While her husband was away, Florence Mary took a flat in Willesden Lane, and Alan Wynn, who was aged nine, began attending Sunbury House School, after a brief experience at another school in the neighborhood.[401] Sunbury House was a preparatory school in Willesden Lane, run by Ernest Dove, and - because of this - was also known as "Mr. Dove's". Ernest Dove (1873-1932) was the son of Henry Charles Dove (1840-1895), a building contractor, and his wife Agnes née

---

[398] Somerset House, Will of Henry Shorter, drawn up 27th September 1911.

[399] **Army List**, August 1918.

[400] Cf. Edwards, T. J., **Regimental Badges**, Aldershot, 1951, pp.210-211.

[401] Lady Margaret School, next door to Sunbury House.

Wreynolds.[402] In 1899, Ernest Dove married Edith Caudwell (1880-1975), the daughter of Francis Caudwell, Vicar of St. Matthias Stoke Newington, and his Cornish wife, Mary née James.[403] Ernest and Edith Dove had two daughters, Joan Mary Agnes (1904-1993) and Helen Mary (1919-1984). A famous near-contemporary of Alan's at Sunbury House School was Sir Michael Redgrave, the actor and film star.

When the First World War ended in November 1918, and Wilfred was demobilized, he and Florence Mary moved to 90, Brook Green, Hammersmith. This was to enable their son to attend St. Paul's School which was then situated in Hammersmith. [404] Alan entered St. Paul's in the summer term of 1919, and his father resumed work at the Stock Exchange.[405] They were still living at Brook Green when Wilfred's mother, Eleanor, made her will in 1924.[406] By 1926, Wilfred Wynn had become a Stock Jobber, operating on behalf of R. B. Pott and Co.[407]

---

[402] One of the founders of the firm of building contractors, Dove Brothers. Cf. Braithwaite, David, **Building in the Blood**, London, 1981, p.12. The author is also indebted to his cousin, Mary Beryl Lea, (the granddaughter of Henry Charles Dove's nephew, Frederick Lionel Dove) for the information contained in her genealogical table of the Dove family.

[403] Francis Caudwell (1831-1920) wrote a manuscript autobiography, which is in the author's possession and which he has transcribed. Francis was a saintly Anglican priest, who did pioneering mission work in London's East End, and built St. Peter's Hoxton Square.

[404] It is now situated in Barnes.

[405] **St. Paul's Registers**, ed. Mead, A.H. **et al.**, London 1990, p.171.

[406] Somerset House, Will of Eleanor Shorter, drawn up 27th December 1924.

[407] **Stock Exchange List 1926-1927**, London, E. Couchman, 1926, **sub** Shorter. Cf. also **Stock Exchange List 1933-1934**, London, E. Couchman, 1933.

Around 1927, Wilfred Wynn and Florence Mary moved to North End Road, Golders Green, near the family home of the writer, Evelyn Waugh. Later they moved to Adelaide Road, London NW3, and then, in the same neighborhood, to 10, Provost Road. This was a large, semi-detached, Edwardian House, with an upstairs sitting-room.[408] Florence Mary was received into the Roman Catholic Church in 1933, shortly after her son. However, he was to live only five more years, and Florence Mary was to nurse him in his final illness at Carshalton.

At the beginning of the Second World War, Wilfred Wynn re-tired from the Stock Exchange, and he and Florence Mary moved to a basement flat in Upper Park Road. The house was situated behind St. Dominic's Priory Church, Malden Road, Haverstock Hill, and Florence Mary's final years were largely focused on the Dominican community and its parish, where she attended daily Mass. She was particularly fond of the saintly, Fr. Vincent McNabb O.P. The couple remained in London throughout the Second World War, surviving the Blitz and the V-1 and V-2 rockets.

Wilfred had several interests. He was a keen gardener, and he was also devoted to his clocks. Besides the grandfather clock he had inherited from Henry (3), he possessed an inlaid chiming clock, by Shapland of Paris; and there were other clocks on mantlepieces and cupboards in the various rooms of the small flat.[409] The ritual of rewinding all the clocks took place on Sunday morning. They were a symptom, perhaps, of his extreme punctuality. Wilfred Wynn was so punctual that, when he traveled, one was obliged to meet the train before. He was sure to be on it.[410]

---

[408] The author remembers visiting it several times, with his father, Alan Wynn.

[409] The grandfather clock was known to his grandchildren as "the teaspoons clock", because of its chime; and the Shapland clock was known as "the diddy-boom clock".

[410] Wilfred Wynn took the family motto **Promptus** very seriously.

In his old age, Wilfred reminisced about the Shorter family. He was devoted to the south-eastern counties where his family originated, always taking his holidays at Margate, Broadstairs and other seaside resorts which had ceased to be fashionable. A saying of his, still current in the family, was "a poke in the eye with a burnt stick", referring to an ungrateful reaction. He had the Shorter characteristics of face and stature, and was a habitual pipe smoker. Wilfred Wynn died on December 22nd, his bronchitis aggravated by the terrible London "smog" of 1952. His funeral took place after Christmas, at Hendon Crematorium.

After her husband's death Florence Mary gave up the flat in Upper Park Road and moved to 26, Dean Road, Willesden, where she lived with her sisters Ethel Georgie Palmer ("Auntie Jo") (1874-1968) and Mabel Evelyn Adams (1878-1963).[411] Her final years were marred by a severe attack of shingles which resulted in the loss of an eye. She died at Sudbury Hill, in the nursing home of the Little Company of Mary (the "Blue Sisters") on April 15th 1956. Her funeral, which took place at her beloved St. Dominic's Priory, was attended by children from the parish school. She is buried in St. Mary's Cemetery, Kensal Green.

Alan Wynn and Joan Mary Agnes

As we have seen, Alan Wynn entered St. Paul's School in the summer term of 1919, at the age of fourteen.[412] The

---

[411] The collection of clocks was dispersed. The Bowra grandfather clock was given to Dr.Harwood Stevenson to present (appropriately) to St. Wilfred's House, Ampleforth School. The author inherited the Shapland clock which is still in his possession.

[412] This section is based on **St. Paul's School Registers**, ed. A. H. Mead **et al.**, London 1990; Blackman, Aylward M., "Alan Wynn Shorter

school was founded by the famous humanist scholar and Dean of St. Paul's Cathedral, John Colet, in 1509. Destroyed in the Great Fire of London, it was twice rebuilt on its original site near the cathedral, before being moved to Hammersmith in 1884.[413] Famous pupils included the poet John Milton, the diarist Samuel Pepys, the first Duke of Marlborough, Edmund Halley the astronomer and - nearer to Alan's time - G. K. Chesterton and Field Marshall Montgomery.[414] When Alan was in the school, the "High Master" of St. Paul's was the redoubtable Dr. Hillard, the classical scholar who had published Latin and Greek grammars that were inflicted on generations of schoolboys and schoolgirls throughout the country.[415] It was not surprising that Alan's desire to switch from a science to a classical specialization was warmly supported by Dr. Hillard. He began his study of Latin and Greek under Dr. Pantin. By this time he had been liberated from his leg irons, but it was too late for him to take a serious interest in sports. Later, at Oxford, he was able to develop an interest in fencing.

During his years at St. Paul's, Alan's imagination was fired by the advances being made in Egyptology. He was commencing his fourth year at school, when Howard Carter and Lord Carnarvon opened Tutankhamon's tomb in the Valley of the Kings at Thebes on November 26th 1922.[416] The young Shorter followed the discoveries avidly, and made his own

1905-1938", **Journal of Egyptian Archaeology**, vol.24, part 2, 1938, pp.211-212; obituaries from **The Times** and **The Daily Telegraph** and other journals; and information within the family.

[413] It moved to its present site at Barnes in 1968.

[414] Weinreb and Hibbert, **op.cit.**, pp.761-762, **sub** St. Paul's School.

[415] "North and Hillard" and "Hillard and Botting".

[416] Carter, Howard, **Tutankhamen's Treasure**, Sphere Books, London, 1972.

scrap-book of newspaper cuttings and photographs.[417] During his last two years at St.Paul's, he began to teach himself Egyptology. His enthusiasm for ancient Egypt was such that Professor Christopher Hawkes, who was later a colleague of his at the British Museum, joked that he had begun "to walk like an ancient Egyptian".[418] With Latin and Greek and a self-acquired knowledge of Egyptian, Alan gained a Classical exhibition at The Queen's College, Oxford in July 1924, and went up to the university in October.

The Queen's College had been founded in 1340, by a chaplain of Edward III's Queen, Philippa of Hainault, mainly for students from the north of England. Its attraction for Alan was the fact that it boasted among its senior members several oriental scholars and papyrologists. The aged Dr. J. R.Magrath, who reigned as Provost for sixty years, still presided over the college.[419] Alan's tutor was Dr. Aylward Manley Blackman, a colorful character, with a lengthy experience of archaeological excavation in Egypt and Lower Nubia. Later, from 1934 to 1948, Blackman was professor of Egyptology at Liverpool University. After winning a college prize, Alan took Classical Honor Moderations in 1926, and Finals in Egyptian and Coptic in 1928.[420]

On coming down from Oxford he joined the Egypt Exploration Society's expedition of 1928-1929 to excavate the Bucheum at Armant, and the palace of the "heretic" Pharoah Akhnaton at Tell el-Amarna. His interests, however, lay more

---

[417] The author made a slide lecture out of the photographs in this scrap-book.

[418] The remark was made to the author in 1954 at Oxford, where Hawkes was Professor of European Archaeology.

[419] He was Provost of Queen's from 1871-1931.

[420] Mead, **op.cit.**, p.171; Blackman, **op.cit.**, p.211.

with philology and papyrology than with archaeology, and, on his return to England in 1929, he accepted the post of Assistant Keeper of Egyptian Antiquities at the British Museum. At that time, Assyrian and Egyptian Antiquities were placed within a single department, headed first by H. R.Hall and later by Sidney Smith. The Assyrian and Egyptian exhibitions were, and probably still are, among the most spectacular sights of the British Museum. While the Keeper of the department was usually an Assyriologist, the Assistant Keeper was an Egyptologist.

Alan was the author of three works on Egyptology for the general reader, published by Kegan Paul, London: **An Introduction to the Egyptian Religion** in 1931; **Everyday Life in Ancient Egypt** in 1932 and **The Egyptian Gods** in 1937. In 1938 he published the first volume of what was to have been a major work, his **Catalogue of Egyptian Religious papyri in the British Museum**.

While Alan was working on his books about ancient Egyptian religion, he began to consider his own religious position. In 1931 he wrote about the coming of Christianity to Egypt: "Soon a new faith was to come, in which all the threads of ancient man's religion were to be gathered up, none being lost".[421] Just as the religion of the Egyptians had been a historical precursor of Christianity, so it was to be a step towards a religious conversion in his own personal life. At Oxford he had frequented the Anglo-Catholic community of Pusey House, and a Catholic contemporary, Reginald Trevett (a founder of the Catholic People's Weeks), was another major influence. In London, he and his fellow Pauline, Harwood Stevenson, fell under the spell of an Anglican Franciscan, the future Monsignor Vernon Johnson, and future Catholic Chaplain at Oxford, who preached at St. Mary Magdalen,

---

[421] Shorter, Alan Wynn, **An Introduction to the Egyptian Religion**, Kegan Paul, London, 1931, p.126.

Munster Square.[422] Alan was also an admirer of Fr. Vincent McNabb O.P. at St. Dominic's Haverstock Hill. Early in 1933, he was received into the Roman Catholic Church, at St.Mary's Cadogan Gardens, Chelsea.

On December 29th 1930, at St. Michael's Camden Town, Alan married Joan Mary Agnes, the elder daughter of his preparatory school Headmaster, Ernest Dove. The couple went to live at 4, Norland Square, Holland Park Avenue, and it was while they were living there that their first child, Aylward Ernest, was born on May 2nd 1932.[423] Aylward was named after Dr. Aylward Blackman, who asked to be the child's godfather. In 1933 they moved briefly to a flat in Adelaide Road, before Crispin Anthony was born on September 24th of that year. Shortly afterwards the young family moved to 7, Rotherfield Road, Carshalton. The house, which was semi-detached, possessed an attic study on the top floor where Alan could work at home. A daughter, Mary Caroline, was born on October 12th 1935, and was baptized in the Catholic Church. Joan and the two boys were received into the Catholic Church on September 29th 1936, at Our Lady of the Rosary, Carshalton Road, (Wallington) Sutton. Finally, Gervase Thomas More was born on February 15th 1938.

The family's stay at Carshalton was marked by a number of memorable national events: the Silver Jubilee of King George V in 1935, his death in the following year, the abdication of King Edward VIII and the accession of King George VI. Also in 1936, the Crystal Palace at Sydenham was burned down, and the fire was visible from vantage points in Carshalton.

In appearance, Alan had all the Shorter characteristics, especially where height was concerned. He was six foot, four

---

[422] Communication from Dr. Harwood Stevenson.

[423] The author; who took the additional name Michael at his Catholic Baptism **sub conditione** in 1936.

inches tall. Like his father, Wilfred, he enjoyed smoking a pipe. Although he had got over his childhood disability, he suffered bouts of ill health at Oxford, as a result of overwork. Barely three months after Gervase's birth, Alan fell ill with pneumonia and died, at the early age of 32, on May 31st 1938.[424] His funeral took place at St. Dominic's Priory, Haverstock Hill, and he is buried at St. Mary's Cemetery, Kensal Green. This grievous loss was keenly felt, not only by his widow and family, but by his colleagues at the British Museum. **The Times** described him as "a man of scrupulous honor, of deep religious conviction, kind-hearted and a pleasant companion",[425] and Aylward Blackman wrote of him:

> Shorter possessed great strength of character and could never be persuaded to put expediency before principle. But he could be a charming and highly entertaining companion, and was at all times and in all circumstances a most faithful and sympathetic friend.[426]

Joan Mary Agnes and her Children

Joan was faced with the daunting task of bringing up a family of small children single-handed. Shortly after Alan's death, she moved to 73, Grosvenor Avenue, Carshalton, a house with a long garden, stretching up to a railway embankment. Aylward and Crispin began kindergarten at St.Hilda's school, and the whole family attended Holy Cross Catholic Church. In the crisis which followed the Munich pact of September 1938, the German army occupied Czechoslovakia. Joan and the children went to Ventnor on the Isle of Wight, in October, for the duration of the crisis. In May

---

424 G.R.O. Deaths Index, Surrey Mid-East, 2a 194, June 1938.

425 **The Times**, June 2nd 1938, Obituary.

426 Blackman, **loc.cit.**

1939 Aylward was sent as a boarder to St. Augustine's Abbey School, Ramsgate. This was a preparatory school founded in 1865 by the Subiacan Benedictine Congregation, with the help of the Gothic revival architect, Augustus Welby Pugin, whose son was the first pupil in the school.

During 1939, Joan moved to Seaford, Sussex, where her mother, Edith Dove, was already living. The house she bought was "Shenstone", 9 Ashurst Road. On September 3rd 1939, the Second World War was declared, and St. Augustine's Abbey School was evacuated to Madeley Court, Hemingford Grey, Huntingdonshire. Aylward continued at the school and was joined there by Crispin in 1941. Gervase also eventually joined the school in 1946. Wilfred and Florence Mary joined Joan and the children at Seaford for Christmas 1939. In May 1940 the family moved to Brympton D'Evercy, near Yeovil in Somerset, the historic stately home of the Clive Ponsonby-Fane family. Here they were guests of the headmistress of Westcroft School which was also evacuated there. The Battle of Britain raged from August to October, and at the end of 1940 Joan and her children moved to a coast guard cottage at Lyme Regis in Dorset. Finally, in March 1941, they were evacuated once more, this time to St. Michael's Cottage, Hyde, near Fordingbridge in Hampshire. The cottage was owned by the widow of Captain Woodgett, who had commanded the famous tea clipper, the Cutty Sark, now preserved at Greenwich, and the house was full of naval memorabilia.[427] Eventually in 1942, the family returned to their house at Seaford, where they spent the rest of the Second World War. After the war, in 1948, they moved to "Windrush", Hartfield Road, also at Seaford.

In 1945, Aylward was sent to the English Benedictine public school at Downside. This school, which was founded at Douai in Flanders in 1614, had reopened at Downside in Somerset in 1814, after a brief sojourn at Acton Burnell in Shropshire. Shortly

---

427 Captain Woodgett's portrait occupies a prominent place in the exhibition aboard the Cutty Sark at Greenwich in London.

after Aylward's arrival in the school, the headmaster, Dom Basil Christopher Butler, was elected Abbot of Downside, and his place as headmaster was taken by Dom Nicholas Wilfrid Passmore.[428] Crispin also attended Downside School from 1947-1951, and Gervase from 1950-1954. All three boys obtained scholarships.[429] Caroline, whose schooling had been disrupted by the family's wartime moves, completed her schooling with the Society of the Holy Child Jesus at St. Leonard's School, St. Leonard's-on-Sea, in 1952.

Joan moved to the Manor Farm House, Gosbeck, Suffolk, in 1950. From 1959-1978 she lived at "The Limes", Ipswich Road, Stowmarket. This was a 16th century frame house, to which a Queen Anne front and porch had been added in c.1702. The first Catholic priest appointed to Stowmarket, after the Reformation, had lived there in the 1870s. The house possessed a large Victorian garden. From 1978-1991, Joan lived at 109, High Street, Needham Market, Suffolk. This was a 14th century frame house which was probably part of a complex associated with the pilgrimage to the shrine of St. Edmund at Bury St. Edmund's. It had been restored and modernized by Eric Sandom, on behalf of Crispin, who was the owner. In 1991, Joan moved to 27A, High Street, Debenham, Suffolk. She died there on March 14th 1993 and is buried with her husband, Alan, in St. Mary's cemetery, Kensal Green.

Aylward

On leaving Downside in 1950, Aylward was called up for military service. He was commissioned a 2nd Lieutenant in the Royal Sussex Regiment, and was seconded to the 3rd (Kenya) Battalion of the King's African Rifles. He served with them in

428 Abbot Butler was later appointed Auxiliary of Westminster and Bishop in Hertfordshire, with the titular see of Nova Barbara.

429 In Aylward's case it was a bursary; Crispin took the scholarship examination from Madeley Court; and Gervase, at Downside itself.

Kenya and in the Malayan war. He was promoted Lieutenant in the Territorial Battalion of the Suffolk Regiment, with which he served from 1952-1955. He read modern history at The Queen's College, Oxford, from 1952-1955, and then studied with the Society of Missionaries of Africa ("The White Fathers") in Ireland, Holland, Canada and Britain from 1955-1962. He was ordained deacon by Mgr. Paul-Emile Charbonneau, Auxiliary Bishop of Ottawa, at Ottawa on June 19th 1961, and was ordained priest by Cardinal William Godfrey, 7th Archbishop of Westminster, at St. Mary Magdalen's Church, Whetstone, London, on June 30th 1962.[430]

After studies in missiology at the Pontifical Gregorian University, Rome, 1962-1963, and social anthropology at Oxford 1963-1968, (including field research in Tanzania 1964-1967), he served as a missionary in Uganda, Tanzania and Kenya from 1968-1988, teaching, writing and researching in various church institutions. In 1988, he was appointed President of the Missionary Institute London, and in 1995, Principal of Tangaza College, Nairobi, a constituent college of the Catholic University of Eastern Africa.

Crispin

On leaving Downside in 1951, Crispin read classics at St. Catherine's College, Cambridge (1951-1954), was a Boxing Blue, and captained the University Boxing Club in his final year. He was called up for National Service in the Fleet Air Arm 1954, and was commissioned an Acting Sub-Lieutenant ([A] [O] R.N.V.R.). On leaving the Navy, he worked with the Metal Box Company in London, and then with Harrison and Crosfield Ltd. in Malaysia, before eventually joining Barber Wilhelmsen shipping agencies in Singapore and becoming their Deputy Managing Director. On February 10th 1968 he married Marjorie (1933-), daughter of Hector Pereira and Frances Mary

---

430 Mgr. Charbonneau became Bishop of Hull-Gatineau, Canada, in 1963.

née Pestana, at the Church of St. Ignatius Loyola, Singapore. Jacqueline was born on January 30th 1970; Georgina on October 10th 1974; Anastasia on November 25th 1975; and Teresa Marie on April 10th 1979.

Caroline

On leaving St. Leonard's school, Caroline attended the Ipswich Art School for two years and then went up to Oxford University to spend a further two years at the Ruskin School of Drawing and Fine Art. On October 22nd 1959, at the Church of Our Lady, Stowmarket, she married Dr. Charles Alan Hutt (1912-1992) of Debenham, Suffolk, and has five children.[431] Caroline's artistic activity has chiefly taken the form of painting, and making masks, hats and bridal headdresses.

Gervase

Gervase left Downside in 1954, and was called up for military service in 1955-1957. He was commissioned a Second Lieutenant in the Suffolk Regiment, seconded to the 5th (Kenya) Battalion of the King's African Rifles, and saw service in the Mau Mau campaign. He read Modern History at the Queen's College, Oxford, from 1957-1960, and qualified as a Chartered Accountant with Derbyshire and Derbyshire, joining Peat, Marwick and Mitchell in 1964, and working with this firm until 1973 in Tokyo, Lisbon, and Rio de Janeiro. From 1977-1982 he was Financial Controller of Wilkinson Match, Brazil. In 1982 he became Financial Director of William

---

[431] William Laurence Hutt, born on August 7th 1961; (Dr.) Edward Charles Becket Hutt, born on December 29th 1962; Giles Joseph Hutt, born on April 1st 1964; Damian Frederick Hutt, born on September 25th 1966; and Cecilia Mary Hutt, born on November 24th 1968. Dr. Edward Hutt married Emma Corp on June 3rd 2000 at the church of his parents' wedding.

Teacher and Sons, Brazil, and then President of Hiram Walker (Allied Distillers), Brazil. He took retirement in Brazil in 1994.

On September 2nd 1961, Gervase married Charmian (born on October 4th 1939), daughter of Derric and Elizabeth Stopford-Adams of Anstey Hall, near Coventry, at St. Peter's, Dormer Place, Leamington Spa. They lived at 73, Cloudesley Road, Islington, from 1961-1965, and their eldest son, Tristram Dominic, was born in London on April 26th 1964. Two sons were born to Gervase and Charmian in Tokyo: Hugo Benedict on August 11th 1966, and Orlando Mark on November 21st 1967. Elizabeth Zoë was born in Brazil on December 19th 1981.

Tristram married Orska Largo Valenzuela (born August 16th 1966) in Rio de Janeiro on December 10th 1988. Of Chilean origin, she was a fellow student at the University of Sao Paolo. Pauline Andrea was born to them on May 31st 1989, Alan Gabriel on May 11th 1992 and Melanie in January 1998. Hugo read Modern Languages at the Queen's College, Oxford, from 1986-1989, and then joined the Foreign Office, London. He married Laura Lindon on April 7th 2001 at the Church of St. Antoine de Braixe, France. After a post-secondary course in Brazil, Orlando came to Britain to study Photography at Salisbury, and then set up his own CD-ROM and video production business in Rio de Janeiro. On January 6th 2000, he married Cristina Neves Passos at the Church of Santo Cristo dos Milagros, Rio de Janeiro, Brazil.

The story of the Shorter family, in one of its lines, has now been told in the first part of this book. Meanwhile, the family took root across the Atlantic in America, and that story must now be told in the second part.

Catherine Lady Walpole,
miniature enameled portrait

Tomb of Catherine Lady Walpole in
Westminster Abbey

Bybrook House as it is today

Robert Shorter, from a portrait
by Sir Francis Grant

Jane Shorter, from a portrait by
Sir Francis Grant

Henry Shorter

Alan Wynn Shorter

PART TWO

THE SHORTER FAMILY IN AMERICA

1635-2001

by

Aylward Shorter with Maggie Price Taylor

CHAPTER THIRTEEN

THE FIRST AMERICAN SHORTER

The Founding of Virginia

In 1606, King James I of England issued a charter to Sir Thomas Smith and his associates, incorporated as the Virginia Company of London.[432] Next year in May, three ships arrived along a marshy peninsula, thirty miles inland from Chesapeake Bay. The travelers went ashore to found the first permanent English settlement in America. The colony was named Virginia after Elizabeth I, the "Virgin Queen", and the settlement, Jamestown, after the reigning King. The Commonwealth of Virginia, also nicknamed the "Old Dominion" and the "Cavalier State", because of its loyalty to the cause of King Charles I, was the first of the thirteen original colonies.

The beginnings of the colony were shaky in the extreme, and it was only the timely arrival of Lord De la Warr with further supplies that prevented the abandonment of Jamestown in 1610. The native American inhabitants of the area were the

---

[432] Information for the background history of the colony of Virginia came from Gentry, Daphne S., **Virginia Land Office Inventory**, 3rd Edition, Richmond VA, 1981, Introduction, pp.vii-xxviii; from notes kindly supplied by Dr. M. P. Taylor and from **Compton's Interactive Encyclopaedia**, Compton's New Media Inc., Cambridge MA. 1996.

Powhatan Confederacy of Woodland Indians. It was from them that the English colonists learned about the cultivation of tobacco and John Rolfe began tobacco planting in 1612. After several years of warfare, the marriage of John Rolfe to Powhatan's daughter, Pocahontas, in 1614 brought a measure of peace, but there were further Indian attacks and massacres of settlers in 1622 and 1644. Having defeated the Indians in 1675, Nathaniel Bacon led a revolt against the tyrannical and extortionate Governor, William Berkeley, the following year, sacking and burning Jamestown. The rebellion collapsed with the death of Bacon, but there were no further Indian attacks, and by 1684 the Indian Confederacy had almost disappeared.

Northumberland County was founded in 1648 and the other original Tidewater counties were founded during the next twenty five years: Westmoreland in 1653, Old Rappahannock in 1656 and Middlesex in 1673. Under Oliver Cromwell's Protectorate, there were twelve counties and by the reign of Charles II there were already twenty-one counties. In the reign of William and Mary there were twenty-four counties. Today, Virginia has ninety-five counties altogether.

Under a new charter of 1609 a vast territory was claimed by Virginia, stretching north, south, west and northwest to the Pacific Ocean. In 1781, the state ceded certain territories northwest of the Ohio River to the federal government, and from this area the states of Ohio, Illinois, Indiana, Michigan, Wisconsin and part of Minnesota were formed. Kentucky was separated in 1791 to form a new state and in 1863, after Virginia itself seceded from the union, fifty counties separated to form the state of West Virginia.

In 1624 the charter of the Virginia Company was revoked and the colony was placed under the immediate jurisdiction of the Crown. Theoretically, it was now part of the royal manor of East Greenwich! In 1699 the state capital was moved from Jamestown to Williamsburg and in 1779 Richmond became the capital, three years after Virginia had declared its independence. During the American Civil War in 1861 Richmond was made the Confederate capital.

Virginia has been associated with some of the most momentous events in American history. The first representative assembly in the New World, the Virginia House of Burgesses, met there in 1619. It was the birthplace of four of the first five Presidents of the United States, including George Washington. The American Revolution ended in the colony, with the surrender of Lord Cornwallis at Yorktown. The American Civil War also ended in Virginia, with the surrender of General Robert E. Lee at Appommatox. Some of the bloodiest battles of that war were fought in Virginia.

The Shorter Family in America

The name Shorter first appears in seventeenth century Virginia, in the records of the Tidewater counties mentioned above, beginning with Northumberland, the original parent county of the colony.[433] The name has spread today throughout the United States. According to a representative sample of the U.S. Census from 1800 to 1850, there were Shorters in New York, Maryland, North and South Carolina, Pennsylvania, Idaho, Mississippi and Arizona, besides Virginia. A present day sample (1998) revealed Shorters living in 47 states and the District of Columbia. Florida had 187 Shorters, Texas 186, Michigan 150, Virginia 151 and Georgia 125.[434]

---

433 For the history of the Shorters in early Virginia I am heavily indebted to William J. Shorter, **The Shorter Family in Virginia - The Early Years,** Unpublished MS, Fredericksburg VA, May 1992; also to notes on her own research supplied by Dr. M. P. Taylor.

434 The calculations were made and kindly supplied by Dr. M. P. Taylor, from information published in Halbert's **Family Heritage**, Bath, Ohio, 1996, (communication of October 3rd 1999). According to the **Encyclopedia of American Family Names**, "Shorter" ranks 3,387.

Arguably, the most famous American member of the family is Frank Shorter (1947-). He was a member of the 1972 and 1976 United States Olympic teams. He won a stunning victory in the 1972 Olympic Marathon in Munich. In that race, he outdistanced the British favorite, the Australian world record holder and the Ethiopian defending champion by over two minutes. The gold medalist was the first American to win the marathon in 64 years (since 1908).

Edward Shorter is another American member of the family, well known to the public from his prolific writing. He is a historian with medical training and most of his books deal with health and the history of medical practice.

Another celebrated member of the family was Rev. Fr. Joseph A. Shorter, a Catholic Priest, born in Kansas City in 1863. Ordained at Innsbruck, Austria, where he studied, in 1889, he was appointed to the parish of Holy Epiphany, Leavenworth, in 1890. For nearly forty years, he was pastor and history teacher in Leavenworth, and was instrumental in setting up schools for colored boys and girls.[435]

Evidence is lacking to link the early Virginia Shorters genealogically, because of the dearth of records. Many of the early records were burned or destroyed during Bacon's rebellion, during the revolutionary war or during the American Civil War. It is chronologically possible to link some of the earliest names, and to make them descend from the first Shorter who is mentioned. Up to 1722, when information becomes more plentiful, such a linkage remains purely speculative, as William J.Shorter, who prefers this hypothesis, concedes. It may be thought more likely that the links between some of the Virginia Shorters existed, not in Virginia itself, but in England

---

[435] William Elsey Connelley, **History of Kansas State and People**, The American Historical Society Inc., Chicago and New York, 1928, Vol. IV, pp.1944-1945.

from which they came. However, it remains a question of probabilities. The first member of the family in Virginia was a John Shorter who sailed to Virginia from London on June 6th 1635, appearing in a list of licensed emigrants. He embarked at Gravesend on a ship called "The Thomas and John", whose master was Richard Lombard, after being examined by the minister of Gravesend, concerning his conformity to the orders and discipline of the Church of England. He was therefore a free man who was given license to emigrate, and not a transportee.[436] His age was given as twenty-six.[437]

On board there were some one hundred travelers, of whom more than half were in their twenties. A quarter of the passengers were teenagers, and the rest were aged thirty and above. There was even one fifty year old. Given the state of many English parish records, seventeenth century passengers bound for America would not have found it easy to furnish evidence of their date of birth, and for many it may have been a question of guesswork. The estimated ages may have been incorrectly recorded, and some passengers may have concealed their real age, in order to appear older or younger. We do not know. If American John's real age was twenty six, then he would have been born in 1609. If this was an approximation,

---

[436] Several Shorters who crossed the Atlantic later in the 17th century were convicted transportees. Such was Henry Shorter of Sevenoaks, for example, a reprieved home circuit prisoner, sentenced to be transported from Gravesend to Barbados or Jamaica, who sailed on 28th February 1690. Cf. Coldham, Peter Wilson, **The Complete Book of Emigrants**, Vol.2, 1661-1699, Baltimore 1987.

[437] Filby, P., William and Meyer, Mary, K, (eds.), **Passenger and Immigration Lists Index**, Detroit 1981; Coldham, Peter Wilson, **The Complete Book of Emigrants 1607-1660**, Baltimore 1987, p.147; Hotten, John Camden, **The Original Lists of Persons of Quality 1600-1700**, New York 1874, p.84.

then his birth would, at any rate, have been some time around the first decade of the seventeenth century.

A John Shorter is named in a Virginia land patent dated November 15th 1638. He appears as a headright of Thomas Clipwell who received 600 acres of land in "James Citty County", in return for the transport of twelve persons, among them John Shorter.[438] No age is given for him. The patenting of lands in Virginia, also called "the headright system", dates from 1634, the year before American John sailed.[439] It was designed to encourage settlement by allocating fifty acres of virgin land to each new arrival. In practice the acreage was awarded to the person who paid the transportation costs, not to the settler himself, who was known as the patentee's "headright". The issue of land patents was a complex process that could even take several years. This, as well as the random recording and haphazard dating of patents meant that the date of issue did not coincide with the date of the settler's journey. The John Shorter, therefore, mentioned in 1638, may well have been American John, who sailed in 1635. Equally, it might have been another person. We simply do not know.

Yet another John Shorter is mentioned in a land patent granted to Moses Spring of Norfolk County, in connection with a grant of 224 acres (either a misprint, or a rare exception to the rule that patents were granted in multiples of fifty acres).[440] It is difficult to imagine that he is the same person as the John Shorter who sailed in 1635 and/or was a headright in 1638. If he was alive in 1695, American John would have been 86 years old.

---

[438] Filby and Meyer, **op.cit.**, ref.27772, p.297.

[439] Cf. Gentry, **op.cit.**, pp.x-xx.

[440] Nugent, Nell, **Cavaliers and Pioneers - Abstracts of Virginia Land Patents and Grants**, Dietz Publishing Co., 1934, Vol.3, p.4.

A "Marie" or Mary Shorter, traveled as a licensed emigrant on July 24th 1635, the same year as American John. Like the latter, her age was also given as 26. Was she his wife or perhaps his sister? She was among forty women who traveled from London in the "Assurance", owned by Isaac Bromwell and George Pewsie.[441] A Mary Shorter or Shorten appears in a land grant of 28th August 1638, as headright of Joseph Moore who received two hundred acres in Elizabeth City County.[442] This may have been the same person. Another "Ma" or Mary Shorter appears in a land patent of 1675/6, but this is probably too late a date to refer to the first Mary.[443]

It cannot be safely assumed that the first Mary was the wife of American John. When wives traveled with their husbands, their names appear in the passenger lists, with the appendage <u>uxor</u>. This would not have been the case when a wife traveled on her own. An informant has claimed, on the basis of oral and handwritten family tradition that American John's wife was a certain Sara, née Mabbe, that they married in England and sailed together.[444] It is further claimed that wives were not registered by name. This is not necessarily true. There is no one called Sara Shorter or Sara Mabbe in the passenger lists of 1635. However, a "Sara Mabb" married a John Ward at Hurstpierrepoint Sussex (England) on June 7th 1631.[445] Also, a John (or "Jon") Ward appears on Virginia land patent grants of 21st March 1633, 12th July 1636 and 17th August 1637, the

---

[441] Coldham, **op.cit.**, p.157; Hotten, **op.cit.,** p.114.

[442] Cf. Nugent, **op.cit.,** vol.1, pp. 19, 45, 65, 96.

[443] Nugent, **op. cit.,** vol.2, p.175.

[444] Communication of Dr. M. P. Taylor, 8th May 2000.

[445] This marriage can be found in Boyd's Marriage Index and the International Genealogical Index.

first time in his own name. No wife appears to have travelled with him. John Ward was evidently a planter in his own right, buying and leasing land in his own name.[446]

A John Shorter married in Canterbury (England) in 1631, but his wife's name is unknown. A son, "John", was born to him there on 27th October 1637. Nothing is known about the further life of this John Shorter, and there are no other Shorter family events in Canterbury.[447]

The Identity of American John

It must be considered likely that American John belonged to the original Shorter family of Chiddingfold (Surrey), Staines (Middlesex) and London (Southwark), for the following reasons:
Firstly, the Staines-London Shorters had commercial interests in the American colonies. This is proved by the transatlantic journeys (described in the next chapter) of the timber merchants, Sir John Shorter (4) and his son, John Shorter (9) of Bybrook.[448] Secondly, during his mayoralty in London, Sir John Shorter (4) issued a testimonial for Lord Culpeper, concerning land in Virginia, dated August 13th 1688.[449] Lord Culpeper was the heir of an original grantee, who had received land in the Northern Neck (the area between the Rappahannock and Potomac Rivers) from the exiled King Charles II in 1649. This may betoken a further interest of the Lord Mayor in

---

[446] Cf. Nugent, **op.cit.,** vol.1., pp.19, 37.

[447] Cf. International Genealogical Index and transcripts of Canterbury Cathedral Registers, Society of Genealogists, London.

[448] These numerals are used in the first part of this book.

[449] Virginia County Court Records, Deed and Will Abstracts of Stafford County, VA., 1686-1689, Deed Book - D, Part 1, p.101.

America.[450] Thirdly, the Staines-London Shorters belonged to the Puritan wing of the established Church and Sir John Shorter (4) sympathized with early Baptists. In fact, (as we have seen in Part I) he was a patron of John Bunyan, author of **Pilgrim's Progress.**[451] Many early American settlers had similar misgivings about the High Church of King Charles I (1625-1649), and this was, no doubt, the reason why licensed emigrants had to be examined by a minister of that Church. Fourthly, in the mid-1630s the Shorters, who lived at Staines and in the neighboring parishes of Colnbrook and Horton, moved out of this royalist enclave and into London (especially Southwark). In the run-up to the English Civil War, and during the war itself (1642-1649), they sided with the London-based Parliamentarians (the Puritans). Fifthly, (as we have already seen in Part I) the Staines-London Shorters were involved with shipping, ship-building, and Thames river traffic. Sir John Shorter (4) had his own dockyard on Bankside and his brother Charles (1) owned wharves on the north side of the Thames and property in Rotherhithe, further down river. John (9) of Bybrook actually died on board ship. If they did not personally own ships, he and his father, Sir John (4), certainly hired them. Sixthly, American John sailed from Gravesend, and it was in the Thames/Medway that the Staines-London Shorters had their shipping interests. Seventhly, the Christian names given by Shorters in America, repeat the naming patterns of the Chiddingfold-Staines-London Shorters: particularly John and William. For all these reasons it is likely that American John belonged to this London-based Shorter family.

In the England of King Charles I (reigned 1625-1649), the Shorter family is to be found almost exclusively in London and the South-East. A search in the parish registers of London, Middlesex, Surrey, Sussex, Kent and Buckinghamshire -

---

[450] Members of the Shorter family were later associated with Culpeper County, VA.

[451] Part One, Chapter Four.

counties in which the Shorter family is known to have resided - reveals five candidates for First and/or Second American John. These five were all born in the first decade of the seventeenth century. None of them was born in 1609 and all except one is a dead end as far as American John is concerned.[452]

Going back in time, the first candidate, John Shorter, son of William and Elizabeth née Priest or Preist, was christened at Chiddingfold on 21st November 1610, but the baby died within two weeks of christening and was buried on December 10th 1610.[453] William and Elizabeth also had a daughter called Mercy, baptized on 15th March 1612 (1611 according to the Julian Calendar). She is mistakenly named "Mary" in the International Genealogical Index.[454] This was the very last Shorter family event ever recorded in the Chiddingfold registers.

Treyford-cum-Didling and Woolbeding are two small villages in West Sussex, situated two or three miles from each other on the Surrey-Sussex border. They are almost equidistant from Chiddingfold, being respectively fifteen and twelve miles away. In both these villages a John Shorter was born to a William Shorter in the year 1606 - at Woolbeding on 13th April and at Treyford on 30th November. No mother's name is recorded in either case. Chronologically it is impossible to

---

[452] The search was made with the help of the International Genealogical Index, and in the parish registers themselves, which have references to the Shorter family. These were seen by me as originals, on microfilm and/or in transcript.

[453] Chiddingfold Registers seen on microfiche and in transcript at Surrey Record Office, Kingston on 21st July 1998.

[454] Study of the actual registers on microfiche revealed the error, which was repeated in Shorter, Aylward, **op.cit.,** pp.18-19. The I.G.I. has, in fact, both a "Mary" and a "Mercy", baptized on 15th March 1611. "Mary" is a misreading and a duplication. Even if her name had been Mary, she would have been only 23 in 1635, too young for "American Mary".

identify them with each other or with the William of Chiddingfold already mentioned above. However, it is likely that they are all part of the Chiddingfold cluster of Shorters. A daughter, Agnes, was born to William of Treyford in 1609 (1610) and christened on 4th February.

There are no extant parish registers of Treyford and Woolbeding for the first decade of the seventeenth century, and no Shorter family events recorded thereafter. The Bishop's Transcripts for 1600-1610 have similarly disappeared, although abstracts were made of them and copies of these are kept at the West Sussex Record Office in Chichester.[455] It is in these that the baptisms of the two John Shorters in 1606 are recorded. The two Johns have therefore disappeared into oblivion and nothing is known of their subsequent life or death. It is also unlikely that American John would have originated in villages as remote as Woolbeding and Treyford.

There remain two further John Shorters: John Shorter (3), son of Henry Shorter of Colnbrook, christened at Horton on 15th July 1604 and John Shorter (iii) ("Jhon [sic], son of Jhon [sic] Shorter Senior" - i.e John Shorter (ii)), christened at Staines on 26th February 1602.[456] A daughter called Martha was christened on 2nd October 1603 and a son with a hitherto illegible name on 14th December 1610. This name has since been deciphered as "Humphra".[457] Finally, another son, Richard, was christened on 22nd January 1613.

---

[455] The "Challen" copies of the "Dunkin" (original) abstracts, mf 398. I am grateful to Ms Frances Lonsdale at the West Sussex Record Office for kindly supplying photocopies of the relevant abstracts.

[456] Staines registers, G.L.R.O., X90/105; Shorter, Aylward, **op.cit.,** pp.26-7. The Greater London Record Office is now renamed the London Metropolitan Archive, but the microfilm reference is unchanged.

[457] I am grateful to the archivist of the London Metropolitan Archive for helping me to decipher the Jacobean handwriting of this entry on 26th May 2000.

Chronologically and genealogically, (taking into account the evidence of pedigrees and wills) John (ii) is not identifiable with John (1) or John (2). He may, however, have been the son of William (ii), born in 1542, to whom we have already referred. William (i) would have been born c.1505, and was possibly a brother of John (i), and an elder son of John, the royal launderer. As we have seen, a son, John (iii) was born to John (ii), baptized on 20th February 1602.

John (3), son of Henry Shorter of Colnbrook, was a first cousin of the Lord Mayor, Sir John Shorter (4). Hitherto, it has been assumed (without evidence) that John (3) was "John Shorter Waterman" whose property in Southwark was disposed of by Sir John (4) in his will of 1688, and whose son Thomas received patronage from Sir Robert Walpole as a relative of his wife Catherine, granddaughter of Sir John Shorter (4).[458] There is no inherent reason why the Waterman should not have been the more distant cousin of Sir John Shorter (4), John (iii). It is known that John (3)'s father, Henry, died on 25th October 1616, and his mother, Margaret, on 6th September 1629. Five years later, John (3), who had been elected collector of the Horton tithe in 1626, sold all his land and property in Horton and disappeared from the area.[459] This looks like the act of a man about to emigrate to America, and it may also have been linked to the authorization of land grants in Virginia in 1634. A revision of the previous hypothesis would therefore make John (3) American John, and John (iii) the Waterman. No supporting evidence has been discovered for either hypothesis.

Nothing is known of American John's life in Virginia. The first member of the family to be born in Virginia was William Shorter, whom we shall discuss in a following chapter. A likely

---

[458] Cf. Shorter, Aylward, **op.cit.** pp. 68, 73.

[459] **Ibid.** p.32.

hypothesis is that this William was born in 1636.[460] If that is the case, it is chronologically possible for him to have been the son of American John, but there is no evidence one way or the other.

---

[460] Information supplied by William J. Shorter. The hypothesis will be argued in a subsequent chapter.

CHAPTER FOURTEEN

THE TRANSATLANTIC JOURNEYS OF SIR
JOHN SHORTER

Unsupported Speculation Concerning Sir John Shorter

The Chiddingfold Shorters were the original glass-making Schurterres, who emerged in the Surrey Weald during the thirteenth century. The Staines Shorters were the family of Sir John Shorter (4) (1624-1688), timber merchant, friend of King James II and Lord Mayor of London, whose descendants were connected with the Walpoles and the Seymour-Conways.[461] The names John and William, and to a lesser extent, Richard, Robert, Henry and Thomas, predominate as the male Christian names of both the Chiddingfold and the Staines Shorters. With the exception of Richard, these names reappear among the Shorters of Virginia, and the first Shorter apparently to have been born there was named William (c.1636-1678).[462]

---

461 Shorter, Aylward, **The Shorter Family: A Preliminary History, London 1992**, pp.16-49.

462 Shorter, William J., **op.cit.,** pp.2, 11-13.

156 The Shorter Family

Further support for the link comes from the transatlantic journeys of Sir John Shorter and his son, John Shorter of Bybrook, whom we refer to as John (4) and John (9) respectively.[463] Before embarking on a discussion of Sir John Shorter's interest in the American colonies, it is necessary to clear up several misunderstandings. These have been caused by the unsupported speculations of George Magruder Battey III in his various publications and papers.[464] This author claimed descent from John Hurt, a son of Benjamin Shorter Hurt, another of whose sons, William Hurt, adopted the style Hurt-Shorter in 1790.

Some, at least, of Battey's speculations about the Hurts appear to be based on four summer vacation visits to Virginia to gather oral information and to examine courthouse records and monumental inscriptions.[465] They are part of a misguided attempt to trace his family line from the Hurts to the Shorters, and thence to link it with various royal genealogies. The following is a critique of assertions made in George Magruder Battey III's **Brief Genealogical Sketch of Alfred Shorter**

---

[463] Cf. Shorter, Aylward, **op.cit., passim,** and Part I of this book. The Roman numerals were given to distinguish descendants of John Shorter (1) of Staines, having the same Christian name.

[464] Battey III, George Magruder: **A History of Rome and Floyd County**, GA, Rome, GA, 1922; The Hurt-Shorter Royal Charts, Rome Ga, 1953; A Brief Biogenealogical Sketch of Alfred Shorter (1803-1882) of Rome, Georgia, Rome GA, 1955; also papers deposited with the Library of Congress, entitled: **More Light on the VA. Shorter Family**; cf. also Library of Congress microfilms, Miscellaneous Monographs and Pamphlets, shelf no.86/5993-86/6016.

[465] Communications of Dr. M. P. Taylor, August 13th 1999 and November 4th 2000, interpreting a passage in a paper by Battey entitled: **Alfred Hurt Shorter (1803)-1882 of Rome, GA, Founder in 1877 of Shorter Female College, Figured As Three Times Great-Grandson of Sir John Shorter, Lord Mayor of London, Eng..** p.2, 1st para., line 4.

(1803-1882) of Rome, Georgia, mimeographed, Nov. 25th 1955.

He begins by confusing the Dukes and Earls of Bedford with the Dukes (sic) and Earls of Hertford.[466] He goes on to state that Sir John Shorter (4) and Dame Isabella (née Birkett) lived briefly "in the historic and magnificent Guildhall".[467] In fact, the Guildhall was not the residence of Sir John Shorter (4). He lived at Grocers' Hall, which was then the official mayoral residence. On the same page he asserts that Sir John Shorter and Dame Isabella had "half a dozen children in the old country". In fact, only two sons are recorded. He then states that John Shorter (9) of Bybrook died in 1724.[468] In fact, he died in 1707. On the same page he claims that John (9) had a son Henry and a daughter Mary. Later, however, he claims that he had "at least three daughters", including a Caroline Shorter who married John Churchill ("Mary" is not mentioned).[469] In fact, John (9) had two daughters and three sons. There was no daughter called Caroline or Mary, and no son called Henry. Neither of his daughters married a John Churchill.

Further on, the author assumes "by surmise, rather than record or other evidence" that Sir John Shorter and Dame Isabella had a daughter called Isabella.[470] In fact, no such daughter is recorded. He then makes out that this fictitious Isabella was Isabella Hurt who married Philip Pendleton in 1680.[471] He says that either she took Hurt "as a covering

---

466 Battey, 1955, **op.cit.,** p.1.

467 Battey, **op.cit.,** p.3.

468 Battey, **op.cit.,** p.4.

469 Battey, **op.cit.,** p.6.

470 Battey, **op.cit.,** p.5.

471 Battey, **op.cit.,** p.6.

name" or this was the name of her first husband. He also assumes falsely that Dame Isabella was a second wife of Sir John Shorter (4), considerably younger than her husband. In fact, according to the recorded inscription on Dame Isabella's tomb in Southwark Cathedral, she was born in 1631, and was thus only seven years younger than her husband. There is, of course, no hint in the records and biographies of Sir John Shorter (4) of his having been married twice. The author also asserts on the same page that Isabella Hurt could equally have been the daughter of his son, John (9). Since he claims that she was born around 1660 and John (9) was in fact also born in 1660, this is obviously impossible.

It is clear that these contradictions and unsupported speculations are designed to identify Isabella Hurt as a Shorter. For this, Magruder Battey adduces no real evidence or proof. His writings abound with anachronisms and inconsistencies, and it would be tedious to record them all. The foregoing is sufficient to disprove the direct genealogical link between the Hurt-Shorters and Sir John Shorter (4), as claimed by Battey.

Sir John Shorter's American Interests

Sir John Shorter (4) and his son John (9) of Bybrook, both dealt in timber for ship-building. John (4) built up a fortune from the trade, contracting with the British navy (whose Lord High Admiral was James Duke of York, the future King James II) in 1665 for masts, yards and bowsprits, and offering other contracts for timber to Samuel Pepys, the famous diarist and naval Clerk of the Acts.[472]

Seventeenth century shipbuilding consumed an enormous quantity of timber. Over two thousand trees were required to

---

472 Cf. Shorter, Aylward, **op.cit.,** pp.37-38. See also Part I, Chapter 4 of this book.

build the hull of a single man of war.[471]   This was the equivalent of sixty acres of forest. The England of King Charles II was already running out of suitable forests and the Royal Navy's main sources for timber at that time, especially for masts, were Scandinavia, the Baltic and America. During the seventeenth century the Scandinavian and Baltic merchants experienced growing competition from America. The hardwoods of the newly founded American colonies were eminently suitable for shipbuilding. These woods were found mainly on the eastern seaboard, but also in the Appalachian Mountains. The white pine of New England was highly prized for masts, and the live oak and white oak from the same area was valued for ship's timbers and decking. Sir John Shorter (4) was called a "Norway Merchant", or sometimes a "Danish Merchant", and he did business mainly with Scandinavian suppliers.[472]   His rival in the timber business, Sir William Warren, did business with the Americans.

The passenger lists suggest, however, that John (4) and John (9) were, for a time, frequent travelers to New England and Virginia. A "John Shorter" sailed to New England in 1664, 1666 and 1672, and to Virginia in 1675.[473] These years correspond exactly to the period when John (4) was building up his timber business, and when Pepys was rebuilding the British navy under James, Duke of York, after the Restoration of the Stuarts.   It must be considered extremely likely that this traveler was John (4) exploring new sources of timber in

---

[471] White, Colin, **HMS Victory**, Royal Naval Museum, Portsmouth, 1994, p.6.

[472] **Notes and Queries**, 2nd s. XII, p.14; Gyll, **op.cit.**, p.274.

[473] Coldham, **op.cit.**, pp.65, 92, 190, 241, 252. There is an apparent overlapping of port records for some of these journeys. Either one carrier was substituted for another, or John (4) did not always travel in person. Another possibility is that there was another unidentified John Shorter traveling. This was presumably not John (9) who was only born in 1660, but it could have been American John himself.

America. Samuel Pepys received a tender for three shiploads of New England masts from Sir William Warren in 1663, and he recorded that four New England ships brought masts to Falmouth in December 1666.[476]

John (4) was knighted by King Charles II on October 29th 1675. In 1677 "Sir John Shorter" is named as a traveler to New England, together with "Sir William Warren" on the **Black Cock**, embarking on 3rd-14th May.[477] The fact that Sir John (4) traveled to America with his great rival in the timber trade leaves very little doubt about the purpose of his transatlantic journeys. Thereafter, "Sir John Shorter" made journeys to New England in 1686 and 1687, the year of his mayoralty. Even in 1688, three months before his death, he was also listed as a passenger.[478] There is no passenger listed as "Sir John Shorter" before his knighthood in 1675 or after his death in 1688. There is, of course, no other "Sir John Shorter" known to history.

John (9) continued his father's timber business. A "John Shorter" (as opposed to "Sir John Shorter") made five transatlantic crossings in the lifetime of Sir John (4). These were in 1679, 1684 and 1685. John (9) would have been nineteen years old in 1679. A "John Shorter" was also listed as a passenger to America after Sir John's death in 1690 and 1694.[479] John (9) died thirteen years later in 1707. There are no more mentions of a "John Shorter" in the passenger lists after

---

476 Wheatley, Henry, B., (ed.), **The Diary of Samuel Pepys**, 6 vols., London 1952, vol. iv, p.103, fn.2, p.106, p.269; vol. vi, pp.84-86; entries for 14th April 1664, 19th April 1664, 14th November 1664 and 2nd/3rd November 1666.

477 Coldham, **op.cit.,** p.284.

478 Coldham, **op.cit.,** pp. 581, 592, 605. It is possible that John (9) took his place for the final journey.

479 Coldham, **op.cit.,** pp.331, 451, 507, 624 and 645.

1694. It must be considered likely that John Shorter (9) of Bybrook was this other "John Shorter".

The interest of Sir John Shorter and his son in America was, no doubt, primarily commercial, However, the fact that a relative had preceded them and had settled there may also have been significant. Sir John (4) was considerably younger than his cousin John (3), whom we are suggesting was American John, and he did not commence a business career until after the English Civil War. The war ended in 1649, fourteen years after his cousin's emigration. However, Sir John (4)'s transatlantic journeys did not begin until the early 1660s, after the Restoration of Charles II. American John, if still alive, would have been in his mid-fifties at that time. It is, perhaps, doubtful that he was alive, when John (4) visited Virginia in 1675. However, William, who may have been American John's son probably had two or three more years of life. He died in about 1678.[480]

---

480 See Chapter Fifteen.

CHAPTER FIFTEEN

WILLIAM SHORTER OF NORTHUMBERLAND COUNTY AND THE VIRGINIA SHORTERS

William Shorter of Northumberland County

Mention was made in Chapter Thirteen of the Northern Neck, the land between the Rappahannock and Potomac Rivers. William Shorter was a planter who lived in this area of Virginia.[481] After the foundation of Northumberland County in 1648, he was a resident of that county. Besides being the owner of several hundreds of acres of land, William possessed enough hogs and cattle to justify the registration of a special livestock mark. Both hogs and cattle had a mark on the ears, while his cattle had "WS" branded on the right horn.[482]

William was reckoned to have been about thirty years old in 1664, by the court clerk of a lawsuit in which he was a witness. He testified that "being at Exeter Lodge at Mr. Gaskin's planta-

---

[481] This account of William Shorter and his descendants is based on William J. Shorter, **op.cit.** and further drafts kindly supplied by this author; also on research notes communicated by Dr. M. P. Taylor.

[482] Virginia County Court Records, p.118; reference supplied by Dr. M. P. Taylor. **Deeds and Wills Abstracts of Northumberland County 1662-1666.**

tion on that day Jonathan Parker was buried...saw Thomas Barrett with his fist strike Miles Miller, servant to Mr.Saffin, at least three times in the house".[483] We do not know the exact date of the incident, but Exeter Lodge Plantation was settled around 1664. If the estimate of his age in 1664 was accurate, then he would have been either forty-one (court date) or forty-three (court testimony) when his will was proved in 1678.[484] If, splitting the difference, he was forty-two, then his year of birth would have been 1636, and he could have been a son of American John. All of this depends on contemporary estimates and guesswork. A difference of only a year or two would throw doubt on his being the son of American John. If his year of birth was c.1630, he could have been born in England.[485] However, there is no emigrant William with which he can be identified, and it looks as if he may have been the first Shorter to have been born in America.

On March 21st 1669/1670, William bought fifty acres of land in Northumberland County, "lying on the Mattoponie" (the Mattaponi River) from James Claughton, an area now known as Lodge Creek.[486] Then in May of the same year, 1670, he was granted one hundred acres "situated at the head of Mattoponie (Mattaponi) River", by Philip Evans and Hugh

---

483 **Northumberland County Record Book No.16, 1666-1672**, 10;Nugent, Nell M., **Cavaliers and Pioneers**, Vol.20, **Northumbria Collectanea, 1645-1720**, (M-Z), 1979, p.607; **Virginia Colonial Abstracts**, Vol.20.

484 William died in Northumberland County. His will was proved on August 21st 1678. **Cavaliers and Pioneers, Northumbria Collectanea, 1675-1720** (A-L), p.539; **Virginia Colonial Abstracts**, Beverly Fleet, Vol.1, Genealogical Publishing Co. Inc., Baltimore, 1988, p.554.

485 William (2) of Colnbrook, was born c.1627. However, the Heralds' Visitation of 1664 (1674) suggests he was present in England at that time.

486 **Northumberland County, Virginia, Record Book, 1660-1670,** p.122; cf. also **Virginia County Court Records**, Deed and Will Abstracts of Northumberland County, Virginia, 1666-1670, p.104.

Harris, being part of a six hundred acre plot held by them under patent.[487]

We know that William's wife was named Ann and that they had more than five children. In 1680, Ann presented an inventory of her departed husband's estate, having five small children, requesting the court to allow her 2,154 pounds of tobacco out of the estate for the clothing of her small children.[488] One of their (older) children was named William. In 1665, William Senior assigned a bill of sale for the purchase of one black heifer "unto my son William Shorter".[489] William Junior purchased land sometime before 1679.[490] In order to do this he would have had to be 21 years old. On this basis, William J. Shorter estimates that William and Ann's children would have been born between 1658 and 1677.[491] However, William Junior could have been slightly older.

William Senior appeared in court on November 23rd 1677 for tax evasion. He was prosecuted for concealing a person for whom poll tax or tithe was payable. When a male reached the age of sixteen, he was supposed to be income producing and

487 **Northumberland County, Virginia, Record Book 1666-1678**, pp.139-140; **Virginia County Court Records**, Deed and Will Abstracts of Northumberland County, Virginia, 1666-1670, pp. 116-117.

488 Northumberland County Virginia Order Book No.4, 1678-1698, Pt.1, 74.

489 Northumberland County, Virginia, Record Book No.15, 1662-1666, 174.

490 February 17th 1679/80, John Claughton is mentioned as having formerly sold William Junior a parcel of land "of Matapony" in Northumberland County._**Virginia County Court Records**, Deeds and Will Abstracts of Northumberland County, Deeds 1670-1672/1706-1711, pp.112-113.

491 From a draft supplied by William J. Shorter.

therefore tithable. William Junior could hardly have been concealed, if he was already around twenty years old or older. The son in question may have been Anthony Shorter, who was born c.1661, but we have no strict evidence that he was the son of William Senior.[492] A second court appearance occurred on December 19th 1677 in which William Senior was allowed in the next levy to pay for the use of a baggage horse for three months.[493]

William Senior died in Northumberland County in 1678 and his will was proved on August 21st of that year.[494] William Shorter Junior makes one further appearance in the historical record, after his father's death. In 1691 he sold fifty acres of land in Northumberland County to William Howard. It was part of the land acquired by his father from Philip Evans and Hugh Harris in 1670.[495]

On August 20th 1682, an Anthony Shorter was named in the records of Old Rappahannock County. He witnessed the signing of a deed by William Underwood Junior. Witnesses to deeds were required to be at least twenty-one years old. This means that Anthony was born in c.1661.[496] It is chronologically possible that Anthony was a son of William Senior and a brother to William Junior, but as William J.

---

492 **Northumberland County Virginia Order Book 1666-1678**, 318;

493 **Ibid.**, 331.

494 **Northumberland County, Virginia, Court Order Book**, No.4, 1678-1698; cf. also **Cavaliers and Pioneers**, Northumbria Collectanea, 1675-1720 (A-L) p.539. **Virginia Colonial Abstracts**, Beverly Fleet, Vol.1, Genealogical Publishing Co. Inc. Baltimore 1988, p.554.

495 **Northern Neck Land Grants**, Vol. II, 1742-1775, by Gertrude E. Gray, Genealogical Publishing Co.Inc., Baltimore, 1988, p.14.

496 **Old Rappahannock County Deeds and Other 1682-1688**, pp.164-167. Cf. William J. Shorter **op.cit.**, p.14.

Shorter remarks, the records provide too little information to make this connection.

At some time in the 1680s or early 1690s Anthony seems to have moved to Dorchester County Maryland. Thereafter his name appears in connection with a number of land transactions, beginning in 1693. He married Susannah, the daughter of Richard and Elizabeth Kendal and part of the Kendal estate, named "Stafford" was given to Anthony's son, William. The latter was not of legal age in 1693 and was probably born c.1683. Anthony had two daughters named Elizabeth and Susannah. He died in 1716.[497]

In 1743 and 1761 there is mention of another Anthony Shorter in Maryland, who was born c.1699. These records reveal that his mother's name was Susannah and that this was also the name of his wife. Presumably he could have been another son of Anthony Senior.[498] We now return to Virginia.

John of Lunenburg County and His Descendants

John Shorter of Middlesex County, VA, and his descendants in Georgia form the subject of the next chapter. Apart from him, the most important Virginian to bear the name Shorter was another John, of Lunenburg County. With him, we now enter

---

[497] Cf. William J. Shorter, **op.cit**, Appendix A, 1-2; **Abstracts from the Land Records of Dorchester County Maryland**, James A. McAllister Jr., Cambridge MD, 1961, vol.3, p.24 (Libers old 4 1/2 - old 5); vol.4, p.71 (liber old 6); **Maryland Calendar of Wills 1720-1726, vol.v, Genealogical Publishing Co. Inc., Baltimore, 1968, p.239; Testamentary Proceedings Dorchester Co. MD**, liber 23, folio 144, p.202; **Abstracts of the Inventories and Accounts of the Prerogative Court of Maryland 1715-1718**, V. L. Skinner Jr., Family Line Publications, Westminster MD. 1994, p.16.

[498] William J. Shorter **op.cit.**, Appendix A, 1-2.

the realms of history, for he heads the well- documented line from whom present day Shorters in Virginia trace their descent.[499] Chronologically, John of Lunenburg County could have been the son of John of Middlesex County, or more probably of the William Junior already mentioned. The evidence, however, is lacking. The wife of John of Lunenburg County was named Kindness and he had at least one son, James Archibald of Charlotte County.[500] He died in 1754. His son James was born about 1747.[501] Evidence shows that Kindness Shorter was a neglectful administratrix of her husband's estate and that the Lunenburg County Court may also have viewed her as an unfit mother. Her case was examined in 1758.[502]

Kindness reappeared ten years later, witnessing a deed in 1678 between her son James, and John Haley and his wife, Mary, of Lunenburg County VA, buying ninety-four acres of land on Juniper Creek on April 14th 1768. This same piece of land James sold on September 7th 1778 to Benjamin Lewis.[503] From 1782 to 1805 James and his wife Lucy farmed in Charlotte County and raised five sons, and at least one daughter.[504] Charlotte County was formed out of Lunenburg

---

499 Two major informants for this history have been William J. Shorter and Michael Woodrow Shorter. They are descended from two great-grandsons of John of Lunenburg County, Woodson Henry Shorter (b.1827) and William Ivan Shorter (1811-1862) respectively. Michael W. Shorter kindly provided the author with his complete genealogy.

500 William J. Shorter, **op.cit**, p.25.

501 The year of his birth is based on the assumption of his legal age when he purchased land in 1768. Cf. William J. Shorter, **op.cit.**, p.26, n.70.

502 See William J. Shorter, **op.cit.** pp.27-28, for a full discussion of the evidence concerning Kindness Shorter.

503 **Charlotte County Deed Book 4, 1777-1782**, 1, pp.212-217.

504 Cf. William J. Shorter, **op.cit.** p.29 and n.81.

County in 1764, and James may have been continuously resident on family land. On two occasions James was appointed a surveyor of the road by the county court in October 1791 and June 1797. His responsibility was to keep the road clear and safe for travelers. He had to clear fallen trees, inspect bridges and call on neighbors to help in the work.[505]

On July 7th 1794, James Shorter was sworn in as constable for Charlotte County.[506] Constables were employed in rural areas which could not be regularly visited by sheriffs. They carried out court orders, served warrants, conveyed vagabonds, deserters and runaway slaves, meted out punishments and inspected tobacco plantings and harvests. They were paid in varying amounts of tobacco.[507] Shortly after this appointment, James became indebted to one Amelia Childrey for sixty pounds of Virginian currency and had to pay it off with much needed property, a stud horse, a mare, eight head of cattle, furniture including two beds and kitchen furniture.

James's sons appear in the Virginia tax records of the early nineteenth century. They are Berry, Robert, Jeremiah, James Junior and John. A daughter, Kindness, is mentioned in Tennessee records. Robert married Sally Kennedy on June 7th 1799. Berry married Simey Stembridge on August 2nd 1802. John married Nancy Palimore on December 11th 1806 and Jeremiah married Betsy Hamlett on April 19th 1810. James Jr. married Margaret Smith in Lebanon, Wilson County Tennessee, on August 18th 1810.[508]

---

505 **Charlotte County Order Book 8, 1789-1792**, 179.

506 **Charlotte County Order Book 9, 1792-1794**, 207.

507 Cf. William J. Shorter, **op.cit.**, pp.30-31.

508 Cf. William J. Shorter, **op.cit.**, pp.32-33, 37.

Little is known about Robert and he had few taxable possessions. Agriculture in Charlotte County depended heavily on slave labor at this time, but Robert was not apparently a slave owner, as were his brothers. He may have been born c.1781. He and his wife Sally had three sons and two daughters. After 1816, Robert no longer appears in Charlotte County, but his widow and her children were enumerated in the Tennessee censuses of 1830 and 1840, living in Hawkins County. In 1850, she was living as a head of a household in Grainger County. Robert may have died at the time of the move to Tennessee.[507]

Berry Shorter was born in Charlotte County around 1779 and probably lived there until some time between 1805 and 1820, when he moved with his family to Wilson County, Tennessee. He and his wife, Simey, had at that time six children, three boys and three girls. At least two more girls were born to them in the 1820s. Besides Berry's family, the 1850 census shows that there were seven other Shorter families living in Tennessee, three of them possibly those of his sons, John W., James, and Benjamin.[508]

James Shorter Jr., son of James Sr. and Lucy, moved to Tennessee sometime in the first decade of the nineteenth century. He and his wife Margaret were living in Lincoln County, Tennessee in 1820. They had one son and one daughter. After 1830, this family disappears from the census records.[509]

The one daughter of James Shorter Sr. was called Kindness and she married Stephen Smart in Lebanon, Wilson County,

---

[507] See William J. Shorter, **op.cit.** pp.34-35, for the details of Robert and his family.

[508] William J. Shorter, **op.cit.,** pp.35-37.

[509] William J. Shorter, **op.cit.,** pp.35-36.

Tennessee on January 24th 1810. James Sr. died between May 1805 and April 1806, at the age of fifty-nine.[512]

Two sons of James Sr. and his wife Lucy remained in Virginia. Jeremiah, born c.1786, remained in Charlotte County. He and his wife Elizabeth or Betsy had seven children, Thomas H., George, William Ivan, Julia (July), Woodson Henry, Mary Jane and Jesse W. Jeremiah remained a farmer all his life and died some time between February 1827 and July 1829. Tax records show that he died before the middle of 1829, but his name appears in February 1827.[513]

John Shorter, son of James Sr. and Lucy, was born between 1782 and 1789 in Charlotte County, Virginia. In 1828, he moved with his wife Nancy and family to Pittsylvania County VA, and thence in 1830/1831 to Franklin County VA. They had six children, Booker Randolph, Frances, James, William, Woodson Alexander and George Washington, who all married in Franklin County. John was a farmer, like his brothers. The 1850 census gives John's age as sixty-four and states that he was unable to read or write. His son, Booker Randolph, became a teacher. At the age of seventy-four, on January 15th 1856, John Shorter married the thirty-six year old Sallie Richardson Perkins. Nancy, his first wife, had died on July 18th 1854.[514] John Shorter's own death is unrecorded.

A documented family line is therefore continuous from John Shorter of Lunenburg County in the 1720s up to Jeremiah Shorter in the 1820s, and from Jeremiah and his brother, John of Franklin County, up to the present.[515] In the next chapter,

---

512 William J. Shorter, **op.cit.,** p.37-38.

513 William J. Shorter, **op.cit.,** pp.38-39.

514 William J. Shorter, **op.cit.,** pp.39-40.

515 **Ibid.**

we shall consider the origins and descent of John Shorter of Middlesex County (d.1728), who represents the other Shorter line of Virginia.

CHAPTER SIXTEEN

JOHN SHORTER OF MIDDLESEX COUNTY
AND HIS DESCENDANTS

The Identity of John Shorter of Middlesex County

On December 23rd 1722 John Shorter married Elizabeth Underwood in Christ Church Parish, Middlesex County, VA.[516] Elizabeth was the daughter of Nathan and Diana Underwood and was born on November 22nd 1700. She was christened a month later on December 22nd in Stratton Major Parish in King and Queen County VA by Reverend Emmanuel Jones, Minister of Petsoe Parish in Gloucester County.[517] We are fortunate in possessing such detailed information about the birth of John's wife. For John, himself, however, there are no details of his birth in Virginia. It is chronologically possible for him to have been the son of William of Northumberland County VA and brother of William Junior and Anthony of Dorchester County, MD. He could have been among William Senior's five small children (presumably under ten years old), mentioned in 1680, but there is no evidence that this is so.

---

[516] Society of Colonial Dames of America in the State of Virginia, **The Parish Register of Christ Church Middlesex County, Virginia, from 1653-1812**, 2nd ed. (Easley SC: Southern Historical Press, 1988), 164.

[517] **Ibid.**

Another possibility is that he was a recent emigrant to Virginia, who was born in England.[518]

A patent was granted in 1702 to James Dabney of Pamunkey Neck, King and Queen County VA, of one thousand acres of land for the transportation of twenty persons, among whom was a John Shorter.[519] This could have been John Shorter of Middlesex Co. Using the mean age for Virginia emigrants at that time, this John would have been in his mid-thirties. There is a possible candidate for this emigrant, John (10), the grandson of John Shorter Waterman of St. Saviour's Southwark, England, a relative of Sir John (4), the Lord Mayor. The Waterman had six children born to him in Southwark. Besides these, another John (7) appears as fathering children in St. Saviour's Southwark. He is almost certainly the eldest son of the Waterman, probably born before the move to Southwark. His wife was named Phoebe, and John (7) himself was clerk or porter to Dr. McQuarrie of Axe Yard. In c.1680, John (7) and Phoebe moved to the parish of St. Benet's Paul's Wharf, in which parish he was buried in 1689.[520]

---

518 The fact that he had sons named "William" and "Henry" favor the hypothesis that he was a son of William of Northumberland County, and that the latter was a son of American John. If American John was John (3) of Horton, then he came of a family where the names "John", "William" and "Henry" were common.

519 **Cavaliers and Pioneers, Abstracts of Virginia Land Patents and Grants**, Vol.3, 1695-1702, Nell Marion Nugent, Virginia State Library, Richmond VA, 1979, p. 58. In 1711 another John Shorter sailed to New York as a transportee. Coldham, Peter W., **The Complete Book of Emigrants 1700-1750**, Genealogical Publishing Co. Inc., Baltimore MD, 1992, p.123.

520 For the story of John Shorter Waterman and his family, see Part I, Chapter 7.

On December 30th 1667, John (7)'s firstborn, John (10), was baptized at St. Saviour's Southwark.[521] He would have been aged thirteen, when his family moved across the river to St.Benet's. In 1702, John (10) would have been aged thirty-five. If he is John of Middlesex County, VA, he would have been aged fifty-five when he married in Virginia twenty years later and sixty-one when he died there in 1728. His will shows that he had had time to build up a considerable estate in the twenty years before his marriage. He was the first member of the Shorter family to own slaves, and the slave registers of Christ Church Parish show that his estate survived for nearly twenty years after his death.[522]

There is no indication, so far, of John (10)'s continuing to live in England, unless he was the John Shorter who married Alice Ashton at St. George's Southwark on September 18th 1685. This is most unlikely, since he would then have been aged only seventeen years and nine months.[523] We have, therefore, two hypotheses for the origins of John Shorter of Middlesex County.

In 1727, there is mention of John Shorter, Commander of the ship Hopewell riding at anchor in the west river of Anne Arundel Co., MD, and intending to export tobacco to Messrs. Daniel Mand and Samuel Hewit, merchants in London. This could have been John Shorter of Middlesex Co. exporting his tobacco to London.[524] To be involved in the shipping, as well as the planting, of tobacco, would be in character for a

---

[521] London Metropolitan Archive, X 39/1b, R/133.

[522] William J. Shorter, **op.cit.,** pp.15-16.

[523] London Metropolitan Archive X/92/30.

[524] **Anne Arundel County, Maryland, Land Records, 1724-1728**, T.L.C. Genealogical, Miami, FL, 1993, p.72.

grandson of the Waterman, reared on the River Thames, among the busy traffic of the port of London.[525]

In 1727 John witnessed a will for William Batchelder, dated May 2nd.[526] Then on July 15th 1728, John Shorter died.[527] On the 6th July he had made his will "being very sick and weak in body". In the will are mentioned his son Henry and his daughter Mary, as being "not yet 17 years old", that is to say, requiring special protection under Virginia law at that time. In fact, Henry was only four years old and Mary may have been younger.[528] John desired his good friend and executor, James Meacham, to bring up his children in the fear of God. This looks as if John had no next of kin in the Shorter family of Virginia to perform this service. The will was proved on December 3rd 1728.

John's young wife was 28 years old when he died, and a year after his death she married again on November 21st 1729. Her second husband was Thomas Walker.[529] John's son Henry was

---

[525] It must be said, however, that the commander of the Hopewell could also have been John Shorter of Lunenburg Co.

[526] "Middlesex County VA Wills 1713-1734", Part II. **The Virginia Genealogist**, Jan-Mar 1961, vol. 5, no.17, p.85.

[527] The Parish Register Christ Church, Middlesex County VA, 1653-1812. "Middlesex County VA Wills and Inventories 1673-1812 and Other Court Papers", **The Virginia Genealogist**, Jan-Mar 1962, vol.6, no.1, pp.9-10.

[528] See William J. Shorter, **op.cit.**, p.15, for a fuller discussion. **Will Book B 1713-1734, Part II, Middlesex County VA Wills and Inventories, 1673-1812 and Other Court Papers**, William L. Hopkins, p.88.

[529] The Parish Register, Christ Church, Middlesex County VA, 1653-1812, p.166.

born on August 8th 1724, but there is no record of the birth or christening of his daughter Mary.[530]

Henry Shorter, Son of John

In 1741 a Henry Shorter appeared in Orange County, VA. This date corresponds with Henry, son of John of Middlesex Co, attaining the age of seventeen and with the last mention of John's estate in Middlesex Co. At the very same time, the name Henry Shorter disappeared from the records of Middlesex County.[531] For all these reasons, it is assumed that they are one and the same person.[532]

On February 25th 1741, therefore, Henry bought one hundred acres of land for "30 pounds current money".[533] The property, which was adjacent to Rappahannock upon Beaver

---

[530] See William J. Shorter, **op.cit.,** p.16. The Parish Register of Christ Church, Middlesex Co. VA, 1653-1812, p.115. The name "Henry" raises a number of speculations. It was rare in the Shorter family of Virginia and Georgia. If American John was indeed John (3), as was suggested in Chapter One, then his own father was called Henry and there were other Henrys in the family. On the other hand, the name William appears sooner in Virginia than Henry. The father and grandfather of John (iii) whom I have supposed to be John Shorter Waterman, were both called William. None of his descendants were called William or "Henry" until more than a century later.

[531] Orange County Deed Book No.5, 1741-1742, 9-10.

[532] Cf. William J. Shorter, **op.cit.,** pp.17-18. Henry Shorter Sr. was the only Henry Shorter, apart from his son Henry Jr., who has been found in the records of Middlesex and Orange counties VA, as well as in Wilkes Co. GA. We can therefore be pretty certain that these are the same person, and the one who was the son of John of Middlesex Co. Thomas Walker, Henry's stepfather was with him in Orange County, when he purchased 100 acres of land there, and was living there with Henry's mother, when he (Thomas) died in 1767.

[533] Orange County Deed Book, No.5, 1741-1742, 9-10.

Dam, was bought from planters named Martin and John Duett of St. Mark's Parish. Three years later in May 1745, Henry sold this acreage to another resident of Orange County, Jonathan Pratt.[534]

Henry's move from the Tidewater County of Middlesex to Orange County in Piedmont was probably part of the general westward migration from the coastal regions in search of more fertile land for tobacco growing. Henry engaged in a great deal of buying and selling of land, and this seems to have been his main interest and his main source of wealth. In 1750 Henry purchased another two hundred acres of land for "five shillings sterling" (or fifty pounds) from Henry Kendall and resold them to William Jackson in 1753.[535] The name of his wife, "Elizabeth", occurs in the record of this transaction, which probably means that Henry married between 1750 and 1753.

Over the next thirteen years Henry appeared as a defendant in several court cases, beginning with a charge of "trespass assault" brought by William Simms. Later charges by other plaintiffs were not specified and were mostly dismissed because of non-appearance or because of a settlement between the parties. On April 25th 1755, Henry was summoned to court twice on the same day. Because of his failure to appear in the first case, he had an attachment issued against him for "ten pounds current money" and costs.[536] The sheriff, therefore, attached "one pair of iron spancels (hobbels), a black horse, a gun, three sheep, eight pewter plates, three pewter dishes, two pewter

---

534 Orange County Deed Book, No.10, 1745-1747, 308-309.

535 Orange County Deed Book, No.11, 1747-1751, 211-212; Orange County Deed Book, No.12, 1751-1754, 166; Orange County Order Book, No.5, 1745-1747, 273, 486.

536 For a full account and references of this litigation, see William J. Shorter, **op.cit.,** pp.19-20.

basons (basins) and one grindstone".[537] After this, Henry was a defendant in yet another lawsuit brought by a commercial enterprise named Lenox and Co. on August 27th 1767. The case was dismissed upon agreement.[538]

Within five years of this lawsuit, Henry had moved to Culpeper County. It is likely that he moved away from Orange County in order to escape his legal problems. Records show him and his wife Elizabeth living in Culpeper County in 1772. On May 18th of that year he bought 329 acres from William and Diana Stanton for 105 pounds.[539] On 30th March 1775 land was surveyed for Henry and a warrant issued for 47 acres of land on the north side of Terrell's Bluff. In the survey, one of the chain carriers was John Shorter.[540] This was probably one of Henry's sons, old and strong enough to carry the chain and to fight as a soldier in the Revolutionary War that broke out in that year. Most probably, he is the John Shorter who is listed in the Seventh Virginia Regiment of the Continental Line in August 1777, located at Wilmington, Delaware, and south of Bethlehem, Pennsylvania, in the following month.[541] In 1777 the Virginia Brigades participated in the defense of Philadelphia and in George Washington's counter-attack at Germantown, PA. During these operations John Shorter fell ill, was hospitalized and died on November 19th 1777.[542]

---

[537] Orange County Order Book, No.6, 1754-1763, 133.

[538] Orange County Order Book No.7, 1763-1769, p.448.

[539] Culpeper County Deed Book F, 1769-1773, 465.

[540] **Abstracts of Virginia Northern Neck Warrants and Surveys 1653-1781**, Vol. V, Peggy S. Joyner 1995, p.95.

[541] **National Archives, Revolutionary War Records; Historical Register of the Virginia Revolution 1775-1883**.

[542] **Ibid.**

Another son who probably served in the Revolutionary War was William. Records show that a William Shorter served in Patton's Regiment, Captain John Keene's Company, Continental Troops in Pennsylvania. His tour of duty lasted from April 1777 to April 1779, and he did not rise above the rank of private. There was, however, another William Shorter living in Dorchester County, Maryland, who could have been this soldier.[543] Henry Sr. was fifty years old when the war broke out and was therefore too old to enlist. However, he was obliged to provide commodities for military use on two occasions. He submitted claims for reimbursement of two lots of beef and several casks of brandy.[544]

The Revolutionary War notwithstanding, on September 8th 1777 Henry paid seventy pounds for another one hundred acres of land.[545] In 1782-1783, the tax records show that Henry had four surviving sons. William was the oldest, followed by James, Jacob and Henry Junior. Georgia records imply that Henry Sr. had other children. Russell Shorter was probably another son and Winny Shorter may have been a daughter.[546] William and Jacob were over the age of 21.[547] In 1787 and 1788, tax records reveal Henry Sr. as possessing 400 acres of

---

543 Cf. William J. Shorter, **op.cit.,** p.23.

544 Public Service Claims, Culpeper County, Commissioner's Book II. 115.

545 Culpeper County Deed Book H, 1775-1778, 123, 620.

546 Little is known about Russell and Winny. In 1804 Russell sold land on Big Beaverdam Creek, where Henry Sr.had bought 200 acres, and the witnesses were James and Jacob Shorter. Winny Shorter witnessed the 1777 will of William Sims in Culpeper Co. She may have been a daughter-in-law.Cf. Coke, Ben, **The Underwood Family from Madison County, Virginia**, Virginia State Library, 1986, p.78.

547 Culpeper County Personal Property Tax Books, 1782-1788, Annual; Schreiner-Yantis, N. and Love, F.S., **The 1787 Census of Virginia**, Springfield VA, Genealogical Books in Print 1987, 726.

land.[548] In 1789, however, six years after Independence, Henry Sr. and Elizabeth sold their initial 329 acres to William Harvey for a profit of fifteen pounds.[549]

We do not know exactly the circumstances of the move of Henry's family out of Virginia, but by August 1789 he is found in Wilkes County, Georgia, where he bought 200 acres of land on the Water Course Beaver Dam.[550] The sons of Henry Sr., William, Jacob James and Henry Jr. appear in the records of Wilkes County, GA during the last decade of the eighteenth century. We do not know the date and place of Henry Sr.'s death. It took place either in Virginia or in Georgia after 1789.[551]

---

[548] Virginia County Court Records, Culpeper County VA, Land Tax Books 1782-1786, p.33 and 1787-1789, p.72.

[549] Culpeper County Deed Book P, 1789-1790, 139.

[550] Cf. Coke, op.cit., p.78. According to John H. McIntosh, **The Official History of Elbert County, 1790-1935**, Supplement, Daughters of the American Revolution, 1940, p.399, the family of Henry Shorter was established in Elbert (Wilkes) County in 1784.

[551] A Henry Shorter who died in Wilkes Co.in 1808 was not Henry Sr., as had been previously thought, but the son of William, and husband of Sarah Gresham. Cf. **Information on Some Georgia Pioneers: Family Heads 1805, Georgia**, p.171; cf. also: Brad Sanders, **Descendants of Joshua Sanders of Columbia Co., Georgia**, RootsWeb.com, Inc., 2000. I am indebted to Dr. M. P. Taylor for these references.

CHAPTER SEVENTEEN

THE SHORTER FAMILY IN GEORGIA

The Shorters of Wilkes County

Virginia and Maryland were colonized from England more or less simultaneously. A generation later, some Virginians settled in North Carolina in 1653. This territory had been granted a charter by King Charles I in 1629, after the earlier episode of the "lost colony" of 1587-1591, founded at the behest of Sir Walter Raleigh. However, it was not until the reign of Charles II that a serious attempt was made to colonize the Carolinas. In 1670, the first English settlement was made at Charleston in South Carolina. In 1712 North and South Carolina were separated, the latter becoming a separate royal province seventeen years later.

In the first half of the 18th century North Carolina was settled by Scots-Irish and Germans from Pennsylvania, also by German Swiss Protestants. At the same time, South Carolina had an unsettled early history, as a result of land battles with the Yamasee Indians, and battles at sea with Spaniards and pirates. In 1732 King George II granted a charter to a group of wealthy Englishmen, headed by James Oglethorpe to found a colony further south, named Georgia. This was the last of the thirteen colonies founded by England. After the trustees surrendered their charter, the colony became a royal province in 1754.

In the 1760s and 1770s a steady flow of settlers moved into Georgia. A proclamation of Governor Wright in 1773 advertised its land opportunities, and the population tripled between 1760 and 1773. Each settler was offered 200 acres of land as his own headright, plus fifty acres for his wife, each child and each slave.[552] The attraction of this offer, coupled with the alien settlement and disturbed condition of the Carolinas ensured that Virginians readily moved into Georgia. Among those who did so were members of the Shorter family of Culpeper Co., VA.[553]

Wilkes County in Georgia originally embraced a very large territory. It had been acquired from the Indians in payment of debts due to early traders and in 1773 it was opened for settlement. In 1777 it was declared a county and named after John Wilkes, the pro-American British parliamentarian. Washington,

---

[552] This historical introduction is based on "Georgia" in **Compton's Interactive Encyclopedia**, Compton's New Media Inc. 1996 and on information supplied by Dr. M. P. Taylor, in her "Updated Chronology of Shorter Records", unpublished notes kindly supplied by the author in 1999. Information on the Shorters in Georgia, given by Ben H. Coke, in **The Underwood Family from Madison County, Virginia**, 1986, McDowell Publications, Utica, KY, is more reliable than many other secondary sources.

[553] Some Shorters moved into North and South Carolina. A William Shorter was recorded in North Carolina in 1738, and petitioned for a land patent in the following year in Bertie Co. In the 1740s and 1750s William and his wife Elizabeth witnessed several deeds in Northampton Co., NC. In his will of 1752, he names his wife Elizabeth and his son Benjamin. In the latter's will, Drury and David are named as brothers. David was recorded in Northampton Co. in 1775 and in the 1790 census of Camden District, Clarendon Co., SC. He moved to SC after his brother, Benjamin's death. A Jacob "Shortner" (or Shorter ?) appears in the 1800 census of Sumter Co., SC. Dr. M. P. Taylor: "Updated Chronology of Shorter Family Records", and personal communication of November 25th 2000. Cf. Also Appendix C of William J. Shorter **op.cit.** John Shorter, William Shorter and David G. Shorter may have been among David's children. A John Shorter, with wife and two children, appeared in Camden Co. in 1810. Cf. Census Rolls of Sumter and Clarendon Counties, SC and Camden Co., NC, cited by Dr. M. P. Taylor , **loc.cit.**

GA was the site of the first colony. The earliest settlers of the county came from North Carolina, but they were followed by large numbers of Virginia families, whose education, wealth and social status were superior to the North Carolinians. As a result, there was considerable antagonism between the two groups.[554]

In the last chapter, we mentioned the purchase by Henry Sr.'s family of land in Wilkes Co., GA at Beaver Dam on the Savannah River. His sons William, James, Jacob and Henry are mentioned in the Wilkes Co. Tax Records of 1790. For 1791 and 1792, Henry, James and Jacob were cited, and for 1793, Jacob, Henry Sr. and William were cited. In contrast to their brothers who owned land on Beaver Dam and held small numbers of slaves, Jacob and Henry did not. In 1795 two landowners called Henry Shorter were listed. One may be the son of Henry Sr. of Culpeper Co., VA, whom we have called "Henry Jr." and the other may be the son of William, who married Sarah, daughter of Edward Gresham, and who died in 1808.[555] Jacob still had no land.

In 1797 Jacob was still without land, but two years later we find him with 280 acres and three slaves. 1799 was the year of his marriage. In the early years of the 19th century, Henry, Jacob, James and Russell figure in the tax records. William had died in 1801. His son Reuben (Clark) Shorter first appears as a landowner in 1805.[556]

---

[554] Otis Ashmore, "Wilkes County, Its Place in Georgia History", **The Georgia Historical Quarterly**, Vol.1, No.1, March 1917, pp.59-64.

[555] In the Tax Record, the elder Henry is called "Henry Sr." It has been thought, by William J. Shorter and others, that the Henry who died in 1808 was Henry Sr. of Culpeper Co., VA. **Information on some Georgia Pioneers: Family Heads 1805, Georgia** p. 171, indicates that the Henry who died was the son of William. (Information supplied by Dr. M. P. Taylor).

[556] Frank Parker Hudson, Atlanta, Georgia, **Wilkes County, Georgia Tax Records**, Atlanta, Georgia, 1996, Vols.1 and 2.

The story of the Shorters in Georgia focuses on Reuben Clark Shorter, his brother Eli Sims Shorter and their first cousin Alfred Hurt Shorter. These three men rose to prominence in the medical, legal and educational fields. All three were orphaned in their early years. Before giving their biographies, it is necessary to disentangle the confused genealogy of the Shorters in Georgia. The confusion has been largely caused by early deaths and the subsequent remarriages of widows or widowers.[557]

William Shorter was born in Virginia about 1758. He married Ann Clark, the daughter of Reuben Clark and Bathsheba Sampson of Culpeper Co.[558] The Decree on Boughan **et al.** vs Beckam **et al.**, Chancery Suit 1820, dividing the property of Ambrose Clark, states that William Shorter's wife was "Nancy Clark". "Nan"/"Nancy" is a variant of "Ann". There seems to be no doubt whatever that Ann Clark married William Shorter.

Ann was the fourth out of twelve children. William and Ann's children were Elizabeth, who married William Strozier, Reuben Clark Shorter, born in Virginia c.1787, Eli Sims Shorter, born in Georgia in 1792, and Bedford Shorter, born in Georgia in 1798. There was also the considerably older Henry, already mentioned, who died in 1808. William died about

---

[557] The outline given here is the result of a copious correspondence in 2000-2001 with William J. Shorter and Dr. M. P. Taylor who has conducted recent research in Georgia and cleared up several mysteries and misunderstandings.

[558] The Clark Family Genealogy (Genealogy of Virginia Families, Vol.3, Genealogical Publishing Inc., Baltimore, 1981) makes the huge error of citing Ann Clark as the wife of Henry Shorter Jr., in spite of quoting the Madison County Court proceeding for a petition of Ambrose Clark's (brother of Reuben Clark) land: Virginia Chancery Suit 9A, Hartsuck vs Blakey, Clark, which clearly states that William Shorter was the husband of Ann Clark and that Reuben Clark Shorter, Eli Sims Shorter and (Elizabeth) Strozier were their children. This error has been copied countless times.

1801, leaving his younger sons aged fourteen, nine and three respectively. Reuben Clark Shorter claimed that he was responsible for sending his teenage brother to (law) school in 1809-1811. Bedford, who was probably named after John Russell, 4th Duke of Bedford, the British Secretary of State 1748-1757, was assigned to Nathan Smith, to learn the trade of a wheel and chair maker until attaining his majority. [559]

In the 1805 Georgia Land Lottery, Eli Sims and Reuben Clark Shorter are cited as orphans of William, but placed under the name of his brother, Henry Jr. (1766-1816). It is possible that Henry assumed responsibility for the care of his brother's children, since he apparently had no children of his own. It is also conceivable - although no evidence of any kind has come to light - that he married his brother's widow, Ann (née Clark), since remarriages were common in the Clark family.[560] In any case, she probably died about 1813, and it is thought that Henry Jr. followed her to the grave in 1816, when Eli Sims was already 24 years of age.

Jacob Shorter

Jacob Shorter was born abt.1760 in Virginia. Having moved to Wilkes County, GA, he married Delphia (Delphy) on October 1, 1799. They had two children, Sarah Shorter (Sally - 1800 - 1841) and Alfred Hurt Shorter (1803 - 1882). It appears that Delphia died in childbirth, having her second child, Alfred. Jacob married again and his second

---

[559] Inferior Court Minutes, 1801-1803, **Early Records of Georgia, Wilkes County**, reference supplied by Dr. M. P. Taylor. Russell Shorter was probably named after the fourth Duke of Bedford also. Cf. James Hagemann, **The Heritage of Virginia**, The Donning Company Publishers, 1986, p.14.

[560] This possibility may account for the error of supposing that Henry Jr. was the father of Elizabeth Strozier, Reuben Clark Shorter and Eli Sims Shorter. Madison County court records show clearly that they were the children of William.

wife was Sarah, daughter of Ambrose Bramblett. Before he died in 1812, Jacob had three more children, Selina M., Elizabeth and Henry A. Shorter. His widow, Sarah, was unable to rear both sets of children. So the two elder ones, Sally aged about twelve and Alfred aged about nine, were entrusted to her sister and brother-in-law, Isaiah Irvin. Sally married, first John Truitt on November 20th 1817 in Wilkes Co., GA and second James Beland. He died on August 22nd 1841 and was buried in Priddy Cemetery, LaGrange, Troup Co., GA.[561]

James Hurt Shorter Sr.

James Hurt Shorter Sr., son of Henry Sr., was born in Virginia in 1773. He would have been barely twenty years old, when he started acting as a county surveyor in Georgia in the early 1790s. In the whirlwind of Georgian land speculation, land grants and lotteries, the name of James Shorter became synonymous with fraud and corruption. Records reveal that he received more than a million acres of land. He and another surveyor, Richmond Dawson, made surveys for each other, or for themselves. For example, James surveyed 52,000 acres for himself in Montgomery Co. on 29th May 1793.[562]

James received enormous grants of land at various times. For example, in 1794 he was granted 280,000 acres in Montgomery

---

[561]This reconstruction was completed by Dr. M. P. Taylor. It is based on court records, monumental inscriptions and computerized information. Cf. Updated Chronology of Shorter Records, and personal communication of December 16th 2000. Cf. also **Some Georgia Pioneers: Family Heads 1805 Georgia,** p.171; and **Early Records of Georgia**, Part I, Wilkes Co., p.181. See also Clifford L. Smith, History of Troup County, 1933, p.261. Dr. M. P. Taylor also received information on Sally from her descendant Mary Spearman Williams.

[562] Farris W. Cadle, **Georgia Land Surveying History and Law**, University of Georgia Press, Athens, GA, 1991, pp. 86-106.

Co., GA, 725,000 acres in 1795 and 21,000 acres in 1797, in the same county; finally in 1799 a grant of 600 acres in Scriven Co., GA.[563] The few hundred acres held by his brothers on Beaver Dam in Wilkes Co. pale into insignificance beside these rolling acres.

James had a brief military career in the Company of Georgia Dragoons, commanded by Captain Joseph Way. In August 1793 he was listed as a private who had deserted.[564] His name also appears in several legal contexts, as witness to deeds or defendant in court cases. He married Dorothy Napier, the daughter of Rene Napier of Elbert Co., GA. and Rebekah Hurt. [565] Their son, James Hurt Shorter, Jr., was born in 1810 and died in 1846. James Jr. married Mary Elizabeth Hargraves, "a great heiress", and had five children. Among these was James Hargraves Shorter (1842-1920), physician.[566] James Hurt Shorter, Sr. died in 1820. According to Maria Teresa Shorter Alexander, the daughter of James Jr., James Sr. died in Virginia, leaving James Jr., then ten years old, in reduced circumstances. It would seem, therefore, that, in spite of his massive land acquisitions, James Sr. did not leave any great

---

[563] Silas Emmett Lucas Jr., **Index to the Headright and Bounty Grants of Georgia 1756-1909**, Georgia Genealogical Reprints, p.592.

[564] America Militia in the Frontier Wars 1790-1796.

[565] Cf. Ben Coke, op.cit., p.79. René Napier and Rebekah Hurt were married in Drisdale Parish, VA, on March 28th, 1765, cf. Dorothy Ford Wulfeck, Marriages of Some Virginia Residents 1607-1800, Vol. II, Genealogical Publishing Company Inc., 1986, p.98.

[566] **National Encyclopedia of American Biography**, XIX, p.316. James Hargraves Shorter had a son, Edward Swift Shorter, living in Columbus, GA. cf. Ben Coke, Ibid.

fortune.[567] It may be that, after he died, his ill gotten land acquisitions were returned to the State.

James Hurt Shorter Jr. settled in Columbus, GA, and an interesting pen-portrait of him appears in the diary of Alexander H. Stephens, later Vice-President of the Confederacy and Governor of Georgia. Stephens traveled with James and his wife Mary Elizabeth (née Hargraves) in a stage coach from Columbus to Washington, D.C. in January 1837. He found Shorter "very precise in his conversation (and I soon had him thus engaged) almost bordering on stiffness". He had visited goldmines in the vicinity of Charlotte on the way. Stephens became more familiar with Shorter later in the journey and "better pleased".[568] James Jr. administered the estate of his cousin and benefactor, Judge Eli Sims Shorter and also acquired land of his own.[569]

Bedford Shorter

Before embarking on the biographies of his more famous elder brothers, it is appropriate to say something more about Bedford Shorter (1798-1866). He was born on February 25th 1798 in Wilkes Co., GA. Living at Monticello, Jasper County. GA, he was involved in several lawsuits in that county. He married Sarah Williams Lemon Riddle on July 21st 1850, in Cherokee County, Texas.[570] Sarah had children by two

---

[567] Annie Kendrick Walker, **Old Shorter Houses and Gardens**, New York, Tobias Wright, 1911, p.53.

[568] James Z. Rabun (ed.), "Alexander Stephens's Diary, 1834-1837", Part II, **The Georgia Historical Quarterly**, Vol. XXXVI, No. 2, June 1952, pp.181-182.

[569] Communication from Dr . M. P. Taylor, January 13th 2001.

[570] His wife's name is variously recorded as "Biddle" or "Riddle".

previous marriages (to Lemon and Riddle). She and Bedford had five children: Modena Anne (b. December 9th 1850), Lucretia Jane (b. April 12th 1853), Melvira H. (b. December 20th 1855), Joseph I. (b. August 1st 1859) and George Marion Shorter (b. August 10th 1862). Bedford died in Cherokee Co., Texas in 1866, and Sarah in 1890. Their last three children were buried in Oklahoma.[571]

In the war of 1812, Bedford Shorter served as a private soldier in Captain John Read's Georgia Militia. He migrated to Texas as a single man and received a succession of land grants between 1838 and 1847.

Reuben Clark Shorter

Reuben Clark Shorter (1787-1853) was fourteen years old when his father, William, died in 1801. He was born on March 13th 1787. According to University of Pennsylvania Records, he attended medical lectures there in 1808 and 1809, when in his early twenties. Although new methods of physical diagnosis were being introduced into medical practice at that time, the two years spent by Reuben Clark in medical school were all that were necessary for him to practice as a physician. He returned to Georgia and began to practice at Eatonton, Putnam Co., GA. His medical practice was immensely successful. He was elected a member of the Central Medical Society of Georgia at its fourth meeting on December 27th 1829.[572] Although he was not a military man, he was accorded the rank

---

[571] This life story is based on information supplied to Dr. M. P. Taylor by Bedford's descendants, and records collected by her - personal communication from her to William J. Shorter of December 7th 2000. Ben H. Coke's statement that Bedford Shorter "died young" is very wide of the mark. Cf. Ben H. Coke, op.cit., p.79.

[572] Cecilia C. Mettler, "The Central Medical Society of Georgia", **The Georgia Historical Quarterly**, Vo. XXIV no.2, June 1940, p.149.

of major-general during the organization of the militia to suppress "Indian troubles", and in the closing years of his life he was always referred to as "General Shorter". Reuben Clark Shorter was a shrewd businessman, who amassed a vast fortune. He also served in both houses of the Georgia State Legislature.

At the age of 25, in 1812, Reuben Clark Shorter married Mary Butler Gill (1797-1868), daughter of John and Martha Gill, and they settled at Monticello in Jasper Co., GA. There they reared a family of twelve children.[573] Emily who married David Kolb, John Gill who married Mary Jane Battle, Sarah who married James L. Hunter, Martha who married William H. McKleroy, Eli Sims who married Marietta Fannin, Reuben Clark Jr. who married Carrie Billingslea, Mary who married William H. Thornton, Sophia who married Col. Tennant Lomax, William who died aged thirteen, Henry Russell who married Adriana ("Addie") Keitt, Sampson who died aged seven and Laura who married Capt. Thomas W. Cowles.

Reuben Clark Shorter was among the very first purchasers of a town lot at Monticello. He served as a Justice of Interior Court from 1829-1832, and was on the board of two academies.[574] Having heard from bankers in Georgia of the land boom on the Chattahoochee River, he moved, with his family in 1836 to the Alabama side of the Chattahoochee, where he bought land and settled at Eufaula. In the next chapter, we shall follow the fortunes of himself and his family,

---

[573] Annie Kendrick Walker, **op.cit**., mentions thirteen children, but other sources e.g. James E. Saunders, Early Settlers of Alabama, New Orleans, Graham and Son Ltd. 1899, list twelve, six sons and six daughters.

[574] Jasper County Historical Foundation, **History of Jasper County, Georgia**, pp.8, 281.

singling out some of his more notable children and descendants.[575]

Eli Sims Shorter

Eli Sims Shorter, as we have seen, was orphaned at the age of nine. His elder brother, Reuben Clark Shorter, helped to pay for his law school education at Yale 1809-1811. He returned to Georgia to practice law in 1812, attaching himself to a local lawyer as his mentor. He established a highly successful practice at Eatonton and, on June 18th 1817, married Sophia Herndon Watkins, daughter of James Watkins, Jr. and Jane Thompson, in Elbert Co., GA. They had four children: Reuben Clark Shorter of Columbus, GA was born in 1818 and married Kate Ward. His children included Dr. Eli Sims Shorter, Jr. of New York and John Urquhart Shorter, a lawyer in Brooklyn, N.Y. The second child of Eli Sims Sr. and Sophia Watkins was Mary Jane, born in 1820 and married to Dr. John A. Urquhart. Their third child was Virginia born in 1821, and married to J. Berrien Oliver. There was also another son called James Watkins Shorter.

In 1822 Eli Sims Shorter was elected Judge of the Superior Court of Flint Circuit, and presided over the first court held in Macon, GA in 1823. As lawyer and judge, Eli Sims Shorter traveled to various parts of Georgia and accumulated a large fortune. In 1832, however, he moved to Columbus, Muscogee Co., GA and acquired thousands of acres there on the Georgia side of the Chattahoochee River. Reuben Clark's mansion at Eufaula, AL was a night's boat-ride down river from his brother's at Columbus. We have seen above that James Hurt Shorter, Sr. died in 1820, leaving his son James Hurt Shorter, Jr. an orphan of 10 years old. At the age of twelve, James wrote

---

[575] Cf. Saunders, **op.cit.**, Annie Kendrick Walker **op.cit.,** Mattie Thomas Thompson, History of Barbour County, Alabama, Eufaula, Alabama, 1939, and notes supplied by Dr. M. P. Taylor and William J. Shorter.

to his cousin, Judge Eli Sims Shorter, asking him to defray the expenses of his education. The judge readily agreed to take on the whole burden of James's education, remembering, no doubt, his own experience as an orphan, as well as an obligation he had to James Sr.

Judge Eli Sims Shorter died at Columbus on 13th December 1836, the year in which his brother, General Reuben Clark Shorter, moved to Alabama. His wife, Sophia, outlived him, dying in 1856.[576]

The story of Alfred Hurt Shorter (1803-1882), first cousin of General Reuben Clark Shorter and Judge Eli Sims Shorter, and the founding of Shorter College in Georgia, belongs mainly to the second half of the nineteenth century, and will be told in the final chapter of this book.

---

[576] This account of the life of Judge Eli Sims Shorter is based on Saunders **op cit.,** pp.245-246; Annie Kendrick Walker, **op.cit.,** pp.16, 53-54; Ben H. Coke, **op.cit.,** p.79; and notes and references supplied by William J. Shorter and Dr. M. P. Taylor. In nearly every case, I have preferred the latter's dates.

CHAPTER EIGHTEEN

THE SHORTER FAMILY IN ALABAMA

The Settlement of Alabama

In the south-western corner of Alabama a neck of land reaches down to the Gulf of Mexico, and is divided by Mobile Bay. It was here that the settlement of Alabama was begun by the French in 1702, with the building of Fort Louis de la Mobile, on the Mobile River. France eventually ceded the region to Britain in 1763, and Britain ceded most of the area to the United States in 1783. Settlement in the east was hindered at first by the Creek Indians who were defeated at the Battle of Horsehoe Bend in 1814 by General Andrew Jackson. In 1819 Alabama was admitted to the Union as the 22nd state. The early years of the 19th century saw extensive cotton planting, but the Creek Indians continued to pose a problem.[577]

In 1832 a treaty with the Creek Indians provided for their eventual removal west of the Mississippi and for the controlled settlement of planters in the Creek territory west of the Chatta-hoochee River. However, people began to move into the area from Georgia and the Carolinas, disregarding the terms of the treaty. The Union Government acted mainly to support the

---

[577] This account of the early years of Barbour County AL is based on Annie Kendrick Walker, **Backtracking in Barbour County - A Narrative of the Last Alabama Frontier**, Richmond Virginia, The Dietz Press, 1941.

pioneers and to organize counties in the ceded territory. The Creek Indians were dissatisfied with the situation and continued their attacks on the settlers. Their power was finally broken in 1837.

Cotton dominated the economy of Alabama. Its production was labour intensive and slavery became an indispensable component in the system. The British and European textile factories, that were part of the incipient industrial revolution, created the growing demand for cotton, and huge fortunes were made by planters in America. By 1860 cotton constituted 57% of the value of all American exports. Cotton production and slavery reinforced each other, and economic advancement seemed to come easily from the simple expedient of increasing the ownership of land and slaves. In reality, slavery was a costly labor system and too much capital was invested in it. When it was abolished after the American Civil War, some planters continued to make fortunes through share cropping or the use of hired labor. Up to that moment, however, most white planters passionately believed in the necessity of the so-called "peculiar institution", and often combined this conviction with a staunch Christian faith.[576]

Reuben Clark Shorter's Move to Alabama

This was the scenario against which General Reuben Clark Shorter definitively moved across the Chattahoochee into Barbour County AL in 1836, with his family and his caravan of retainers and slaves.[577] He and his brother Judge Eli Sims

---

[576] Cf. William Warren Rogers **et al., Alabama - The History of a Deep South State**, University of Alabama Press, 1994, pp.93-112; Bruce Catton, **The Civil War**, New York, Fairfax Press, 1971, pp.1-5.

[577] The biography of Reuben Clark Shorter is based mainly on Annie Kendrick Walker, **Old Shorter Houses and Gardens**, New York, Tobias A. Wright, 1911, and on Mattie Thomas Thompson, **History of Barbour County Alabama**, Eufaula, AL, 1939. 1836 is the date given for Reuben

Shorter had already acquired land on either side of the river. In fact, downstream from Columbus there was a landing stage named Shorterville. Here William Irwin, an early pioneer and trader, had a settlement. Twenty miles north of Shorterville, Irwin had established a village called Irwinton, on the site of an old Creek settlement, known as Eufaula. The town's name reverted to Eufaula in 1843. This was where Reuben Clark Shorter established himself and his family.

Reuben Clark Shorter built himself a magnificent mansion in the colonial style on the Chattahoochee Embankment or Bluff, where he maintained his family in absolute luxury and entertained his friends on a lavish scale. The house overlooked the river, where the steamboats plied up and down. Surrounding the mansion was a famous garden. Later it became fashionable to leave the vicinity of the river and move to the "hill". The historic house was demolished and the material used in the construction of Shorter Opera House on Broad Street. This Opera House had a lengthy and interesting history. Today, the Eufaula Hardware Company occupies the site.

Reuben Clark Shorter, a religious man, was a founding member of the First Baptist Church at Eufaula, along with his son Colonel Eli Sims Shorter, and his daughters Mary Battle Shorter Thornton and Emily Frances Shorter Kolb. The church was constituted on June 24th 1837 in the Male Academy. Later, a spacious wooden building was erected on the Bluff and this was dedicated in 1841. The present church was begun in 1869 and rebuilt in 1907, after being struck by lightning. The new organ was presented by Mrs. Eli Sims Shorter II. Reuben Clark Shorter was among the first Deacons of the church, as was his eldest son, John Gill Shorter. The latter even officiated as

---

Clark Shorter's move to Eufaula. The 1833 census, however, already shows that he and his family were present in Barbour County. Helen S. Foley, **Alabama State Census 1833, 1850, 1860** copied 1976.

Deacon in the administration of the Sacraments, when Governor of Alabama, on Sunday April 12th 1863.[580]

On January 13th 1849, four years before his death, General Reuben Clark Shorter drew up a will, disposing of his immense property, personal, real and movable, to his wife, children and grandchildren. He bequeathed to them more than a hundred "negro slaves", eighty-four of them being mentioned by name.[581] Also in the will were his Eufaula mansion and summer residence, his lands in Barbour County and river plantation in Randolph County, Georgia. He also bequeathed to his lawyer son, Colonel Eli Sims Shorter, his half interest in the Eufaula law firm of Shorter and Brothers.[582]

General Reuben Clark Shorter died on July 14th 1853, aged 66 years and five months. He was laid to rest, according to his wish, in the beautiful Shorter Cemetery at Eufaula. Already buried there were two sons who died young, two daughters Sophia Herndon Lomax and Emily Frances Kolb, as well the latter's husband, David Cameron Kolb.[583]

---

[580] Mattie Thomas Thompson, **History of Barbour County Alabama**, Eufaula, Alabama, 1943, pp.274-279; Annie Kendrick Walker, **op.cit.**, 1941, p.196.

[581] In fact he bequeathed thirty-three more negro slaves than he had, so that the three younger children, when they came of age, would each receive eleven slaves, like his other children.

[582] Photocopy of the probate January 17th 1854, supplied by Dr. M. P. Taylor.

[583] Richard Price, **Shorter Family Cemetery**, survey made April 22nd 2000.

Governor John Gill Shorter

Reuben Clark Shorter's first and most famous son was John Gill Shorter, who was born at Monticello in Jasper County, GA, on April 23rd 1818. He graduated from Franklin College, Athens, now the University of Georgia, in 1837. After a course of Law studies, he was admitted to the bar in 1838, and started to practice law at Eufaula, to which his family had moved two years previously. In 1842, Governor Fitzpatrick of Alabama appointed him solicitor of his judicial district. In 1845 and 1851 he was elected Senator for Barbour County. In the latter year, Governor Collier appointed him Judge of the Circuit Court, to which office he was re-elected in 1852 and 1858.

John Gill Shorter was both a lawyer and a planter. In 1843 he married Mary Jane Battle, the daughter of Dr. Cullen Battle of North Carolina, whose wealthy and socially distinguished family had moved to Eufaula in the same year as General Reuben Clark Shorter. Their daughter, Mary Jane ("Mollie") married first T. J. Perkins, and later, after many years of widowhood, B. L. Willingham, who also predeceased her. John Gill Shorter built, for his wife, one of the first residences on the "hill" at Eufaula. Later, he built further out an imposing mansion called Monterey. The wedding, at Monterey, of his daughter to T. J. Perkins was the most brilliant event in the social history of the county to date. John and his wife had other children who died in infancy. The Treadwell family purchased his first house, and built a new mansion, "Buena Vista", on the site. This eventually passed through marriage to the family of John's brother Henry Russell Shorter.[584]

Judge John Gill Shorter had, by common consent, an attractive personality. No superlatives were apparently too great, to describe his moral courage and noble traits of character. He had a remarkable command of language in public speaking. "Gentle, refined, highly cultured, modest, he was yet

---

[584] Annie Kendrick Walker, **op.cit.,** 1941, p.138.

a firm and faithful official. His presence produced an atmosphere of purity, and provoked the profoundest respect. His life was a living sermon."[585] Judge Shorter was as pious as he was wealthy. He once publicly declared: "There is truth in religion; it is all true; and there is a power in the atonement of Christ. It is a glorious reality."[586] On his death bed, he was asked: "How is your faith?" He replied: "My faith, did you say? Did you ever see the sun shine? It is as strong as the everlasting hills."[587] He was, however, also an implacable secessionist, who once declared that he "hoped that the State (of Alabama) would remain separated from the Union, as if a wall of fire intervened".[588] Such was the Alabama patriot, who became the man of the hour in 1861.

The American Civil War

The legislative wrangling of the 1850s between those who advocated the abolition of slavery and those who supported its retention, and even extension in the new territories, resulted in a hardening of positions between North and South. The election of Abraham Lincoln as President in 1860 and his refusal to countenance the extension of slavery to the new territories brought matters to a head. Southerners were convinced that the abolition of slavery would entail the collapse of their whole economy and way of life. They also had before their eyes the bogey of possible slave rebellions and general mayhem. In the last phase of the secession movement Judge John Gill Shorter,

---

[585] B. F. Riley, **Makers and Romance of Alabama History**, no publisher shown, 1915, pp.185-189.

[586] Riley, **op.cit.**, p.188.

[587] Annie Kendrick Walker, **op.cit.** 1941, p. 287.

[588] Annie Kendrick Walker, **op.cit.** 1941, p. 163.

and his brothers, Colonel Eli Sims Shorter and Henry Russell Shorter, joined the political oligarchy known as the "Eufaula Regency", which was the most vocal lobby for secession in south-east Alabama. As early as 1850, the Regency had petitioned Governor Collier for the secession of Alabama from the Union. But it was not until January 1861 that the Secession Ordinance was finally passed, and the Republic of Alabama was proclaimed. John Gill Shorter was appointed commissioner in the Secession Convention of Georgia and then a representative in the provisional Confederate Congress in both Montgomery and Richmond, resigning his judgeship for the purpose. It was while carrying out this duty that he was elected fifteenth Governor of Alabama.

Alabama was the heart of the Confederacy, and although it saw relatively little fighting compared to other states, it suffered very considerable hardship, both because of the blockade of imports from the industrialized north and because of harsh laws enacted by the Confederate Congress. The burden of taxation was increased. Defenses had to be put in place, especially at Mobile. Conscription to the army was introduced. Medical services for the wounded and financial support for bereaved families, and those with members serving at the front, had to be found. The great houses of Eufaula were deserted. No fewer than fifty-seven members of the Shorter family served in the Confederate Army; while in the army of the Union there were fifty-one colored soldiers with the name of Shorter.[589]

It was inevitable that Governor Shorter should meet with opposition and unpopularity, especially when the tide of war turned against the South, as it began to do in 1863. For Alabama, the climax came with the Battle of Mobile Bay in 1864, won by the Union Forces. Great firmness and strength of

---

[589] Janet B. Hewett, (ed.), **Roster of Confederate Soldiers, 1861-1865**, Vol. XIV, Broadfoot Publishing Company, Wilmington NC, 1996; **Roster of Union Soldiers, 1861-1865, United States Coloured Troops**, Broadfoot Publishing Company, Wilmington NC, 1997.

mind was required of Alabama's War Governor, and John Gill Shorter rose to the occasion. However, when his term came to an end in 1863, he was not re-elected. Most of Alabama escaped the ruin and destruction that spread throughout the South at the close of the Civil War. This was certainly true of Eufaula, where Governor Shorter retired to continue his practice of law and to run his estates, after the ending of slavery. In 1867 he was running two plantations, one with hired men and the other on a sharecropping basis.[590] Governor Shorter died of bronchitis at his home in Eufaula on May 29th 1872. His death has been described as "triumphant". After quoting a couplet from a favorite hymn, he added: "I want to be off", and died.[591] He was buried in the Shorter Cemetery at Eufaula. His wife died on January 20th 1879 and was laid beside him.[592]

Colonel Eli Sims Shorter

Colonel Eli Sims Shorter (not to be confused with his uncle, Judge Eli Sims Shorter, of Columbus, GA) was the second son of Reuben Clark Shorter and was born at Monticello in 1823. He graduated from Yale in 1843, delivering the salutatory address. On returning to Eufaula, he began to practice law, and then decided to enter politics. He became the first Democrat to represent his Congressional District and was re-elected to Congress in 1857. He married Marietta Fannin, the daughter of Colonel Fannin of Alamo fame. His family mansion stood across the road from his brother's home, Monterey, until it was destroyed by fire. Next to the site stands Highland View ("the

---

[590] Annie Kendrick Walker, **op.cit.** 1941, p.248.

[591] Riley, **op.cit.,** p.189.

[592] Cf. Price, **op.cit.** The town of Shorter, west of Montgomery, AL, is presumably named after Governor Shorter.

Leftwich Place"), the beautiful home he built for his daughter, Annie Shorter Leftwich.

During the Civil War, Colonel Eli Sims Shorter fought on the plains of Shiloh in April 1862, when the Confederacy made its supreme bid to regain western Tennessee. It was a bewildering and bloody battle in which 13,000 Federals died and 10,000 Confederates. In the aftermath of the Civil War, during the so-called Reconstruction period, political intimidation of voters reached its height at Eufaula during the 1874 polls with the so-called Spring Hill Riot. During the riot an attempt was made on the life of the Eufaula City Judge, Elias M. Kiels, a Radical leader of the Negroes; and his son was shot dead. Colonel Eli Sims Shorter and his brother Major Henry Russell Shorter, who was accidentally shot in the arm and left side during the affray, appeared as witnesses during the congressional committee hearings which followed the riot. Colonel Eli Sims Shorter's health declined after the death of his eldest son William, and he died in 1879.

Of his two other sons, Clement Clay Shorter became Speaker of the Alabama House of Representatives at the age of 26, and Eli Sims Shorter II became well known as a gifted public speaker and student of literature. Eli Sims Shorter II married Wylena Lamar and built a palatial mansion at Eufaula in the Corinthian style. This descended to their daughter Mrs. Fanny Upshaw, and is at present in the hands of the Eufaula Heritage Association as the "Shorter Mansion Museum". Eli Sims Shorter III continued to manage his father's businesses and was a noted philanthropist. He died in 1934.

Henry Russell Shorter

Major Henry Russell Shorter was Reuben Clark Shorter's youngest son, born at Monticello on February 28th 1833. In 1849 he entered the University of North Carolina, from which he graduated in 1853. He then read law with his brother

Colonel Eli Sims Shorter at Eufaula and was called to the bar in May 1854. He practiced law at Eufaula in the firm of Shorter and Brothers and became one of the best known civil and criminal lawyers in the state. He was also a planter.

At the outbreak of the Civil War, he enlisted as a private in the Alabama Volunteer Infantry in 1861 and served for a year. He then joined the army of northern Virginia, with the rank of first lieutenant and aide-de-camp on the staff of Brigadier-General Cullen A. Battle, where he remained until the end of the war. He was wounded on May 5th 1864, during the battle of the Wilderness and left the service with the rank of major, acting adjutant and inspector-general. General R. E. Rhodes offered him the rank of lieutenant colonel on his staff, which he refused. When General Battle was severely wounded at the battle of Cedar Creek, VA, Major Henry Russell Shorter accompanied him home to Alabama.

After the war, he returned to Eufaula to resume his law practice and was appointed president of the railroad commission of Alabama, a position he held until 1897. As we have already seen, he was wounded in the Spring Hill Riot between Democrats and Radicals in 1874. In the last year of his life he represented the interests of several large loan corporations. Unlike his brothers, he was not a Baptist but an Episcopalian.

On May 9th 1854 he married Adriana Keitt, the daughter of John Keitt and Mrs. A .B. Treadwell. They had four children, including Henry Russell Shorter, Jr. who eventually became insurance commissioner of Alabama and Alice, who married William Dorsey Jelks, Governor of Alabama. Henry Russell Shorter, Sr. died at Eufaula on November 28th 1898.[593]

---

[593] These biographies of Colonel Eli Sims Shorter and Major Henry Russell Shorter were compiled from: Annie Kendrick Walker, **op.cit.,** 1911 and **op.cit.,** 1941; Thomas McAdory Owen, **History of Alabama and Dictionary of Alabama Biography**, The Reprint Company, Spartanburg SC., 1978; Thompson, **op.cit.,** 1939; **Northern Alabama Historical and**

Daughters of Reuben Clark Shorter

General Reuben Clark Shorter's daughter, Emily Frances, married David Cameron Kolb, who was engaged in general merchandising and the Cotton Commission business in Eufaula. He died at the early age of 31 on August 11th 1841. His wife predeceased him, dying on May 13th 1839, soon after the birth of their son Reuben Francis Kolb. Both are buried in the Shorter Cemetery at Eufaula.

Captain Reuben Francis Kolb was born on April 16th 1839 and graduated from the University of North Carolina in June 1859. He first enlisted in the Confederate Army as a sergeant in the Eufaula Rifles, and then raised and commanded "Kolb's Battery of Artillery". After the war, he was engaged in farming in Barbour County and was commissioner of agriculture from 1886-1890. In 1890 and 1892 he ran unsuccessfully for Governor of Alabama. He married Mary Caledonia Cargile, daughter of Thomas and Ann Louise Cargile of Eufaula, on January 3rd 1860, and had three children, Emily Frances, Reuben and William Howard. He featured in General Reuben Clark Shorter's will, mentioned above.

Martha Gill Shorter, another daughter of General Reuben Clark Shorter (died September 6th 1855), married William Henry McKleroy. Their daughter, Sarah Sophia McKleroy, married Alfred Alexis Couric, son of a French stowaway immigrant, called Charles Mathurin Couric, who became a wealthy cotton planter. Their house at Eufaula is one of the finest surviving examples of the Alabama classic revival, and their great grand-daughter, Katie Couric, is the famous television presenter, co-host of the Today show. Her sister,

Biographical, The Reprint Company, Spartanburg NC, 1976; **Memorial Record of Alabama**, Brant and Fuller, Madison WIS, 1893.

Emily Couric, was elected Senator of the State of Virginia, 25th District.[594]

Finally, another of General Reuben Clark Shorter's daughters, Sophia Herndon Shorter (1830-1850) married Tennent Lomax, but died soon after their marriage, aged only 20. In 1857 he was married a second time to a widow, Mrs. Carrie A. Shorter of Georgia. Colonel Tennent Lomax had been Military Governor of Orizaba during the Mexican War. During the American Civil War he served with distinction as Colonel of the Second Volunteer Regiment of Alabama and then of the Third Volunteer Regiment. He was killed in action at the Battle of Seven Pines in Virginia, on June 1st 1862. [595]

---

[594] Annie Kendrick Walker, **op.cit.,** 1941, p.146 and **passim**; MSNBC, **On Air**, "The Smallest Gift from France", interview with Katie Couric, April 28th 1999, "Exploring Our Roots Home Page".

[595] **Northern Alabama Historical and Biographical, op.cit.**

CHAPTER NINETEEN

AFRICAN AMERICAN SLAVERY AND THE SHORTER FAMILY

The African American Shorters

The African American story is, without exaggeration, one of the great epics of humankind. It records the triumph of the human spirit over one of the most appalling experiences that people have inflicted on each other, the trans-Atlantic slave trade. The violent capture of innocent people, the trauma of the march to the African coast, the horrors of the middle passage, the indignity of the slave block, the sentence to life-long hard labor in conditions resembling a prison farm in a foreign land, the violent punishments and the horrific retribution meted out to rebels and runaways - all of this was the crucible in which were fashioned the heroism and spirituality of African American people.

Although some African Americans emerged from slavery with professional skills, they had, as a rule, to take their own education in hand and struggle to make their own way in American society and in the long battle for equality and civil rights. They did this in such fields as the Church, the entertainment industry, and eventually in public service and government. African Americans bearing the name of Shorter, and their descendants, have distinguished themselves in these fields. Bishop James Alexander Shorter of the Methodist Episcopal Church; Wayne Shorter, the acclaimed jazz saxophonist; and Shorter descendants such as Raven Symoné the child TV star and Dr. Maggie Price Taylor, with a distinguished record of service in United States Government Departments, are but a few examples.

How did African slaves acquire the name Shorter? The records suggest that slave owning families used Christian names for their slaves and were not interested in whether or not they possessed a surname. Slave-owning white Shorters were no exception. Sometimes slave-owners resented the use of the family name by their African slaves, since it suggested that miscegenation had occurred. In fact, this was often enough the case. In other instances, the slaves themselves, if they had been badly treated, were reluctant to use their master's surname.[596] African Americans using the name Shorter, however, seem to be fairly numerous, and there is plenty of evidence for slaves and free persons of color using the name Shorter long before the general assumption of surnames by ex-slaves after the passing of the Thirteenth Amendment in 1865.[597] We know that miscegenation probably did occur between a white Shorter and a slave, and that descent from a white mother was a pretext for the manumission of enslaved Shorters.[598] Manumissions and certificates of freedom were issued to enslaved Shorters

---

[596] Cf. Edward Ball, **Slaves in the Family**, New York, Ballantine Books, 1998/1999, pp.105-109, 368-374, and **passim**, for a discussion of such cases.

[597] Dr. M. P. Taylor: "Free People of Color (FPC) in America", Unpublished Essay, 30th January 2001.

[598] Elizabeth Shorter, a white woman, allegedly married a black slave named "Little Robin" around 1702 in Maryland, and this was the basis for petitions for freedom by their descendants. Court records cited by Dr. M. P. Taylor in her "Slave Chronology", for 1793. Cf. also "Free People of Color (FPC) in America" by the same author.

during the era of slavery itself.[599] Many slaves received help from their former masters on gaining their freedom at the end of the American Civil War. Among these were some who took, or who retained, the surname Shorter.[600] Besides African Americans, there are even Native Americans who use the name Shorter today. For example, the ancestors of Charles Benjamin Shorter (c.1907-2000) and his daughter Charlotte Shorter Shelton were from the Blackfoot tribe and the Cherokee Indians, who came from the Carolinas in the 1830s, when their people were being forcibly re-settled beyond the Mississippi. They sailed up the Potomac River and hid in caves in order to escape this horrific "Trail of Tears".[601]

The most important reason why African slaves took the family name of their masters - possibly without their knowledge or consent - was simply to hold their families together and to keep track of relatives. Africans then, as now, had a strong sense of family and of ancestry. The use of a western family surname replaced their clan and descent names, and served a similar purpose of family solidarity.

In this chapter a general history of the trans-Atlantic slave trade and of slavery in North America will be followed by an account of the first African slaves owned by white Shorters and of free persons of color who used the name Shorter. The following chapter will give a further account of African American families named Shorter, with biographies of some of their more notable members and descendants.

---

[599] Dr. M. P. Taylor, **Ibid**.

[600] Cf. Anne Kendrick Walker, **Backtracking in Barbour County**, Richmond, VA, Dietz Press, 1941, pp. 247-252.

[601] Charles Benjamin was a school teacher in D.C. for 57 years. His family possesses an Indian club handed down from father to son for over 300 years. Communications with Dr. M. P. Taylor, October 3rd 1999 and February 16th, 2001.

The African Slave Trade

The African slave trade in Europe began as an incident in the commercial expansion of Portugal and its exploration of the African coastline. Prince Henry the Navigator imported ten African slaves to Lisbon in 1442, and two years later the Portuguese Company of Lagos imported two hundred. The colonization of the Spanish West Indies in 1502-1503 created a demand for African slave labor and the traffic was undertaken by Spain, England and France. By the end of the seventeenth century all European nations with any extended commerce were engaged in the trade.[602]

John Hawkins was the first English slave-trader. In 1562, with a fleet of three ships and a mere one hundred men, he managed to capture 300 Africans in Sierra Leone and sell them in Hispaniola, the island which today is divided between Haiti and the Dominican Republic.[603] By this time, some 4,000 miles of West African coast, stretching from the Gambia to Angola, had been opened up by western traders, and dotted with forts, bases and slave castles from which to operate the trade. In 1663 the Royal African Company entered the field and was given a monopoly of the British trade. However, it had soon become clear that capturing slaves was not possible without the co-operation of Africans themselves.

When the trans-Atlantic trade began, there were already various forms of slavery that were endemic to Africa. The Islamic trans-Saharan slave trade was centuries old and there were different types of domestic slavery, as well as the enslavement of

---

[602] Cf. James Benson Sellers, **Slavery in Alabama**, London and Tuscaloosa, University of Alabama Press, 1950, pp.22-3.

[603] James Walvin, **Black Ivory - A History of British Slavery**, London, Fontana Press, 1993, p.25.

war captives. The trans-Atlantic trade transformed the shape of African slavery beyond recognition. In the first place, it was fuelled by inter-ethnic and inter-state wars. In the second place, it encouraged widespread kidnapping. About 70% of all slaves were kidnapped. African rulers thrived on the slave trade, and the great kingdoms of Ashanti and Dahomey owed their wealth and influence to it in large measure.

Mortality among the slaves was horrendous. Many died on the way to the African coast and many more during the sea passage. It is reckoned that about 24 million Africans were enslaved in Africa itself during the period of the trans-Atlantic trade, but that only 11 million survivors were eventually deposited in the Americas. Even then, around 25% of the arrivals died within the first three years.[604]

Newly founded Virginia first solved its labor problems by means of indentured servitude. Working class people from England, seeking to escape poverty in their home country, bound themselves in service to settlers. Conditions were harsh and indentured servants were bought, sold and beaten like slaves. The system also proved expensive. Not surprisingly, it declined. In 1619 twenty African bondsmen, enfranchised and baptized ex-slaves, arrived in Virginia. Although not technically slaves, they were not in fact free.[605]

---

[604] Walvin, **op.cit.,** pp.36-37, 136.

[605] This general account of slavery and the slave trade is based on the following sources: Dr. M. P. Taylor, "Slave Chronology", unpublished, 2000; James Walvin, **Black Ivory - A History of British Slavery**, London, Fontana, 1993; Nigel Tattersfield, **The Forgotten Trade**, London. Jonathan Cape, 1991; James Benson Sellers, **Slavery in Alabama**, London and Tuscaloosa, University of Alabama Press, 1950; William Warren Rogers **et al., Alabama - The History of a_Deep South State**, London and Tuscaloosa, University of Alabama Press, 1994; Edward Ball, **Slaves in the Family**, New York Ballantine Books, 1998.

Slavery in Virginia

Ten years later slaves, in the strict sense of the term, began to be imported into the British West Indies in order to facilitate the large-scale production of sugar. From there slaves began to be re-exported to the North American colonies. In Massachusetts, slavery was made legal in 1641. By this time also slavery had gained a foothold in Virginia and, in 1662, was recognized in law. Between 1640 and 1700 some 264,000 slaves were imported to the British West Indies, and from there, a growing number were re-exported to North America. In the first decades of North American slavery, the re-export of West Indian slaves was favored. In the West Indies, slaves were "seasoned", that is to say, they were "broken in" to work in the fields and they acquired a knowledge of the English language. Slave ships sailed from virtually all the ports of England: Deal, Portsmouth, Southampton, Cowes, Weymouth, Bristol, Lyme Regis, Exeter, Dartmouth, Plymouth, Bideford, Falmouth, Whitehaven, Minehead, Bridgewater and Barnstaple, as well as from London and Liverpool. All the country's commercial outlets were involved in, and prospered from, the trade. The ships sailed first to the Guinea Coast, the Gold Coast and the coasts of modern Nigeria and Angola. From there, they went to the Caribbean and on to such destinations as Virginia (Rappahannock), the Potomac River, Charleston and New York.[606]

As the European demand for Virginian tobacco increased, the number of slaves grew in Virginia. However, although the cultivation of tobacco swelled the state's slave population as a whole, it did not involve huge slave gangs in the fields, as did the large-scale commercial cultivation of rice, cotton and sugar further south. In 1650 there were no more than 500 slaves in Virginia, but between 1690 and 1770, 100,000 slaves were

---

[606] Tattersfield, **op.cit.,** pp.380-382.

imported. In 1775, Virginia and Maryland between them exported 220 million pounds of tobacco. It was soon found that the growing demand for tobacco could no longer depend on slave re-exports from the West Indies and on their natural increase within the colonies. From 1703 onwards, direct shipments of slaves took place to North American ports. By 1708, Virginia had 12,000 slaves and by 1782, a black population of 260,000.

Slavery in Georgia

At its foundation, the trustees of the new colony of Georgia opposed slavery and forbade slaveholding in the territory. However, they permitted slave labor in the building of Savannah. A few years later, the oppressive Negro Act of 1740 imposed the carrying of passes, the wearing of certain types of clothing and the restriction of movement for blacks. With the establishment of a plantation economy in Georgia, slavery was legally sanctioned in 1751. The stage was then set for the importation of slaves from or via the West Indies, as well as directly from West Africa. By the time the Revolutionary War broke out in 1775, Georgia already had 10,000 slaves.

During the war, in spite of George Washington's efforts to bar slaves from military service, there were 5,000 blacks in the continental army. The British saw blacks as potential allies and offered them their freedom if they joined their side. Some 13,000 did so in South Carolina. In 1783, the defeated British took some 3,000 ex-slaves with them to Nova Scotia, whence many went back to Africa (Sierra Leone). In 1776 the Continental Congress banned the importation of slaves to any of the thirteen colonies, but abolition did not find its way into the Declaration of Independence, despite the ideals of the American Revolution.

While in Britain pressure was mounting for abolition, in the United States the last two decades of the eighteenth century saw the north and the south move in directions that were inexorably opposed. "Conscience and virtue came easily where slavery was not economically profitable."[607] One northern state after another passed legislation freeing their slaves, but, under pressure from the labour hungry planters in the south, the new constitution of 1787 prohibited Congress from outlawing the slave trade for twenty years. During the two decades that followed, more slaves entered the United States than in any similar period in history. In 1807 the British Parliament passed the Slave Trade Act, making it henceforth illegal for British ships to carry slaves. In the following year legislation came into effect in the United States officially outlawing the slave trade.

However, there was still a massive demand for labor in the burgeoning cotton plantations of Georgia and Alabama. Although some 15,000 Africans were smuggled in over the next eight years, an internal slave trade continued unofficially in the United States. In the 1830s, while the British "Reform" Parliament debated the legislation that ended slavery in Britain and its colonies, thousands of slaves were carried from one American coastal port to another, or marched overland in coffles. The name Shorter occurs in several ship's manifests of human cargo during these years. Slaves were drained away from the declining rice fields of South Carolina to the expanding cotton fields of Georgia. Some unscrupulous traders even kidnapped free blacks to sell in the slave states. Many slaves, however, moved with their masters into the newly developed areas of commercial farming, and when emancipation finally came in 1865, 99% of all southern slaves were American born.

---

[607] William Warren Rogers **et al.**, **op.cit.,** p.94.

Enslaved Shorters

The first slave-owning Shorter was John Shorter of Middlesex County, Virginia, whose story has been told above in Chapter Sixteen. The parish registers of Christchurch Parish, Middlesex Co. record the family of his slave, Kate. Her children were Venus (b.20 August 1722), Judy (b.17 December 1723), Tamar (b.26 April 1725), Jack (b.27 August 1727) and Glasgow (b.15 July 1741). John Shorter's will, dated July 6th 1728, bequeaths Kate to his wife Elizabeth and Judy and Jack, together with the hitherto unmentioned Nan, to his son Henry. Tamar (Thamar) was willed to his daughter Mary. Glasgow was not yet born, and Jack died on November 16th 1734.[608]

First generation slaves in America often kept their own African names and gave African names to their children. However, white masters transformed and shortened them, turning them into English forms. Venus was a common version of the Akan name "Abena", meaning a child born on Tuesday. Judy was a transformation of the Ewe name Ajowa, meaning a child born on Monday, or the fourth female child. Jack was the English form of another Ewe name, Kwakow, for a child born on Wednesday and Nan was a form of the Akan name Anan, the fourth born child. The Akan peoples (including Ashanti and Fante) are found in Ghana. The Ewe are in Ghana and across the border into modern Togo. It would seem therefore that the slaves of John Shorter of Middlesex Co., VA came from the region of modern Ghana.[609]

---

[608] Dr. M. P. Taylor's "Slave Chronology", quoting **Christchurch Parish Registers 1653-1812**, National Society of Colonial Dames of America, Richmond VA, 1897; and **The Virginia Genealogist**, Jan-Mar 1962, "Middlesex County Wills 1713-1734", Vol. 6, no.1, pp. 9-10.

[609] Dr. M. P. Taylor, "Slave Chronology", quoting Marvin L. Michael Kay and Lorin Lee Cary.

A property tax list of 1783 names a slave owned by the family of John's son Henry, in Culpeper County, Virginia, as "Pett".[610] When the family moved to Wilkes County, Georgia, they held small numbers of slaves on their Beaver Dam property. The tax records reveal William with one slave and James with three in 1790; James with three slaves in 1791 and three in 1792; Henry Sr. with three in 1793; Henry with eight in 1794, three in 1795 and 1797, and two in 1799; Jacob with three in 1799 and Russell with one in 1804 and 1805.[611]

The Henry Shorter who died in 1808 (see Chapter Sixteen) had owned slaves named Abraham, Daniel and Dangerfield. A slave named Ruth was given by Russell Shorter to Reuben Clark Shorter, and Jacob Shorter bought Daniel and Abraham. Dangerfield was bought by a certain Burwell. Russell Shorter is also recorded as buying "one Negro" from Beaufort District, South Carolina.[612] The name Daniel may be a transformation of the Ghanaian name Danuwa or Danuor.[613]

Free Persons of Color

Meanwhile, in the 1790s, particularly in Maryland, a number of enslaved Shorters obtained their freedom.[614] This did not

---

[610] Cf. Essay of Dr. M. P. Taylor: "Slavery and the Shorters", 2nd February 2001.

[611] Frank Parker Hudson, **Wilkes County Georgia, Tax Records, 1785-1805**, Vols. 1 and 2, 1996.

[612] **Early Records of Georgia**, Vol. II, p. 286, Inventory of December 19th 1808; Dorothy W. Potter, **Passport of Southeastern Pioneers 1770-1823**, Baltimore, Gateway Press Inc., 1982, p. 269.

[613] Aylward Shorter has known personally a Ghanaian called "Danuor". Kay and Cary **op.cit**, pp. 227, 268-275, believe it to be originally a Hausa name.

[614] The account that follows is based on Dr. M. P. Taylor's essays: "Free People of Color (FPC) in America", 30th January 2001; "Slavery and the

happen primarily because of the benevolence of the white slave-owners, but because of a strong judicial challenge mounted by the slaves concerned. Under state law every free person of color had to have a white guardian responsible for him or her, who acted for the person in legal matters, who paid the annual registration fee, the taxes and the fines which might have been incurred.[615] A free person of color who taught a slave or another free Negro to read or write could be fined or flogged. The existence of free persons of color was highly precarious, since they were seen as a threat to the institution of slavery. Frequently, they were re-enslaved, and some were even known to have returned to slavery in order to enjoy greater security.

Freedom could be obtained when there was proof of descent from a white mother. The slave Henrietta Shorter filed such a petition in 1790, but it was not until three years later that her master posted the required recognizance bond, after being cited for contempt of court. She was then judged a free woman. Another petitioner who encountered a similar delay was the slave Teresa Shorter, who brought a suit in 1792. Slave owners delayed proceedings because they had to pay fees and wages to successful petitioners. The mulatto Shorter slave family that originated in St. Mary's County, MD eventually won their case, based on the claim that their progenitor was a slave called "Little Robin" who had married a white servant named Elizabeth Shorter around 1702. Other members of this family, led by Basil Shorter, walked free in 1794.

Certificates of freedom were issued to persons of color who could establish that they were born free or had been

---

Shorters", 3rd February 2001; and her earlier "Slave Chronology" of 11th February 2000.

[615] David Shorter of Clarendon Co., SC (mentioned above in Chapter 17, note 557), was made guardian of a free man of color, named Black Jamey Pearson, in 1800. Silas Emmett Lucas Jr., **Some South Carolina County Records**, Vol.2, Southern Historical Press, Inc., 1989, p.387.

manumitted by their owners. Between 1806 and 1849 the State of Maryland issued such certificates to sixteen men and women named Shorter. They bore the following Christian names: Dolly, William, Jim, Eliza, John Williams, Rachel, Joseph, Charlotte, Lewis (1), John Henry, George, Sarah Jane, Mary Alice, James Sidney, Clinton and Lewis (2).

Slaves were also manumitted by free family members who saved the money to purchase their freedom. By 1840, there were even 454 black slave masters, many of whom had simply purchased their own kinsfolk. Between 1780 and 1810 the number of freed blacks surged in Virginia, reaching 30,570 in 1810. However, many freed Shorters lived in Washington, DC, because of a law that re-enslaved any emancipated person who remained in the Commonwealth of Virginia for more than twelve months after gaining his/her freedom. After 1800, free persons of color named Shorter occur as family heads with their households in the census lists of Maryland and Washington, DC, and the marriages of many free persons of color named Shorter were registered in both places.

CHAPTER TWENTY

AFRICAN AMERICAN SHORTER FAMILIES

Slave Families of Reuben Clark Shorter

As we have seen, white Shorters usually had small numbers of slaves. However, when the brothers, General Reuben Clark Shorter and Judge Eli Sims Shorter, took up large-scale cotton planting, they needed bigger numbers of slaves to work the plantations. We know some of the names of Eli Sims Shorter's slaves. His wife Sophia received in her father's will in 1824 slaves called: Jim, Dragon, Joe, Charlotte, Charity and Mary. When Judge Eli Sims Shorter himself died at Columbus, Muscogee County, GA in 1836, his slaves were hired and some sold for the benefit of his heirs. There were slaves with the names of Jacob, Nelson, Clarissa, Kate, Ben and Jerry, Dave, Joe, Osborne, Isaac and Jane. After the eventual sale in 1840 the balance of slaves were retained as house servants.[616]

General Reuben Clark Shorter, as we have seen in Chapter Eighteen, was both a planter and physician. He was one of the founders of Eufaula Town, Barbour County, AL, where he first arrived in 1833 with his family and twenty slaves. At his death in 1854, he possessed two plantations, one near his mansion in

---

[616] Information for the slaves of Reuben Clark Shorter and Eli Sims Shorter comes from Dr. M. P. Taylor, "Slavery and the Shorters".

Eufaula and one across the Chattahoochee River in Randolph County, GA. As his will of 1853 shows, his slaves were both house servants and field hands. Ben was his carriage driver, Cathy was his cook and Yellow Jim was his carpenter. Slaves not only worked in the cotton fields, but they also built and decorated the magnificent mansions, many of which still stand. They themselves lived at some distance from the master's house, in a slave quarter consisting of rough bark or log cabins. There is no need to indulge the plantation myth of the "Gone with the Wind" variety. The life of the slaves was harsh, particularly at the hands of the whip-carrying overseers in the fields, some of whom were themselves blacks. The white Shorters conformed to the accepted social patterns, but were certainly no worse than other slave-owners, perhaps considerably better. At least, there is no record of unkind treatment cited against them, and no known advertisements for runaway Shorter slaves.

Reuben Clark Shorter's will bequeathed over one hundred slaves to members of his family, eighty-four of them being mentioned by name. It is noteworthy that he tried to keep the various slave families together. We shall follow the fortunes of one of these families, that of Nathan Shorter, his wife Molly and their five children Martha, Daniel, Nancy, Nathan and Frankey, later in this chapter. Reuben Clark Shorter's family had enough respect for their slaves to bury them, albeit in unmarked graves, in the Shorter family cemetery at Eufaula, near the site of the original mansion.

The care of sick slaves was the concern of the plantation's mistress. Mary Jane Battle, wife of John Gill Shorter, used to care for them in a room off her kitchen.[617] A spontaneous tribute was paid to her husband by an ex-slave called Julius Caesar Shorter in the Reconstruction period after the Civil War. Before a pro-Republican Congressional hearing at Montgomery, investigating alleged southern atrocities by

---

[617] William Warren Rogers **et al., op.cit**., p.106.

whites, this erstwhile body servant of the Governor, now a Democrat like his former master, declared: "I knew the best friend I had was John Gill Shorter".[618]

A slave census of Barbour County, taken in September 1850, reveals that Reuben Clark Shorter held 17 slaves in Eufaula; John Gill Shorter held 11 and Colonel Eli Sims Shorter held 44. Ten years later, in 1860, Henry Russell Shorter held 38 slaves, Mary Battle Shorter held 22 and Colonel Eli Sims Shorter held 80. Shorter slave owners continued to buy, sell and bequeath slaves almost up to the end of the Civil War.[619] Although slavery helped to lay the foundations of the white Shorters' cotton fortune, they made their really big money in the 1870s and 1880s, after slavery had ended. It is also worth remembering that 200,000 colored soldiers, among them 51 Shorters, served in the Union Army during the Civil War. Thirty-eight thousand colored soldiers gave their lives and twenty-four received the Congressional Medal of Honor.

A sad commentary on the aftermath of the Civil War is provided by the story of William Shorter, a nineteen year old African American who was lynched at Winchester, VA in 1892. He had been arrested and charged with attempted rape, but the sheriff and jailor failed to protect him from the lynch mob, in spite of the precautions taken by the court.[620]

One of the adaptive mechanisms that helped in the social integration of freed slaves was Freemasonry, in the shape of African Lodge No.459, founded by a West Indian black, a

---

[618] Anne Kendrick Walker, **Backtracking in Barbour County**, Richmond VA, the Dietz Press, 1941, p.248.

[619] From photocopies of census material, bills of sale and probate, supplied by Dr. M. P. Taylor.

[620] T. K. Cartmell, **Shenandoah Valley Pioneers and their Descendants - A History of Frederick Co. VA**, Berryville VA, Chesapeake Book Co., 1963, pp.122-123.

Methodist Minister named Prince Hall, in 1787. However, far and away the most important adaptive mechanism was Christianity itself. Religion was important in African culture, and Biblical themes associated with the Exodus were emphasized in the spirituality of the slaves. A Eufaula ex-slave named Jerry Shorter was a Baptist preacher and gave evidence concerning the Spring Hill riot in 1874.[621]

Bishop James Alexander Shorter

Probably, the most distinguished African American churchman named Shorter was Bishop James Alexander Shorter of the Methodist Episcopal Church. Bishop Shorter was born free in Washington, DC on February 14th 1817. His father, Charles Shorter, was in the oyster business and his mother, Elizabeth, kept a food stall. In 1838 James Alexander was sent to be a barber's apprentice in Pennsylvania. After attending Methodist General Conferences in Washington 1846 and Baltimore 1847, he was ordained deacon in 1848, and met his wife Julia Ann at another General Conference in Philadelphia. She died, leaving him with three small children, two sons and a daughter. In 1851 he married Maria Kerr in the Israel Church, Washington, DC, and by her had two daughters. He was appointed successively to the Bethel Church and the Ebenezer Church in Baltimore.

In 1857 Bishop Shorter settled at Wilberforce University, Ohio, to which he made benefactions on behalf of his wife and himself. By 1887, he was seventy years old and a Bishop of the African Methodist Episcopal Church. A year later, and shortly before his death, he was chosen to represent his Church at the Ecumenical Missionary Conference in London, one of the meetings that paved the way for the Edinburgh World

---

[621] Anne Kendrick Walker, **Backtracking in Barbour County**, Richmond VA, the Dietz Press 1941, p.274.

Missionary Conference of 1910.[622] A brick administration building at Wilberforce University, Ohio, was named "Shorter Hall" in his honor, as well as the Shorter AME Church, in Denver, CO.

The Family of Nathan Shorter

We now return to the family of Nathan and Molly and their five children.[623] Nathan and Molly were born in South Carolina c.1807 and c.1810 respectively. Their children also seem to have been born in South Carolina. They would have joined Reuben Clark Shorter's workforce sometime in the 1840s. This family was bequeathed to General Reuben Clark Shorter's grandson, Reuben Francis Kolb, to be delivered to him by the executor, John Gill Shorter, on arriving at lawful age. "Old" Nathan and Molly died in about 1855 before this could happen. All the children were handed over to Reuben Kolb in 1860, with the exception of young Nathan.

The latter, whom we shall now call "Nathan Senior" was born in South Carolina in about 1840. After the mention in Reuben Clark Shorter's will, we next hear of him in the 1880 census of Eufaula, fifteen years after Emancipation. He was a farmer and his wife Betsie Dent-Bigham was a housekeeper. Nathan Sr. had eight children of his own and three step-children from his wife's former marriage. Betsie died c.1885 at Eufaula. Not long afterwards, Nathan Sr. and his family moved across the Chattahoochee River from Eufaula into Quitman County, Georgia. Here he married Annie Ellison

---

[622] Dr. M. P. Taylor in her essay, "Free People of Color", following Alexander W. Wayman, **The Life of Rev. James Alexander Shorter, One of the Bishops of the African M. E. Church**, Baltimore, J. Lanahan, 1890, gives the date of the London conference as 1889. In fact, it met in 1888.

[623] This account of Nathan Shorter's family is based on references, photocopies, genealogies and personal notes supplied by Dr. M. P. Taylor.

in 1886, and became a founder of Morris First Baptist Church in 1895. After twenty-five years of slavery, Nathan Sr. started his life of freedom with no house, no money and no education. Six of his children were under the age of thirteen. Then he lost his wife Betsie. After his move to Georgia and his remarriage there, his children were able to grow up in the Church and receive a grammar school or other education. All of them managed to survive and lead very productive lives. His son John purchased a farm and his other sons, Roland, Samuel and William purchased their homes which are still in the family. Johnnie, son of John, was a pioneer worker with voter registration and was former NAACP President in Dawson GA.[624] Some of Nathan Sr.'s descendants served in the military in two World Wars and in the Korean and Viet Nam Wars. Nathan Sr. died before 1919 and was buried in a cemetery near the First Morris Baptist Church.[625] Nathan Sr. has over 1,100 descendants, who reside in sixteen states and the District of Columbia.[626]

Nathan Sr.'s children were: Roland (1870-1961) whose first wife was Edna Greer and lived to be 91; Samuel (1871-1940) who married Laura Price; Clifford (1872-1934) who married Wilson Price, Sr.; William (1876-1956) who married Willie Brown; Anna (1878-1930) who married Charles Smith; Nathan Jr. (1879-1969) who married Paralee Price; John (1882-1944) who married firstly Eva West and secondly Dixie Davenport and Mollie (1884-1913) who married Neal Jenkins.

---

[624] National Association for the Advancement of Colored Peoples (NAACP).

[625] At the time of writing, the author has not yet obtained information about the date of Nathan Sr.'s death.

[626] A few of his descendants still live in Alabama. The majority resides in Georgia, Florida, Maryland, Virginia, North Carolina, South Carolina, Connecticut, Pennsylvania, New York, New Jersey, Illinois, Texas, Michigan, Kentucky, Louisiana, Ohio and the District of Columbia.

Around 1879/1880 the Shorter, Price and allied families were founders of the Pleasant Hill Missionary Baptist Church in Randolph Co., GA. Through the years they have been devoted members of the Church. Randall P. Shorter chairs the Board of Trustees and others are Deacons of the Church. The children of these families and Randall himself received their primary education in the historic Mitchell Grove Grammar School, a little wooden school house near Cuthbert, maintained by their families with some county funds through the 1950s when the schools were consolidated in Randolph Co., GA. Randall is the only surviving child of Samuel and has over 140 descendants in six states.[627]

Roland Shorter's daughter Jessie (1900-), who married Robert Lemon, celebrated her one hundredth birthday on March 4th 2000.[628] John Shorter's great, great, great granddaughter is Raven Symoné, the well-known child TV star. Her TV career has included The Cosby Show and Hangin' with Mr. Cooper. A millionaire at the age of five, she is also a singer, film star and stage actress.[629]

Clifford Shorter Price's son, Rev. Nathan Thomas Price (1893-1974), a Baptist Minister, married Maggie Lee Johnson (1911-1997). Their daughter Maggie Henrietta Price (1936-) married James Taylor (1936-1981). Maggie Henrietta Price Taylor has enjoyed a distinguished career in the Federal Service, starting as a clerk and moving up the ladder to

---

[627] At the time of writing he is 96 years old and lives Randolph County, GA.

[628] "Happy Hundredth Birthday", **The Southwest Georgian**, Vol.62, no.21, March 9th-16th 2000, p.1.

[629] Cf. **People Weekly**, June 26th 2000, and notes of Dr. M.P. Taylor.

senior-level competitive positions at the Department of Commerce, National Institute of Education, Department of Education, and the Department of Energy. From 1979-1996, she served in the Department of Housing and Urban Development in various top managerial capacities, and received a number of awards for outstanding performance. She retired after 39 years of U. S. Federal service.[630]

Mollie Shorter Jenkins' great, grandson, Bobby T. Jenkins, is the superintendent of the Randolph County, GA School System, of some 2000 students housed on three separate school campuses.

Clifford Shorter Price's great, granddaughter, Andrea R. Price was promoted to Executive Vice-President and Chief Operating Officer of the Hurley Medical Center in Michigan, overseeing over 800 full-time members of staff and managing several millions of dollars in operational revenue.

Nathan Sr.'s daughter Anna Shorter Smith had a son named Nathan (1903-2000). He was a Baptist Minister, who founded and organized the First Grace Baptist Church in Chicago and was its pastor for 39 years. He retired in 1995. His son (by his second wife), Nathan Joseph, is also an ordained minister of the Gospel.

Other African American Shorters

Wayne Shorter is considered one of modern Jazz's most influential saxophonists and among its most original composers. He was born on August 25th 1933 and grew up in Newark, New Jersey. He studied music and education at New

---

[630] Cf. Entries in **Who's Who of American Women**, 13th edition, 1983-1984, Chicago and **International Who's Who of Intellectuals**, Cambridge U.K. 1987; also autobiographical notes supplied by Dr. M. P. Taylor herself.

York University, and, after serving in the U.S. Army 1956-1958, was invited by Art Blakey to be musical director of the Jazz Messengers. He traveled around the world with the group. In 1970, together with Joe Zawinul, he founded Weather Report, a jazz fusion group, but broke away in 1985 to found his own group. He has received numerous awards, including a Grammy Award in 1987 for best jazz instrumental composition. A practicing Buddhist, Wayne Shorter resides, with his wife Anna Maria, in Los Angeles, CA.

Mention should also be made of Dr. Fred Shorter, who practices dentistry in Lathrup Village, Michigan. His father, Frank Shorter (1910-1987) was the son of James Shorter and Sophy Crosby. The family migrated from the town of Shorter, near Montgomery, AL, named after John Gill Shorter.[631]

The United States of America is a great nation today because Africans and African Americans helped to make it that way. In spite of the destructive effects of slavery, enslaved Shorters, free people of color who bore the name Shorter and the Shorter descendants of both these categories, made, and continue to make, a great contribution to the American Nation.

---

[631] Information supplied to Dr. M. P. Taylor by Dr. Fred Shorter, April 1999, and communicated to the author, February 16th 2001.

CHAPTER TWENTY ONE

ALFRED HURT SHORTER AND SHORTER COLLEGE

Early Life of Alfred Hurt Shorter

The story of Alfred Hurt Shorter (1803-1882) is an inspiring one. It is the "rags to riches" story of a poor orphan who became a wealthy merchant, farmer and philanthropist. In Chapter Seventeen, we mentioned that Alfred Hurt Shorter was the son of Jacob Shorter (c.1760-1812) and Delphia Bankston Shorter. Alfred was born in Wilkes Co., GA on 23rd November 1803. His mother died at the time of his birth and Alfred was aged nine when his father died in 1812. His father's second wife Sarah Shorter (née Bramblett) entrusted Alfred and his sister, Sally, to her sister and brother-in-law Isaiah Irvin to rear.

Alfred's family was poor, and, as an orphan, he was at a serious disadvantage. He received no formal education, but moved around to the homes of his relatives in Wilkes Co., Georgia and Eufaula, Alabama, working in a series of general stores. In spite of his lack of education, he developed an acute business acumen. In 1819, at the age of sixteen, he left Alabama, carrying all his worldly possessions, a travel bag in one hand and a pet cockerel under his arm. He made his way to Monticello in Jasper Co., GA, where his cousin, General Reuben Clark Shorter, was then still residing. Alfred began working for Reuben Clark Shorter and in the same year 1819 his sister Sally and her husband John Truitt also moved to Monticello.[632]

At Monticello Alfred later found employment as a clerk in a store owned by John Baldwin, eventually becoming his partner. John Baldwin died on 19th October 1831, and his widow assumed control of the estate. Martha Baldwin (née Harper) was a devout Baptist, whose piety was afterwards the inspiration for successive religious activities and fellowships at Shorter College. Alfred Shorter, four years her junior, became her financial advisor and firm friend. In 1834 they married. Alfred was then 31 years of age. With her encouragement, Alfred invested the forty thousand dollars, left to her by her first husband, in real estate in Georgia, Alabama and Mississippi. They had no children of their own, but brought up a neice and nephew of Martha's.

In 1836, after Reuben Clark Shorter's definitive move from Monticello to Eufaula, Barbour, Alabama, Alfred and Martha Shorter also moved to Alabama, staying for a year in Barbour and Macon Counties. In the following year, 1837, they moved back to Georgia and took up residence in Floyd County. At this time Alfred profited from the boom in Cotton and established extensive plantations, notably in Floyd County and in Thomas County, GA, on the borders of Florida. He had a large work force of slaves.

Alfred Shorter was a businessman, as well as a farmer, trading in other forms of merchandise besides cotton and also in real estate. He became a part owner of numerous businesses, including a local steamboat line, banks, an insurance company, iron mines, a salt factory and a hotel. He was president and

---

[632] This biography of Alfred Hurt Shorter is based on Robert G. Gardner, article in Kenneth Coleman and Charles Stephen Gurr, **Dictionary of Georgia Biography**, Vol.2, Athens, University of Georgia Press and **On the Hill - The Story of Shorter College**, Rome GA, Shorter College 1972; also Jasper County Historical Foundation, **History of Jasper County Georgia**, p.281.

principal investor of the Rome Railroad Company, which ran a locomotive between Rome and Kingston, named the "Alfred Shorter". For almost twenty-five years he was co-owner of two bridges over the Etowah and Oostanaula Rivers in Rome, GA, which provided him with a regular income from toll fees.

Alfred and Martha Shorter moved to Rome, Floyd, Georgia in 1847. Here they built a fine white mansion called "Thornwood", a mile outside the town on the Alabama Road.

When the American Civil War broke out, Alfred Shorter, at 58, was well past the age for military service. Although he was referred to as "Colonel Alfred Shorter" in his later years, he does not seem ever to have held any position that would justify such a title. Towards the end of 1863, Alfred Shorter was a signatory to a letter of protest addressed to General Braxton Bragg, the commander of the Confederate Army of Tennessee, deploring abuses of the Impressment Act. Shorter, however, was a staunch supporter of the Confederacy, both morally and financially.

In 1863 Alfred and Martha Shorter left Rome for their plantation in Thomas County, southern Georgia. They stayed there until the end of the war in 1865. In the meantime, they allowed their houses in Rome to be requisitioned as military hospitals, offices and stores.[633] In spite of his lack of education, Alfred Shorter read widely and was especially fond of the novels of Charles Dickens, several of whose narratives resembled his own life story. His modesty and placid manner often made him seem unapproachable, but those who knew him well found him gentle, wise and deeply pious. He was quietly active in the Rome Baptist Church and made financial

---

[633] Receipt Roll Voucher 124, February 29th 1864, photocopy from the National Archives and Records Administration (NARA), Washington, D.C., supplied by Dr. M. P. Taylor.

contributions to it and to other churches. He and his wife, Martha, regularly occupied their pew on the extreme right hand side of the Church.

The Founding of Shorter College

In August 1873, Reverend Luther R. Gwaltney, founded the "Cherokee Baptist Female College" at Rome, GA, and Alfred Shorter became president of its Board of Trustees. Gwaltney described the institution as "a college for the daughters of Cherokee, Georgia". This did not mean that it was intended for native American women. "Cherokee" in this connection had a geographical, rather than an ethnic connotation. Although, the Cherokee nation had possessed its own constitution, government, schools and churches, the entire Cherokee population had been moved to reservations west of the Mississippi River in the late 1830s. After three years, the new college was still struggling to survive and it became clear that its future could only be assured by a bigger student enrolment. For this, more facilities were needed. Early in 1876 Gwaltney wrote to Shorter asking him to make a generous contribution to the college. Shorter did not reply until June. It seems that his first thought was to use his money to establish an orphan asylum, however he was eventually prevailed upon to adopt the Cherokee Baptist Female College. Accordingly, he summoned Gwaltney and announced his intention of rebuilding the college with a donation of 20,000 dollars. This sum was to be raised in part by the sale of some of Shorter's residences, the college land title being made over to Shorter himself.

A conference of the Rome Baptist Church was hastily summoned and Alfred Shorter's intention was made public. The conference proposed that the college should be named "Martha Shorter College", but Mrs. Shorter did not favor this. Alfred Shorter was equally opposed to its being called "Alfred Shorter College". It was eventually decided to commemorate them both by naming it "Shorter College", and, as one conference member punningly observed, this was more appropriate because it was "a shorter name". The departure of Gwaltney shortly after the conference immediately plunged the project into a state of uncertainty. However, Alfred Shorter became increasingly committed to the proposal. Towards the end of 1876 he told Gwaltney's successor about his determination to found a much bigger and more expensive college. It was no longer a question of restoring the ailing Cherokee College. He also revealed that his wife was the only other person who knew of this determination.

In view of this remark, it is perhaps appropriate to ask what role may have been played by Martha Shorter in the genesis of the planned college. It has already been noted that the name that was first proposed was "Martha Shorter College". It is also a fact that Martha Shorter has been commemorated far more explicitly at Shorter College than her husband. Not only has there been a Martha Shorter Memorial Chapel and a Martha Shorter Memorial Window, but there is also a Martha Shorter Missionary Society, a Martha Shorter Prayer Room and even a Martha Shorter Tea Room. This nomenclature is explained in part by the fact that Shorter College was an exclusively female college for most of its existence. However, it may also be that the College knew of, or guessed at, Martha's influence on her husband.

We have seen that Alfred Shorter was slow to respond to Gwaltney's first appeal and that he had other ideas in mind for spending his wealth. When he finally adopted the project, his commitment grew progressively throughout 1876 and 1877. Martha Shorter was a quiet, retiring person, but nobody was in any doubt of her Christian principles. She was also popular with the college students whom she regularly entertained at Thornwood. It is therefore very likely that her Christian allegiance also included a commitment to the Christian education of women, and that she helped Alfred to make up his mind. She may also have been aware of her approaching death, and therefore have wanted to see the project begun. In this she was disappointed, for Martha Baldwin Shorter died on March

22nd 1877, at the age of 78. She was buried at Myrtle Hill Cemetery, Rome, with the faculty and students of the college present at her funeral.

It is said that Alfred Shorter's first choice for the location of his college was the so-called Maplehurst site, west of Thornwood, on which "Greater Shorter" was later constructed in 1911. To build there in 1877 proved impossible, and so the site of the original college was leveled and enlarged. The cornerstone of the first building, known as "the College Edifice" was laid at elaborate ceremonies on October 18th 1877. Alfred Shorter's modesty did not permit him to attend. Instead, he spent the day on one of his nearby plantations.

The new building was for both administrative and teaching purposes and the Memorial Chapel, with its Memorial Window, was an integral part of the building at the rear. The chapel could seat up to eight hundred people. The walls and ceiling were frescoed and the Martha Shorter Memorial Window illustrated the theme of "the life and reward of a good woman". The building cost Alfred Shorter about thirty thousand dollars.

In May 1878 foundations for a dormitory were laid and the old Cherokee College building was razed the following month. This four story building contained the president's office and apartment, the kitchen, dining-room, laundry, ironing room. parlors, music room, thirty-six bedrooms and "bathing tubs and every other modern appliance for...comfort and convenience".[634] It was lighted by gas and heated by steam. The cost of this building was also thirty thousand dollars and it was named for the superintendant of construction, C. M. Pennington, "Pennington Hall".

The college continued to expand and in March 1880 a three-story brick building was constructed behind Pennington Hall. It

---

[634] Quoted in Gardner, **op.cit.** 1972, p.33.

was known as the Music and Art Building. It was completed in the summer of 1881, and the cost was again in the region of thirty thousand dollars. Alfred Shorter also contributed to the current expenditure of the College, and, at his death, left it a sizable endowment of forty thousand dollars. Probably, he contributed around two hundred thousand dollars in all to the college.

Death of Alfred Shorter and Subsequent History of the College

After months of declining health, Alfred Shorter died on July 18th 1882. In his wallet was found the following text: "I commend my soul into the hands of God my creator, hoping and assuredly believing, through the only merits of Jesus Christ my Savior, to be made partaker of life everlasting, and my body to the earth whereof it is made." He is also on record as saying: "I can but wonder why the Lord allowed me, a poor boy, to make all this money. He must have intended that I use it for his glory, and I know of no better use to which I may put it than in building a school where God's name may be honored and where young women may be fitted to occupy stations of honor and usefulness, and thus make the college a blessing to humanity and a glory to God."[635]

Alfred Shorter was laid to rest beside his wife in Myrtle Hill Cemetery, where a great nephew, the grandson of his sister Sally, was also later buried.[636] His estate, reliably estimated to be worth about seven hundred thousand dollars, was divided among his relatives, friends and Shorter College.

---

[635] Gardner, **op.cit.,** p. 47.

[636] Shirley Foster Kinney and James Paul Kinney Jr., "Myrtle Hill Cemetery Obituaries and Interments", **SFK Genealogy**, Rome GA, 1997, vol. X, pp., 39, 371.

In 1909, a local merchant and real estate developer, J. L. Bass, donated his house "Maplehurst" and its surrounding thirty acres to Shorter College. The site was increased to 155 acres by purchases of adjacent land. This was the site said to have been Alfred Shorter's first choice for the college. A funding drive was launched, and in January 1911 the construction of "Greater Shorter" began on what came to be known as "Shorter Hill". This was the beginning of the truly magnificent campus which constitutes Shorter College today.

After the college moved to its present location, "Old Shorter" became a public high school. However, in 1924 the Academic and Chapel building was destroyed by fire and not even the memorial window was saved. Alfred Shorter's other two buildings survived, though Pennington Hall lost its towers and top story.

Shorter College continued to thrive at its new location, becoming effectively co-educational in the 1950s. Though still basically Baptist, there was even a small number of Catholics, a Catholic Club and eventually a "Newman Club". The College celebrated its centenary in 1973 and continues to grow in numbers, facilities and achievements. Alfred and Martha Shorter had no children of their own, but their benefaction ensured for them a posterity - generations of alumni who praise and perpetuate the name of Shorter.

"Shorter, Shorter is our cry: V-I-C-T-O-R-Y!"
(A Shorter College cheer.)

Governor John Gill Shorter, portrait in the Shorter Mansion

The Shorter Mansion Museum at Eufaula, AL

Bishop James Alexander
Shorter, contemporary etching in
Wayman, 1890

Clifford Shorter

Nathan Shorter Senior

Alfred Hurt Shorter

Shorter College, Rome GA

APPENDIX ONE

MAPS

Map 1: Shorters in Surrey, Middlesex and London Area

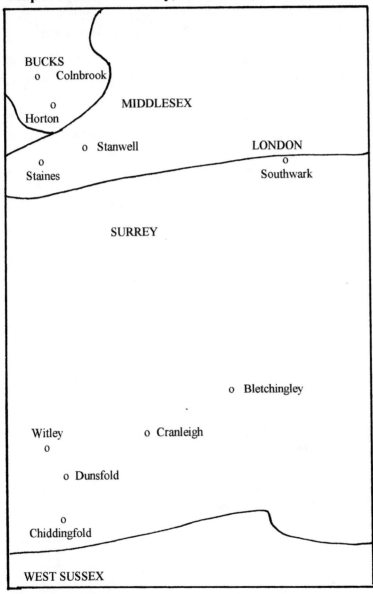

Map 2: Shorters in East Sussex and Kent

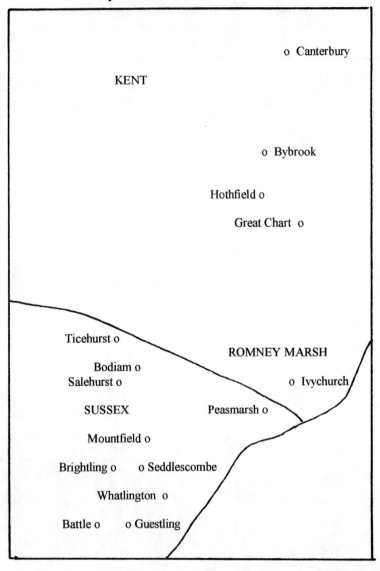

Map 3: Shorters in Virginia Counties

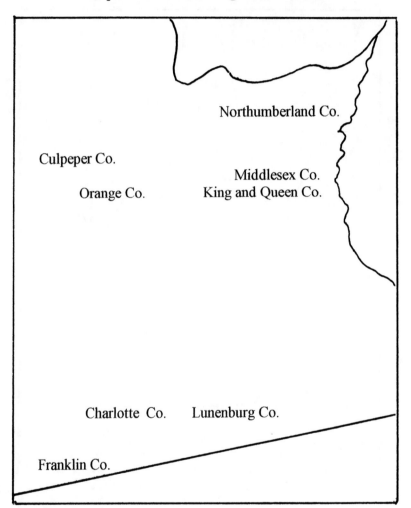

Northumberland Co.

Culpeper Co.

Middlesex Co.

Orange Co.   King and Queen Co.

Charlotte Co.   Lunenburg Co.

Franklin Co.

Map 4: Shorters in Georgia and Alabama Counties

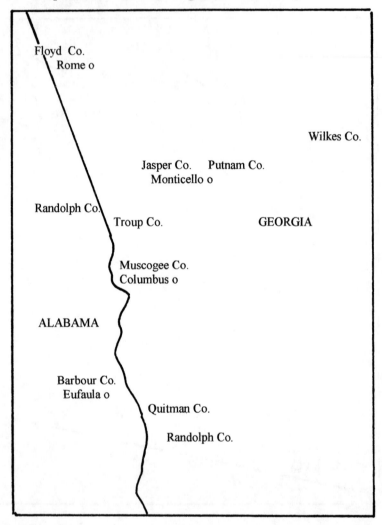

APPENDIX TWO

TABLES

TABLE 1
The Shorters of Chiddingfold and Staines

```
                    John Schurterre (i) of        Joan
                         Chiddingfold         ==
                         d: Abt. 1369

                              |
                         John Schurterre
                              (ii)
                         b: Abt. 1365

                    ?

          Peter Shortere
             fl.
            1400

                    ?

Richard        Elizabeth      Robert Shorter of Cranleigh    Thomas Shorter of Bletchingley
Shortere       Peytowe                  fl.                           fl.
          ==   m: 1475                  1481                       1488 - 1495

                              John Shorter Yeoman of the Crown
                                          fl.
                                       1483 - 1490
```

TABLE 1.1
The Shorters of Chiddingfold and Staines Continued

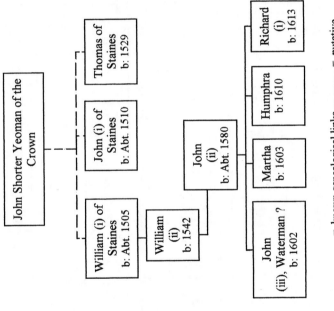

John Shorter Yeoman of the Crown

Thomas of Staines
b: 1529

John (i) of Staines
b: Abt. 1510

William (i) of Staines
b: Abt. 1505

William (ii)
b: 1542

John (ii)
b: Abt. 1580

John (iii), Waterman ?
b: 1602

Martha
b: 1603

Humphra
b: 1610

Richard (i)
b: 1613

―――― = known genealogical links - - - - - = putative genealogical links. The series of Arabic numerals are given for those who are not descended from John (1) .

TABLE 1.2

The Shorters of Chiddingfold and Staines Continued

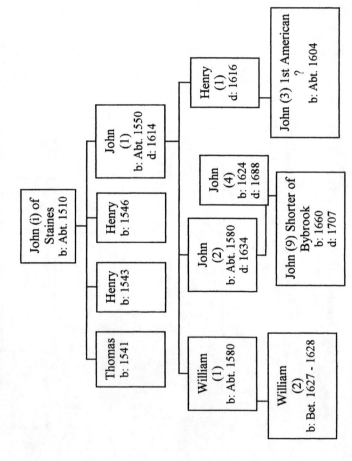

Table 2

The Shorter Families of Staines and Colnbrook (Horton)

TABLE 3

Henry Shorter of Colnbrook (Horton) and his Descendants

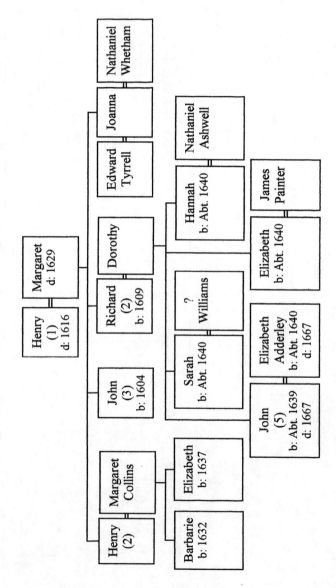

Sir John Shorter and his Descendants

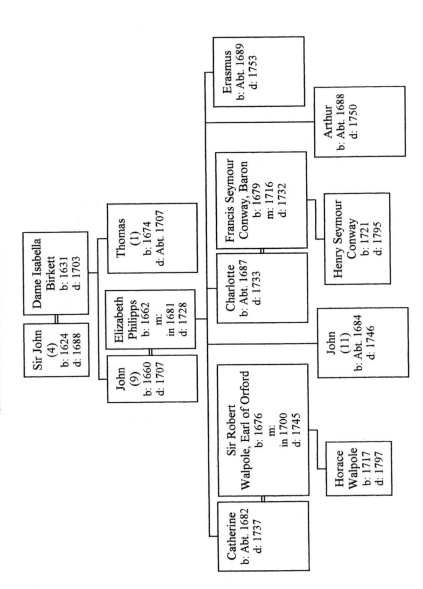

TABLE 5

The Family of Richard Shorter of Southwark

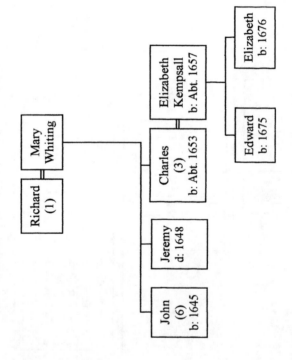

TABLE 6
The Family of Charles Shorter of Southwark

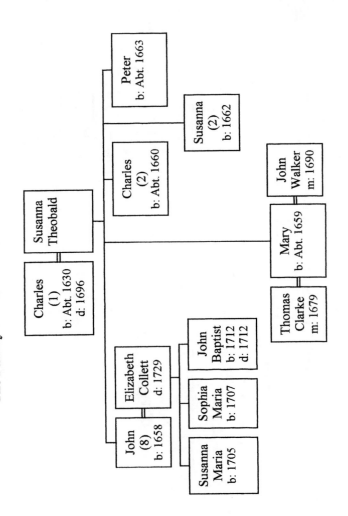

TABLE 6.1

The Family of Charles Shorter of Southwark Continued

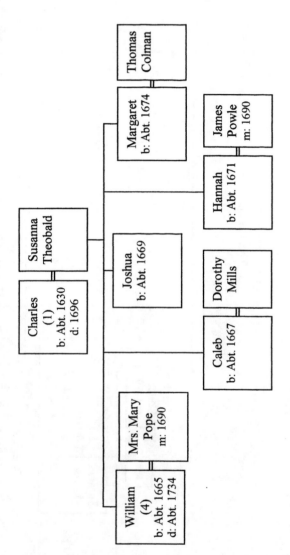

Charles and Susanna Theobald Shorter had ten children.
Table 6 displays the first five children, and Table 6.1 displays
the last five.

TABLE 7

The Family of John Shorter, Waterman

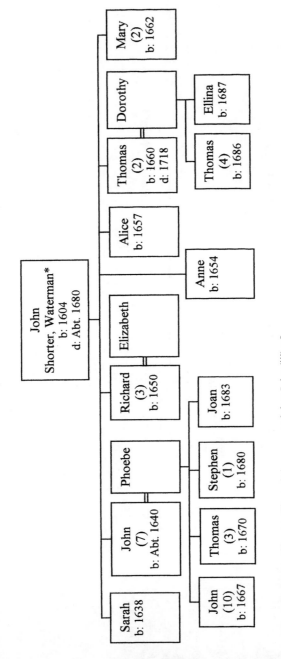

*As explained in Chapter Three, it is suggested that John (iii) of Staines, third cousin of Sir John Shorter (4), was John Shorter, Waterman. Arabic numerals have been retained for his descendants, for ease of reference.

TABLE 7.1
The Family of John Shorter, Waterman Continued

Richard (3) b: 1650	Elizabeth

Esther b: 1677	Elizabeth (6) b: 1680	Richard (4) b: 1683	John (12) b: 1688	Mary (3) b: 1689	George (1) b: 1694	Mary

Mary (4) b: 1717	Elizabeth (7) b: 1722	Richard (5) b: 1724	Thomas (5) b: 1727

TABLE 8

The Family of Richard Shorter of Mountfield

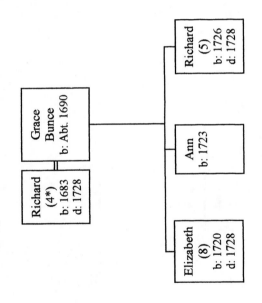

TABLE 9

The Family of John Shorter of Ivychurch (Romney Marsh)

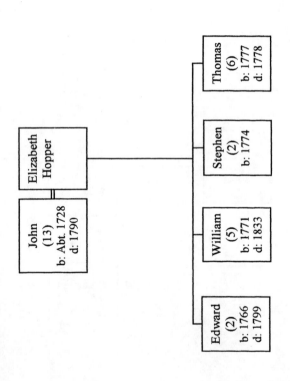

TABLE 10
The Shorters of Mountfield

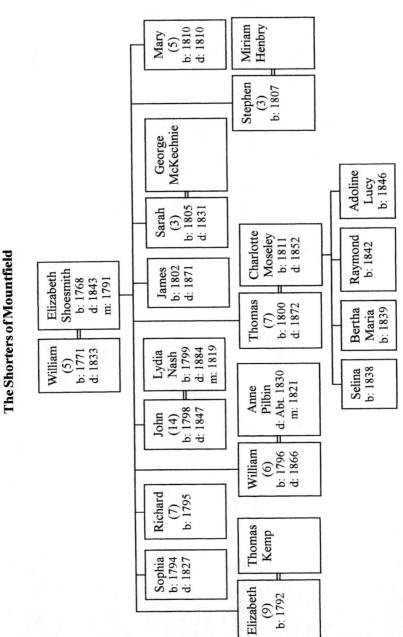

TABLE 11
The Shorters of Mountfield and London (1)

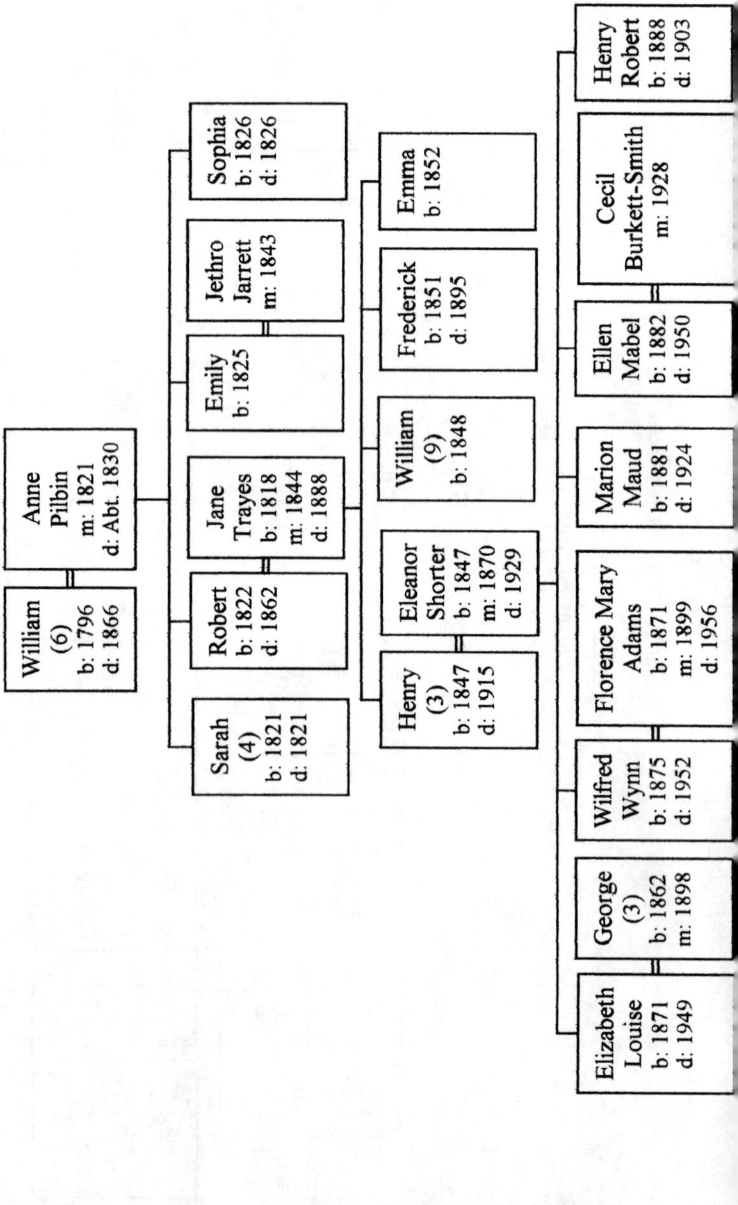

TABLE 11.1
The Shorters of Mountfield and London (1) Continued

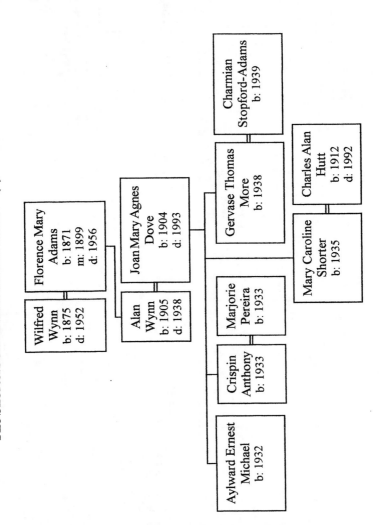

TABLE 12
The Shorters of Mountfield and London (2)

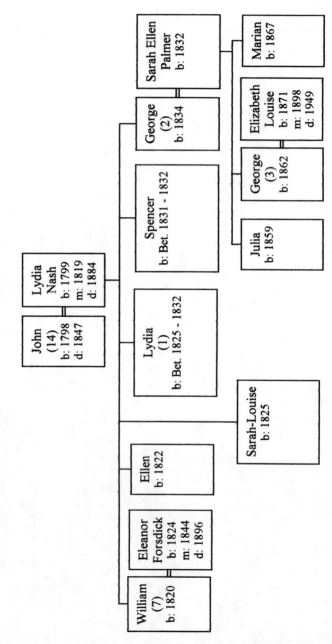

TABLE 12.1
The Shorters of Mountfield and London (2) Continued

TABLE 12.2
The Shorters of Mountfield and London (2) Continued

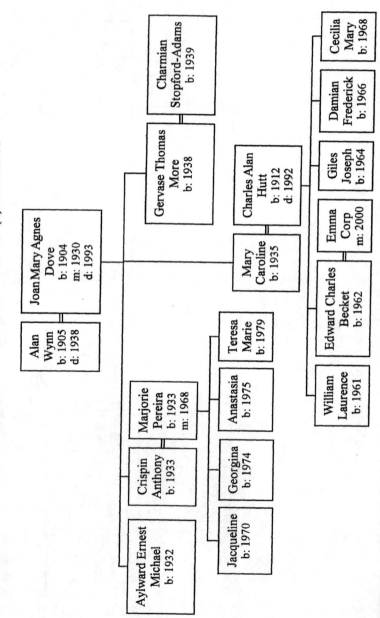

TABLE 12.3
The Shorters of Mountfield and London (2) Continued

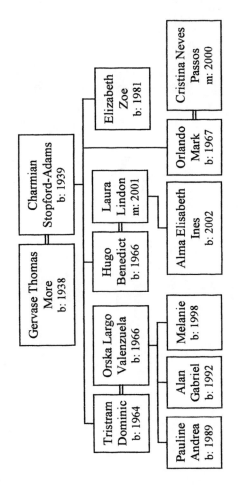

TABLE 13

Shorter Descent of Diana Princess of Wales and the Royal Princes

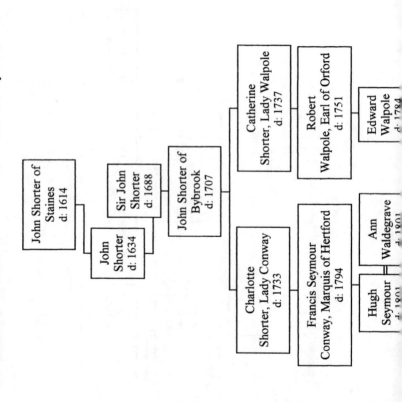

TABLE 13.1

Shorter Descent of Diana Princess of Wales and the Royal Princes Continued

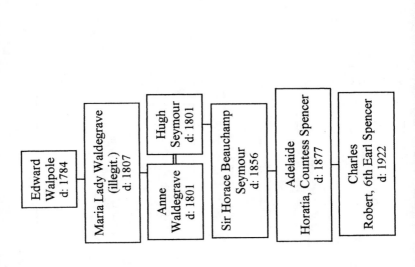

TABLE 13.2

Shorter Descent of Diana Princess of Wales and the Royal Princes Continued

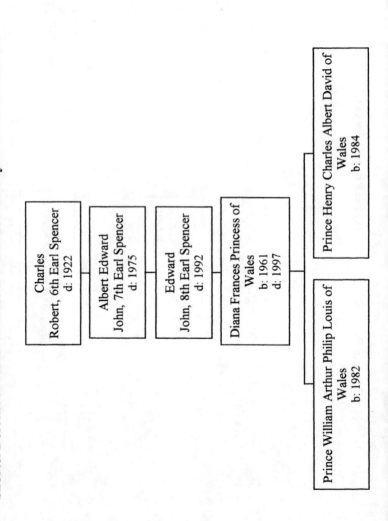

Charles
Robert, 6th Earl Spencer
d: 1922

Albert Edward
John, 7th Earl Spencer
d: 1975

Edward
John, 8th Earl Spencer
d: 1992

Diana Frances Princess of
Wales
b: 1961
d: 1997

Prince William Arthur Philip Louis of
Wales
b: 1982

Prince Henry Charles Albert David of
Wales
b: 1984

TABLE 14
Selected Pedigree of the Shorter Family in Virginia

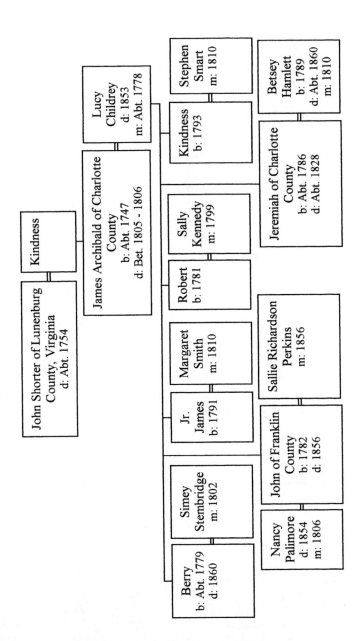

TABLE 14.1

Selected Pedigree of the Shorter Family in Virginia Continued

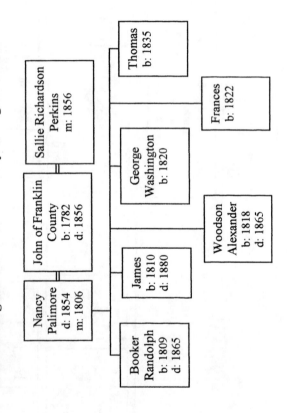

TABLE 15
Descendants of John Shorter of Middlesex County Virginia

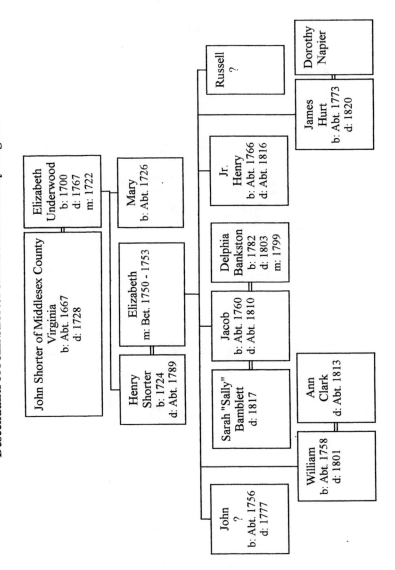

John Shorter of Middlesex County Virginia
b: Abt. 1667
d: 1728

Elizabeth Underwood
b: 1700
d: 1767
m: 1722

Mary
b: Abt. 1726

Elizabeth
m: Bet. 1750 - 1753

Henry Shorter
b: 1724
d: Abt. 1789

Russell
?

Henry Jr.
b: Abt. 1766
d: Abt. 1816

James Hurt
b: Abt. 1773
d: 1820

Dorothy Napier

Delphia Bankston
b: 1782
d: 1803
m: 1799

Jacob
b: Abt. 1760
d: Abt. 1810

Sarah "Sally" Bamblett
d: 1817

Ann Clark
d: Abt. 1813

William
b: Abt. 1758
d: 1801

John
?
b: Abt. 1756
d: 1777

TABLE 15.1

Descendants of John Shorter of Middlesex County Virginia Continued

TABLE 15.2

Descendants of John Shorter of Middlesex County Virginia Continued

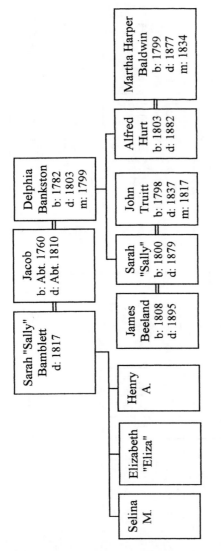

NB: John Shorter, Middlesex Co., could have descended from
Wm. Shorter, Northumb. Co., (c1636-c1678) and/or Anthony
Shorter (b.c1661). It is equally possible that he was John (10).
No evidence found for either hypothesis. Cf. Chaps. 7 and 15.

TABLE 16
Descendants of Reuben Clark Shorter

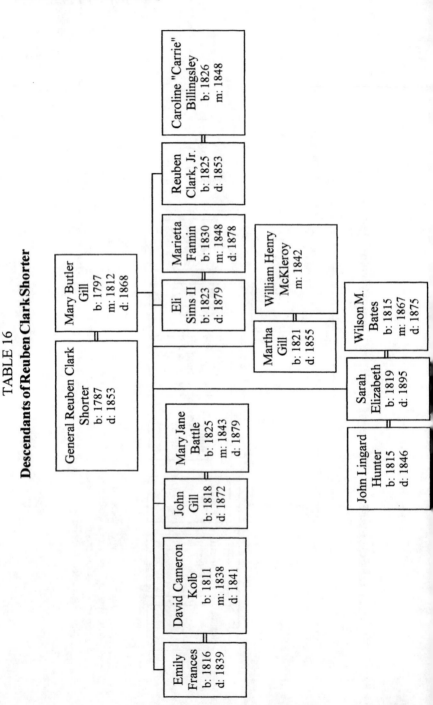

TABLE 16.1
Descendants of Reuben Clark Shorter Continued

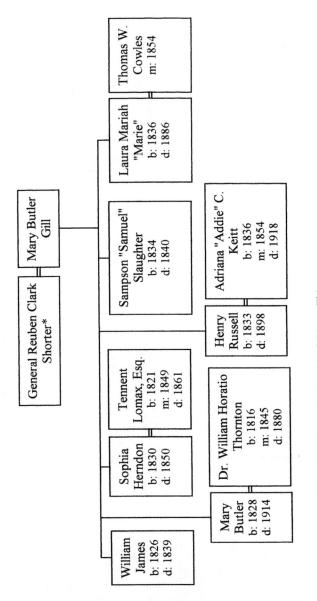

Reuben Clark and Mary Gill Shorter had twelve children. This table displays their last six children.

TABLE 17
Descendants of Nathan Shorter

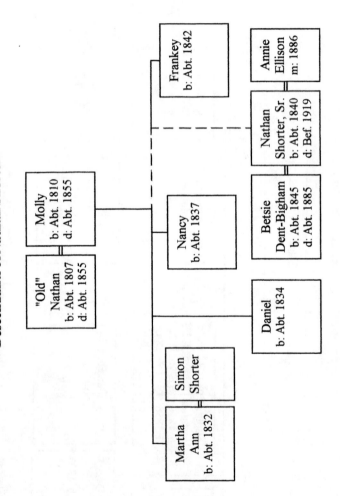

= known genealogical links - - - - - - = putative genealogical links. Information from photocopy of the Will of Reuben Clark Shorter, Eufaula, Barbour, AL. Probate Court,

TABLE 17.1
Descendants of Nathan Shorter, Sr.

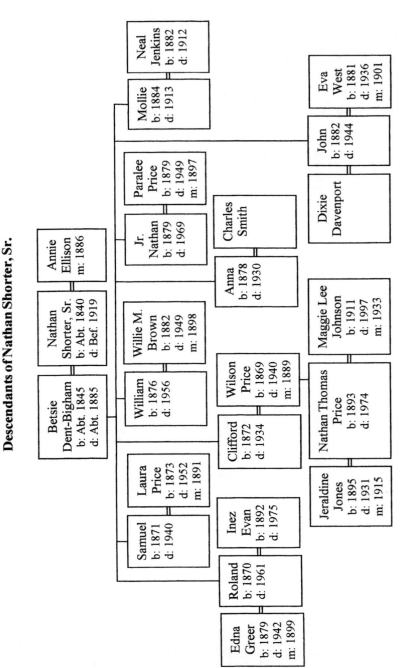

Photo Credits

Frontispiece: Sir John Shorter, from the Sutherland Collection at the Ashmolean Museum, Oxford, U.K.

Plate 1: Catherine Lady Walpole, miniature enameled portrait by C.F.Zincke, at the Ashmolean Museum, Oxford, U.K., no.3.

Plate 2: Tomb of Catherine Lady Walpole in Westminster Abbey. Photo by Aylward Shorter.

Plate 3: Bybrook House as it is today. Photo by Aylward Shorter.

Plate 4: Robert Shorter, from a portrait by Sir Francis Grant.

Plate 5: Jane Shorter, from a portrait by Sir Francis Grant.

Plate 6: Henry Shorter, photo in the possession of his family.

Plate 7: Alan Wynn Shorter, photo in the possession of his family.

Plate 8: The Shorter Mansion Museum at Eufaula, AL. Photo by Maggie Price Taylor.

Plate 9: Bishop James Alexander Shorter, contemporary etching in Wayman, 1890.

Plate 10: Governor John Gill Shorter, portrait in the Shorter Mansion. Photo by Maggie Price Taylor.

Plate 11: Alfred Hurt Shorter, portrait at Shorter College.

Plate 12: Shorter College, Rome, GA, official photo.

Plate 13: Nathan Shorter senior. Photo in the possession of Maggie Price Taylor.

Plate 14: Clifford Shorter. Photo in the possession of Maggie Price Taylor.

For the Tables in this book FTM Software was used.

INDEX

MAGGIE PRICE TAYLOR

Following her retirement of thirty-nine years of
federal government service, and eleven years of
college teaching as an adjunct associate professor of
business at the University of the District of
Columbia, Maggie Price Taylor has been engaged
in researching her family tree. From 1979 to 1996,
she served in several managerial positions in the
Department of Housing and Urban Development,
Washington, DC, retiring as director of the Office
of Special Needs Assistance Programs. During her
career, she received numerous honors and awards
from the public and private sectors. She is published
in *Who's Who of American Women*, and the
International *Who's Who of Professional and
Business Women*, Cambridge England. In 1978,
Maggie received a doctorate in educational
administration, with a concentration in public policy
analysis from the George Washington University,
Washington, DC. She was born in 1936 and was
reared in Atlanta, Georgia. An author of career
booklets, she is the first time co-author of a book.
She is currently devoting her time to genealogical
and historical research.

AYLWARD SHORTER

Aylward Shorter was born in Britain in 1932. He studied Modern History and Social Anthropology at Oxford University and Missiology at the Gregorian University, Rome, after which he carried out doctoral fieldwork in southern Tanzania. A priest of the Society of Missionaries of Africa (White Fathers), he has held teaching posts in Kenya, Uganda, Tanzania and Britain. He is the author of a number of books on Social Anthropology, Ethno-History and Missiology. From 1988-1995 he was President of the Missionary Institute London, which is linked to Middlesex University. From 1995-2002 he was Principal of Tangaza College in the Catholic University of Eastern Africa. He was recently awarded an honorary doctorate in Educational Leadership by Saint Mary's University, Minnesota. He is currently engaged in researching the history of The Society of Missionaries of Africa.